P9-EAO-917

An Introduction to Interactive Multimedia

Stephen J. Misovich

University of Hartford

Jerome Katrichis

University of Hartford

David Demers

University of Connecticut Health Center

William B. Sanders

University of Hartford

Boston   New York   San Francisco
Mexico City   Montreal   Toronto   London   Madrid   Munich   Paris
Hong Kong   Singapore   Tokyo   Cape Town   Sydney

Executive Editor and Publisher: *Stephen D. Dragin*
Editorial Assistant: *Barbara Strickland*
Marketing Manager: *Tara Whorf*
Editorial-Production Administrator: *Anna Socrates*
Editorial-Production Service: *Omegatype Typography, Inc.*
Composition and Prepress Buyer: *Linda Cox*
Manufacturing Buyer: *JoAnne Sweeney*
Cover Administrator: *Kristina Mose-Libon*
Electronic Composition: *Omegatype Typography, Inc.*

LTC
QA76.76
I59 I594

For related titles and support material, visit our online catalog at www.ablongman.com.

Copyright © 2003 Pearson Education, Inc.

All rights reserved. No part of the material protected by this copyright notice may be reproduced or utilized in any form or by any means, electronic or mechanical, including photocopying, recording, or by any information storage and retrieval system, without written permission from the copyright owner.

Many of the designations used by manufacturers and sellers to distinguish their products are claimed as trademarks. Where those designations appear in this book, and Allyn and Bacon was aware of a trademark claim, the designations have been printed in initial or all caps.

To obtain permission(s) to use material from this work, please submit a written request to Allyn and Bacon, Permissions Department, 75 Arlington Street, Boston, MA, 02116 or fax your request to 617-848-7320.

Library of Congress Cataloging-in-Publication Data

An introduction to interactive multimedia / Stephen J. Misovich . . . [et al.].
    p. cm.
   Includes bibliographical references and index.
   ISBN 0-205-34373-2 (alk. paper)
   1. Interactive multimedia. 2. Performing arts. I. Misovich, Stephen.

QA76.76.I59 I594 2003
006.7—dc21

2002016324

Printed in the United States of America

10 9 8 7 6 5 4 3 2 1   07 06 05 04 03 02

Communication browser window © 1999 Netscape Communications Corporation. Used with permission. Netscape Communications has not authorized, sponsored, endorsed, or approved this publication and is not responsible for its content.

Microsoft screen shots reprinted by permission from Microsoft Corporation.

Figures 5.2 and 5.6 © Sinauer Associates, reprinted by permission.

To my wife, Kelly
  —Stephen J. Misovich

To my wife, Chris
  —Jerome Katrichis

To my wife, Dianna
  —David Demers

To my wife, Delia
  —William B. Sanders

CONTENTS

PREFACE

Multimedia implies motion, sound, graphics, film, and photos all working together. Interactive multimedia brings together the interactive elements of social behavior and the technical aspects of multimedia. As an educational and training tool, interactive multimedia is invaluable because it introduces more than a single dimension to a subject. Because most topics are multidimensional, having access to the key and primary tools for multimedia means having the key to education and training. Long before desktop computers and multimedia software were available, multimedia has been available. Good educational films have been using multimedia for years, and different types of training simulators are nothing new. However, such films were hardly interactive. Students would passively sit and watch.

Interactive multimedia has been around at least since before World War II. The military used Link trainers to acquaint pilots with the flying characteristics of aircraft. When the student pilots correctly maneuvered the controls, feedback from the trainer would indicate a correct movement, and when they made mistakes, the errors were shown as well. These trainers helped pilots get the feel of flying airplanes, and although they pale in comparison to modern flight simulators, they were able to give pilots simulated interactive multimedia flying lessons.

So understanding interactive multimedia is neither mysterious nor new. What is new is the incredible power computer-enabled multimedia possesses and the ease with which individuals can create multimedia. This book explores four different types of interactive multimedia. Each type is unique in that it has a specific applied purpose, but all four have the common denominator of multimedia application. Included in this examination are the following:

- Microsoft PowerPoint — Presentation multimedia
- Macromedia Director — CD multimedia
- Macromedia Flash — Web multimedia
- JavaScript — Web multimedia

Each of the four has its own special use. The first chapter provides an overview of interactive multimedia and how to use it from a general perspective. The next twelve chapters each provide a functional introduction to the four different multimedia applications. The last chapter gives an overview of organizing an interactive multimedia project and what each application best accomplishes. In addition, all program listings are available at www.sandlight.com.

1 An Invitation to Interactive Multimedia

Interactive multimedia implies both an exchange between the viewer and the media as well as more than a single medium. Many types of interactive multimedia exist, and they generally fall into one of three general categories:

- Education
- Games
- eBusiness

Educational multimedia ranges from flight simulators whereby pilots learn instrument controls in the virtual reality of flight to an online quiz whereby students engage a question–answer sequence with an online exam. Multimedia in education is used in traditional classroom settings, business training, distance education, and self-learning activities.

Games, which are sometimes used in an educational process, emphasize a range of interactivity from arcade-style games, in which the interaction is fast and reflexive, to games involving the virtual search for a goal while being led through a maze of clues and markers. Many traditional board games such as chess have used interactive multimedia to enhance the game's ability to serve as a proxy for a human counterpart so that a player can practice playing against a computerized opponent. Many of the historical military simulation games have migrated to interactive multimedia technology to better simulate the simultaneous movement of armies. This provides both a realistic re-creation of historical events and history lessons at the same time.

Finally, eBusiness and e-commerce have adopted interactive multimedia. Virtual malls provide sales, service, and just about anything that can be bought or sold in a bricks-and-mortar environment. Three-dimensional moving objects simulate the actual objects in all but the tactile senses. The interactive exchanges in eBusiness involve sales, marketing, product and service searchers, as well as help desk and ordering services.

Multimedia and People

In everyday life people are bombarded by multimedia that includes everything from a tea kettle's whistle to the flickering images on their television sets. Usually people's thoughts of multimedia are in terms of video, film, sound, music, and slide shows—manufactured multimedia. However, a walk in the woods can be a multimedia event with the sounds of different birds and water rushing down a stream; the sights of the sunlight reflecting off of leaves, water, wood, snow, and earth; and the feel of the breeze. Hence, rather than being inherently manufactured, multimedia is a naturally occurring event.

Multimedia, whether manufactured or naturally occurring, is rich in information compared to a single medium. A single medium can produce only one type of information, and that information, while having *something* to tell, is limited. The story of the blind men and the elephant serves to illustrate a single-medium approach to information. Each of the blind men who felt a different part of the elephant came away with very different impression of what the elephant truly was. The man who felt only the tail believed the elephant to be a small furry-headed weasel. The man who felt the legs believed the elephant to be a very tall, skinny animal, and the man who felt only the trunk believed the elephant to be not unlike a boa constrictor. By the same token, a single medium limits what one understands to be the essence of a phenomenon or the understanding of a concept. A person with all of his or her faculties lives in a world of multimedia, and manufactured multimedia is simply an attempt to provide all of the different types of media exposure that people are used to in their everyday experience.

One especially important element of multimedia is the *interactive* component. As noted, some kind of exchange is expected in an interactive environment. If your neighbor says, "Hello," to you, you say, "Hello," to him. You exchange greetings. A question by one person expects an answer, or at least a response, from another person. Because you live in a world rich in both multimedia and interaction, good interactive multimedia stems from everyday experiences in life. These life experiences serve as a resource for creating and understanding interactive multimedia. All multimedia simulations are representations of some real-life events. Buying a book online simulates interaction with a clerk in a store, and a multimedia dissection of a frog simulates dissection of a real frog in a lab.

Technology of Multimedia

Multimedia technology today typically is tied to computers and digital sound and graphics. All of the multimedia discussed in this book—PowerPoint, Director, Flash, and JavaScript— are tools used to create multimedia, and all require a computer. Interactive multimedia is especially dependent on computers because they are the only machines that have both the speed and the flexibility to generate feedback to the user in a way that indicates the response is a *response to the user's action.* Before World War II, the Link trainer was a barrel-shaped mechanical device that simulated some of the variables in flight, and it served as a simple simulation for relatively simple airplanes in simple conditions. Compared with the fully visual, audio, and tactile experience airline pilots use today to simulate flying a Boeing 777 in all kinds of weather and mechanical conditions, the early mechanical efforts of the Link trainer seem to be primitive. As interactive multimedia, indeed they were.

The digital technology that drives multimedia keeps growing at exponential rates. Not long ago, the growth rate of computer technology was estimated to be doubling every eighteen months. That rate of growth is incredible, but the fact of the matter is that the *growth rate is much greater.* The speed of microprocessors once measured in kilohertz (thousands) are now measured in megahertz (millions) and gigahertz (billions). Likewise, consider that state-of-the-art home computer disks held 145K in 1980. By 2000, a CD-ROM in a home computer with a storage capacity of 600Mb contained over 4 million times as much storage capacity. Had storage capacity in a disk *doubled every year* between 1980 and 2000, the CD-ROM would have had only about 76Mb in 2000. The greater the capacity of computers means that more detailed multimedia can be developed and presented, and interactive multimedia becomes more realistic or more fantastic, with the option up to the developer.

The Art of Multimedia

Creating multimedia should not be left to technologists. To create a great piece of multimedia requires artists, designers, programmers, project managers, coordination, cooperation, good social and behavioral science, and excellent content. The carpenter who builds a piano is not expected to know how to play it, nor is the pianist expected to know how to build a piano. By the same token, the concept of *interaction* belongs to the art of charm, etiquette, empathy, and wit, while the science of interaction belongs to sociologists and social psychologists. Knowing how to work with the technology of interactive multimedia is *only the first step* in creating good multimedia.

Hillman Curtis (2000) wrote of *motion design*—design work that requires an understanding of what to do with motion in multimedia. Static graphics have been with humans since the time of prehistory when evidence of civilization could be found only in drawings on cave walls. Later, more portable art was available through the use of paper, papyrus, and canvas. However, the art and graphics were essentially static.

The evolution of art was transformed dramatically with cinema and later video graphics. Dynamic motions that previously had to be frozen in static art could be animated through filming actions. Animators took static art and created fantastic scenes depicting human qualities in animals and other nonhuman elements—singing trees and talking rocks to take two examples. Later, when sound was added to film, a true multimedia evolved. By using special effects, editing, and a quickly emerging art form with its own bag of tricks, film could tell a whole story in a transportable format.

The problem with film multimedia, both live and animated, and later multimedia in video was that the expense was prohibitive for all but a few well-organized and well-funded companies. However, with the advent of the personal computer and the Internet, the hardware and software for creating sophisticated multimedia are well within the reach of the average consumer. Furthermore, creating good multimedia no longer requires either sophisticated computer skills or a design background. Rather, the requirements are an understanding of what the software can do and how to use it. Programs such as PowerPoint make the creation of a very sophisticated live multimedia presentation so simple that even the most computer-phobic, artistically challenged person can put together a presentation with a decent design with very little knowledge of either design or computers. The software has built-in features that help the user with design by providing ready-made templates with appropriate color combinations, object balance, and font selection. Using icons and point-and-click operations, the computer knowledge is limited to turning on the computer and following the prompts to complete the design.

However, the more one learns about design and using the many options the technology has to offer, the more that can be done with all of the software discussed in this book. The art not only involves the art of graphics and design, it also includes the art of using technology. Writing code may not seem like an art, but just as one needs to have technical abilities to create a painting, one needs some coding skills to carry out what resides in the developer's imagination. The *art of writing a program* has all of the same requisites as required for creating a sculpture or painting. JavaScript is purely a coding language that you can embed in HTML, Lingo is Director's language, and ActionScript is the underlying language of Flash. You don't have to know very much of any of these languages, but learning even a little of each can help you create the kind of multimedia first conceived in pure imagination.

Multimedia and Learning

The past decade has seen a great increase in the use of computer-assisted learning in all fields. Traditional and nontraditional students alike have been shown to benefit from computer-assisted learning using multimedia. One significant factor contributing to the effectiveness of multimedia-based learning and instruction involves the interactivity that is potentially available through advanced multimedia software such as PowerPoint, Director, Flash, and JavaScript-based applications. Computer-based animated and interactive experiences have been found to be far more effective in promoting learning, compared with the relatively static or noninteractive experiences provided by textbooks or videotapes (cf. Meyer et al., 1991). In addition, the incorporation of computers into training programs of many varieties has had the added benefit of improving computer literacy itself among learners (e.g., Hall, Hall, & Kasperek, 1995).

Past research has demonstrated that computer-assisted instruction has been evaluated positively by students and has in some instances led to higher levels of learning than a parallel curriculum incorporating only lecture formats. For example, evaluations of computer-assisted instruction have found that for quantitative topics, adding a computer-based element to a traditional in-class lecture format course improves attitudes toward using computers for statistics, and may have indirectly increased learning in the course (Varnhagen & Zumbo, 1990). Similar programs designed for training mathematics over the Web have also shown to be evaluated positively by students (Vanhagen, Drake, & Finley, 1997).

Research also suggests that using computer-based training, as opposed to traditional lecturing techniques, may be especially beneficial for participants who are low scorers initially (Lee, Gillian, & Harrison, 1996). Technology available today allows for the development of a curriculum that will enhance the learning of students with varied backgrounds and different learning styles (e.g., Brown & Campione, 1986; King, 1993, 1994; Thomas & Rohwer, 1986; Wittrock, 1990). The use of multimedia computer-based instruction may be beneficial for students with limited language proficiency, in that content can be delivered at a consistently appropriate reading level. In addition, multimedia learning can provide multisensory communication, so that students are not forced to rely on a single form of delivery (e.g., Soska, 1994).

Providing experience with computers may also increase long-term success in science for women. This outcome is expected because lack of computer experience has been found to be associated with female attrition in computer-related college majors (e.g., Bunderson & Christensen, 1995), and increased exposure time with computers is associated with success for younger women (e.g., D'Amico, Baron, & Sissons, 1995). Integrating computer technology into content areas, and ensuring that the technology is gender neutral, may also help increase women's long-term success in computer-related fields (e.g., Valenza, 1997).

Related research suggests that minority students derive the same benefits. Increasing the use of virtual interaction (e.g., email and online discussion) increases active learning and reduces gender- and minority-related problems associated with classroom learning, such as dominance issues and social barriers that may be present for underrepresented groups (cf. Seagren & Watwood, 1997).

Overall, strong evidence exists that multimedia applications increase learning across populations, across subject areas, and with the advent of broadband online services, across the entire world. The future of learning lies in multimedia applications, such as the ones discussed in this book.

REFERENCES

Brown, A. L., & Campione, J. C. (1986). Psychological theory and the study of learning disabilities. *American Psychologist, 41,* 1059–1068.

Bunderson, E. D., & Christensen, M. E. (1995). An analysis of retention problems for female students in university computer science programs. *Journal of Research on Computing in Education, 28,* 1–18.

Curtis, Hillman (2000). *Flash Web Design: The Art of Motion Graphics.* Indianapolis: New Riders.

D'Amico, M., Baron, L. J., & Sissons, M. E. (1995). Gender differences in attributions about microcomputer learning in elementary school. *Sex Roles, 33(5–6),* 353–385.

Hall, C. W., Hall, T. L., & Kasperek, J. G. (1995). Psychology of computer use: XXXIII. Interactive instruction with college-level science courses. *Psychological Reports, 76(3, Pt. 1),* 963–970.

King, A. (1993). Making the transition from "sage on the stage" to "guide on the side." *College Teaching, 41,* 30–35.

King, A. (1994). Guiding knowledge construction in the classroom: Effects of teaching how to question and how to explain. *American Educational Research Journal, 31,* 338–368.

Lee, A. Y., Gillan, D. J., & Harrison, C. L. (1996). Assessing the effectiveness of a multimedia-based lab for upper-division psychology majors. *Behavior Research Methods, Instruments & Computers, 28,* 295–299.

Meyer, G. E., Rocheleau, D. J., McMullen, J., & Ritter, B. E. (1991). The use of Macintosh 24-bit color and animation programs in undergraduate research and visual perception courses. *Behavior Research Methods, Instruments and Computers, 23,* 166–182.

Seagren, A., & Watwood, B. (1997). The virtual classroom: What works? In *Walking the Tightrope: The Balance between Innovation and Leadership.* Proceedings of the Annual International Conference of the Chair Academy (6th, Reno, NV, February 12–15, 1997).

Soska, M. (1994). An introduction to educational technology. *Directions in Language and Education, 1,* 1–10.

Thomas, J. W., & Rohwer, W. D. (1986). Academic studying: The role of learning strategies. *Educational Psychologist, 21,* 19–41.

Valenza, J. K. (1997). Girls + technology = turnoff? *Technology Connection, 3(10),* 20–21.

Varnhagen, C. K., Drake, S. M., & Finley, G. (1997). Teaching statistics with the Internet. *Teaching of Psychology, 24,* 275–278.

Varnhagen, C. K., & Zumbo, B. D. (1990). CAI as an adjunct to teaching introductory statistics: Affect mediates learning. *Journal of Educational Computing Research, 6,* 29–40.

Wittrock, M. C. (1990). Generative processes of comprehension. *Educational Psychologist, 24,* 345–376.

2 Introducing Presentation Multimedia

What Is Presentation Software?

Presentation software was originally designed for the creation of charts, tables, and graphs for use as aids in presentations and includes such packages as Microsoft PowerPoint, Corel Presentations, Harvard Graphics, Lotus Freelance, and many others. Presentation software is the easiest and least technical method for creating a multimedia product. It requires no programming knowledge or experience because the package creates the actual code for you. Although there are abundant choices in the selection of a presentation software package, this and the next two chapters deal specifically with Microsoft PowerPoint. This package was selected more because it is the most popular than because of any specific feature set or functionality. Most of the other packages, with few exceptions, share the same features as PowerPoint.

What Is a Presentation?

A presentation is quite simply the transmission of some stimulus or message from one individual or group of individuals (the presenter) to another individual or group of individuals (the audience). Presentations are used in order to inform, educate, or persuade the audience.

A presentation can be given to an audience of one or an audience of thousands. Salespeople make one-on-one presentations all the time. Chiefs of state give presentations that are frequently broadcast to millions, if not billions. People have been giving presentations for centuries. Presentations are common in education, government, research, and all phases of business. What you are reading now is actually a written presentation.

The use of visual aids has long been considered to add to the effectiveness of presentations. The use of charts, tables, pictures, and graphs can be an extremely effective way to get your point across. Although every picture may not be worth a thousand words, the use of visual aids allows the presenter to get additional meaning across in a short period of time. It allows the presenter to direct the attention of the audience to a specific point. It strengthens and reinforces the presenter's arguments by appealing to the visual senses in addition to the auditory senses. Of course, the presenter engages the auditory sense mainly by the use of his or her voice. Visual aids allow a presenter to exploit the human ability to process multiple forms of input simultaneously.

The message of a presentation can really be transmitted through information directed at any of the five human senses. Because individual audience members can have different information-processing styles, information directed at different senses will tend to have varying effects on audience members. Some people are more visual than verbal and vice versa. Utilizing multiple senses in a presentation is one way to accommodate different information-processing styles and reach more of the audience.

In fact, presentations derive some of their effectiveness from exploiting multiple types of human memory. A presentation is effective partially because it becomes an episode or event about the topic that you remember. This is stored in what is referred to as your episodic memory. This is distinct from your semantic memory, or your memory for meanings. Ideally, the two forms of memory will reinforce each other, making the message more memorable.

Some speakers are very dynamic when they give presentations, and of course some are not. Visual and audio assistance can make an average presenter a fairly good one, and even the best speakers are more dynamic when they have visual and audio assistance to bring their points across. You can think of presentation effectiveness as lying on a continuum from least effective to most effective. The following list shows presentation methods ranked from least effective to most effective.

1. Audio only—fixed speed
2. Multimedia only—fixed speed
3. Written only—self-paced
4. Multimedia only—self-paced
5. Live speaker—no assists, no interaction
6. Live speaker—black-and-white visuals, no interaction
7. Live speaker—color visuals, no interaction
8. Multimedia only—self-paced and interactive
9. Live speaker—black-and-white visuals, interactive
10. Live speaker—color visuals, interactive
11. Live speaker—color visuals with motion, interactive

Notice that a live speaker in general outperforms other methods of delivery, but an interactive delivery method always outperforms a noninteractive method. Of course these rankings assume that everything is done pretty well. A poorly executed presentation will not be effective regardless of how it is delivered.

Presentations can be local (audience present) or remote (audience at some other location). They can also be live or recorded. Because methods for transmitting or recording taste, smell, or touch data have not been determined, presentations requiring the engagement of those senses are required to be both local and live. Although there are some limited methods for engaging those senses with large audiences, their use tends to be restricted to local, live presentations with small audiences. Because our culture seems to place the greatest importance on information received through our auditory and visual senses, most presentations limit themselves to the engagement of those senses.

The Original Purpose of Presentation Software

Like most major categories of software, presentation software has evolved considerably over time. Presentation software began to become popular in the mid-1980s. This early presentation software appeared well before the popularity of portable computer projecting devices. It really even appeared prior to the widespread acceptance of portable computers. The primary purpose for presentation software at that time was to assist in the preparation of charts and graphs. The ability to store charts and graphs in an electronic form added convenience appeal to these products.

The primary output modes for presentation software were on a computer monitor and either opaque or transparent printed hard copy. Output could also be obtained in the form of 35 mm slides either by having slide printing equipment or by sending your presentation software files to a slide preparation service.

The most popular portable presentation devices of the time were the overhead projector and the 35 mm slide projector. Formal presentations were accomplished by physically assembling a number of slides, either acetate overhead transparencies or 35 mm slides, into the order required for the particular presentation. The software was intended primarily to assist in the development of these slides.

Designers of the software really used the 35 mm slide show as their development metaphor. Even early versions of most presentation packages allowed the user to display the slides in a slide show format. This was effective only for presentations at which you could get the audience to the computer, because it was often impractical to get the computer to the audience.

For small audiences hard-copy printout of the slides was a viable alternative. At the time, color printing technologies were somewhat limited in terms of both market acceptance and economic feasibility, so the hard copy seldom looked like the picture on the computer screen.

No consideration was given to audio or multimedia capabilities in presentation software. Those capabilities were beyond the ability of the personal computers of the day.

How That Purpose Has Changed

With the growing capabilities of personal computers, presentation software capabilities have expanded considerably. Four technological developments were key in the development of presentation software. Those developments included the increased popularity of computer projection devices, the increased popularity of portable computers, the addition of multimedia capabilities to personal computers, and the growth in the popularity of the Internet.

Because 35 mm slides or color overheads are fairly expensive solutions for showing color, the popularity of computer projection equipment has grown tremendously recently. With the increased popularity of computer projectors of various types, it was no longer necessary for presenters to utilize the presentation software as merely a slide preparation device. This made the slide show capabilities of the software even more important. It was no longer necessary for the presenter to prepare acetate transparencies or slides for use on an overhead projector or 35 mm projector. Portable computers made it quite simple to take considerable presentation power with you to the audience.

The portable computer and computer projection capability also allow the presenter to utilize different views of the presentation during the presentation. For example, you could show your slides to the audience through the projector and have your notes and outline in front of you on your portable computer screen.

With the addition of multimedia capabilities to personal computers came a number of developments in presentation software packages. The ability to add sound or music to slides was a huge development. With this ability to include sound, a speaker no longer had to be actually present to deliver a presentation. Most packages now include narration capabilities so that you can time the narration in a slide show to parallel the showing of specific slides. This allows for the creation of presentations that you can distribute and allow to be freely browsed by others. You can also create what is referred to as a kiosk show. A kiosk show is a presentation that runs by itself and loops endlessly. This is popular for product demonstrations and trade shows.

With the introduction of multimedia capabilities to personal computers also came a host of multimedia authoring packages such as Authorware or Director. Over the years, presentation packages have attempted to incorporate some of the functionality of these types of authoring packages. They have met with some success, although a more purely "multimedia" product can also be produced with those types of packages.

Like most procedures that were once carried out manually and are now more automated, presentation software has now greatly impacted the quality of presentations. Because presenters have such better tools than they once had, the quality of presentations has increased substantially over the past two decades.

Moving Presentations to the Web

With the growing popularity of the Internet, several changes have occurred with respect to presentation software. First, all of the major packages have incorporated the ability to create web presentations. Second, all of the major presentation packages allow for web collaboration. That is, you can go live with your coworkers on the Web to work on preparing your presentation.

Probably the biggest impact that the Web has had on presentation packages is that designers have had to incorporate some of the functionality of the Web into the presentation package itself. This is most noticeable in the inclusion of navigation elements into the presentation, which allows for some interactivity to be incorporated into a presentation. You can now include action buttons and hyperlinks within any part of your presentation. This enables you to navigate to a specific slide or a specific URL.

Elements of a Presentation

Static Elements: Titles and Text

Probably the most common type of visuals to see a presenter use today are simply the projected image of words onto a screen. In other words, title charts and text charts are the most popular. They are the most popular because literally every presentation uses them. Regardless of whatever other types of visuals and multimedia elements are utilized, a presentation will still usually have to have words. Slides are there to support what you are doing with the other elements of your presentation. They are not there to be supplementary. When information is cognitively consistent, it is much easier for the audience to process the information presented. Decide on the points you want to make in your presentation and use a slide for each point. If it is a live presentation, do not let the slide make the point for you. You will need to make the point by using the slide.

Every presentation should begin with a title slide. The title slide should, of course, indicate the title of the presentation and the name of the presenter. Choose a title for your presentation that is as short and as descriptive as possible for what it is you will be presenting. In a live presentation, this would be when the speaker would also describe the purpose of the presentation. If it is a recorded or automated presentation, a slide with a purpose statement could follow. When convenient, the date of the presentation should also be indicated on the title slide. If you plan on utilizing the same presentation many times, leave the date off. If you are using PowerPoint to project your live presentation, the date will be automatically updated if you created your slides with a template with the date on it.

Following this introduction and description of purpose should be a slide with a description of the structure of the presentation. This allows the audience to believe that you will be accomplishing the purpose and lets them know what to expect.

Like all elements of a presentation, text charts should be kept as simple as possible. Whenever possible, a text chart should contain a maximum of twenty-five words. Remember that the use of visuals is effective because it directs the attention of the audience. If your text charts have too many words, you are going to have to fight your own charts for the attention of the audience. They will be reading and not listening. Although fewer words will still attract the attention of the audience, they will not attract their attention for long.

Text charts are made up of either a bullet list or a short text message. Bullet lists are lists of items the speaker is planning to address and are almost always used in live presentations. Short text messages are appropriate in only two circumstances. The first circumstance is when it is important that the audience have the message verbatim. This is rarely important except in cases of specific definitions or mission statements of organizations. The other circumstance occurs when the presentation is automated and it contains voice-over narration. If the message is complex, and there are no other visuals, it can be helpful if you display the words used in the narration while the narration is occurring. For most messages, a bullet list will be more appropriate.

Because a text chart should have few words, those words can and should be large. If you are using projection equipment, a minimum font size of 18 points is recommended. Use larger type for titles and other important elements. Avoid mixing many styles and sizes of fonts. Try to be as consistent as possible with your text elements from slide to slide in order to give the overall presentation a consistent look.

Static Elements: Tables, Charts, and Graphs

Tables, charts, and graphs are effective means of getting across a considerable amount of information in a short period of time. They can be inserted by selecting the Insert command on the menu and then selecting either charts (for charts or graphs) or tables.

Tables are an excellent way to organize information in order to make it more meaningful. Keep in mind that you do not want to overwhelm your audience visually or fight your own slides for audience attention. Keep in mind the twenty-five-word maximum rule of thumb for any particular slide and apply it to tables as well. If the table contains numbers, consider each number (not each digit) as a word. If the table is too complex to present on one slide, split it into two or three. If you must present a more complex table, give the audience extra time to process the information both before and after you make your point about it in your presentation. Even the most complex table is there to make one or possibly two points.

PowerPoint refers to all graphs and charts as charts. Although there are seven different graph types and seven different chart types available with PowerPoint, all are variations on three simple visual devices. All seven of the graph types are variations on a simple line graph. The following list summarizes the different types of graphs available.

1. Line graph—The standard two-dimensional plotting device from mathematics
2. Surface graph—Same as a line graph with a third dimension
3. Scatter plots—Simply points, not connected with lines
4. Bubble plots—A scatter plot with the size of the points having significance
5. Stock chart—Simply a line graph that displays ranges instead of points
6. Radar graph—Same as a line graph except that the *x*-axis circles around the *y*-axis
7. Area graph—Simply a line graph with the area under the line filled in

The seven different chart types available in PowerPoint are all variations on either a bar chart or a pie chart. Five of the chart types are different display formats for bar charts. The column chart is simply a vertical bar chart. Cylinder charts, cone charts, and pyramid charts are simply bar charts with different-shaped bars. All of the bar chart types as well as the graph types are useful for displaying relationships between one variable and another. A very common relationship to show with a variable is time. That is, all of these types of charts are useful in showing the relationship of a variable with time. Radar charts are useful for showing the relationship of a variable with a particular time cycle, such as a twenty-four-hour period. For example, plotting average temperature by time of day would be a natural to display on a radar chart, as shown in Figure 2.1. As you complete the cycle by going around the *y*-axis instead of perpendicular to it, you are back at the beginning of the cycle.

Pie charts and doughnut charts are identical except that the doughnut has a hole in the middle. Doughnut charts are excellent for displaying process-type cycles such as those used

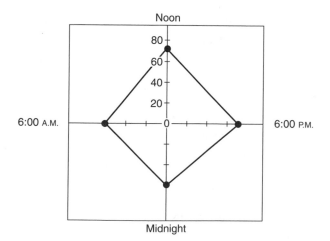

FIGURE 2.1 A Radar Chart of Temperature by Time of Day.

in industrial production. Each section of the doughnut chart can include a step in the cycle that returns you back to the beginning of the cycle.

Each of these fourteen different graphs and charts includes a number of different layout options. Overall, with the layout options, PowerPoint allows for seventy-three total different graph or chart layouts. If you allow for the other appearance and formatting options available, the variations are virtually infinite.

Multimedia Elements: Pictures

PowerPoint can import pictures from a variety of file formats including JPEG, GIF, TIF, CGM, and other bitmap graphics, as well as pictures created in a variety of drawing programs using vector graphics. PowerPoint does have some limited ability to manipulate pictures that have been imported. You can alter brightness and contrast, crop and resize the picture, and set any picture color as transparent. For some file formats you can also recolor the picture. In general, drawing and picture programs are far more powerful than presentation software in terms of the ability to manipulate pictures, so it is best to have the picture looking the way you want it to look before importing it into the presentation software.

PowerPoint allows for multiple layers or "stacking" of pictures, charts, or any graphic object you would like to include in a slide. If you would like to move an object in the stack of graphics on any particular slide, select that object and right click your mouse. Then select Order and move the object to the desired location in the stack.

Multimedia Elements: Sounds

You can include three types of sounds in a PowerPoint slide show: sound effects, music, or narration. PowerPoint comes with sound effects in its clip art gallery, or you can use any of the sounds provided with your operating system. If a particular sound file type is not compatible with PowerPoint, you can select it to be played by the media player that comes as part of your operating system. Within PowerPoint, there are two ways of playing music. You can either have a particular slide trigger an audio CD track in your computer's CD player, or play music as a media clip through your operating system's media player. When playing a music clip, you have the option of either starting it automatically when the slide it is embedded in is shown, or requiring a mouse click on its icon. You have the further option of either letting it continue to play after the slide has been shown or cutting it off with the next slide.

Background music is rarely utilized in live presentations, so the use of short media clips of music is much more common. Background music could be more suitable for a kiosk-type show.

If you are giving a live presentation that is manually timed, there is no way to time music to play in a synchronized way throughout the presentation. Having a presentation that structured would preclude the speaker from engaging in any interaction with the audience. If you are giving a live presentation and would like music running in the background that is not synchronized to the presentation, it is better simply to play that music using some other application while you run your slide show. This is where more multimedia-oriented packages such as Director or Flash have clearly superior capabilities.

You can record voice-over-type narration for your entire presentation using PowerPoint directly. Once your slides are prepared, click on the Slide Show menu item and then select Record Narration. Then simply go through your slides and narrate. You will, of course, need a sound card and a microphone for this. If you would like to put sounds or comments on a single slide, go to the Insert menu and click Record Sound.

In PowerPoint, narration takes precedence over any other sounds present in the slide show. So if you are playing narration, no other sounds will play. If you want other sounds to play during the narration, you must record them as background noise while you are recording the narration. If you would like music in the background for an automated slide show that includes narration, you must play the music in the background while you are recording the narration.

Multimedia Elements: Animation

There are basically three ways to create animated effects in PowerPoint. You can animate entire slides through the use of transition effects, you can animate any or all of the objects in a slide with similar transition effects, and you can add animated objects through the insertion of media clips.

In order to include transition effects, click on the Slide Show menu tab and then select Slide Transitions. PowerPoint offers a number of different wipes or fly ins for slides. In all there are forty-one different transition effects that you might use for the slide transitions. When selecting a transition, you can choose to apply it to all slides in the slide show or have separate transitions for each individual slide.

You can also add animation effects to any of the objects in a slide. An object could be text, a table, a chart, a picture, or a media clip. There are thirteen preset effects and eighteen custom effects that you can apply. You can apply the same effects to each object or have different animation for each effect. Unlike strictly multimedia packages such as Flash or Director, PowerPoint does not allow for layering of animation effects. That is, PowerPoint will apply animation to only one object at a time. It does allow you to select the ordering of the objects for their animation, and you can group the items together and create a single animation effect for what would then be a single object.

The third approach to creating animation effects in your presentation is to include media clips as objects in your slides. This is covered in the next section on video.

Multimedia Elements: Video

PowerPoint can include most kinds of media clips that you can play on your computer. It does not support Real Player files. The procedure for inserting media clips is identical to inserting sound clips. Click on Insert and then select Movies and Sounds. You have the option to play the video automatically as the slide is presented, or you can require a mouse click to activate the clip.

Interactivity with PowerPoint

With the addition of weblike enhancements to presentation software, the potential for interactivity has increased tremendously. PowerPoint is capable of a number of levels of interactivity.

First is a level of interactivity during a live presentation. There are a couple of features in PowerPoint that allow for the presenter to interact more effectively with the software than ever before. One of the major criticisms of using presentation software during a live presentation was the inability to remove all images from the screen during a presentation. For instance, take the case of a speaker addressing an audience and using an overhead projector. When the speaker is done with a slide, but is not ready to move on to the next slide, it is generally good presentation practice to remove the slide from the projector so as not to distract the audience. The inability to do this was always considered one of the key drawbacks of the 35 mm slide projector. With presentation software, the presenter could follow one of two options in the past. He or she could either toggle the computer display off so no image would be sent to the projector or include blank slides in between each actual slide. The latter tends to be awkward because you have to show a blank slide in between every slide whether you need it or not. With action buttons, the speaker now can place a blank slide at the end of the presentation with an action button to return to the previous slide. Then an action button can be placed on each slide in the presentation to go to the last (blank) slide in the presentation. This is a much neater approach to removing images from the screen.

The ability to show multiple displays during a presentation also allows for greater activity with the presenter. Utilizing this feature, the audience could view the slide show, while the speaker can take notes about questions or comments during the presentation.

PowerPoint can virtually create well-featured interactive multimedia deliverables such as training or education software, complete with exercises and responses for students, but it is somewhat awkward. In order to accomplish this, a number of presentations would have to be created, linked to each other with action buttons. When students are asked questions, the presentation would have to end. Answer buttons would be action links to separate feedback presentations for correct and incorrect responses. The feedback presentations would have to then again link back to a second main presentation for the continuation of the lesson. This is certainly awkward, and it only allows for true-or-false or multiple-choice types of interactivity. PowerPoint does not allow for the wide range of interactivity available with java-type applets discussed in later sections of this book.

Structure of a Presentation: The Inherent Linearity of Presentations

Presentations are essentially linear phenomena. That is, they begin at the beginning and move step by step through to a conclusion. They are highly structured and must follow this linear path. Because presentations are designed with objectives in mind, they need to stay focused on those objectives and progress through the logical steps to their conclusions. In this way, creating presentations for the Internet would have to be very different than creating presentations that can be placed on the Internet. It is a subtle but important distinction.

The Internet is by its nature a tree-structured phenomenon. It is best suited to exploration, with users being able to move in whatever direction they see fit. This is the Internet's key interactive feature and goes a long way in describing why it is so attractive to so many. Although presentations do have some navigation capabilities, they are fairly limited compared to those of other applications.

What Presentation Software Is Best Suited For

Presentation software is best suited for offering an extremely powerful tool to presenters in situations in which they are giving live presentations. It offers presenters a wide array of tools for providing outstanding service to their audiences. It can create great slides with a broad range of terrific animation and multimedia effects, notes to use as handouts, and the ability to post the presentation on the Internet. It can be used as a vehicle to show media of virtually any type. Presentation software can also be utilized to create fairly simple interactive multimedia products and excellent fully automated noninteractive multimedia products. For someone without highly developed technical skills who would like to develop simple multimedia applications, it is ideal.

What Presentation Software Is Not Meant to Do

Presentation software is not the answer to the typical web developer's prayers. It has limited interactivity and navigation characteristics. It has less flexibility than other multimedia platforms with regard to issues such as sound and animation. It tends to be relatively slow when used as a web platform. It seems its web capabilities are more geared to being a convenience for presenters than they are a true web development tool.

It also has some limitations with respect to live presentations. With power there is always temptation. With the power of today's presentation software packages comes the temptation to put the chart before the horse so to speak. The software should not be the goal, but it should serve some other goal. That goal, of course, is to get the point across. Presenters have to resist the urge to obscure their point by using vast amounts of video clips and sound clips and animation and overly complicated slides. It is great to have that power available, but the presenter must use sound judgment to decide when it will help get the point across and when it will not. After all, there has to be time left for the presentation.

3 Using Presentation Multimedia

Using presentation packages to produce multimedia is by far the easiest alternative, especially if you have limited technical skills but have some familiarity with the basic functionality of most other Windows and Apple-based software. The interface is very intuitive, and most functions work the same as in other popular software packages. Inserting and deleting elements, moving and sizing, and editing all work the same as in literally hundreds of other software packages. This makes preparing presentations quick, fun, and easy. In fact, the biggest problem is more likely that you will find it too easy. It will be hard to resist the temptation to add too much dazzle, leaving your audience confused and irritated, if not overstimulated.

PowerPoint Basics: Exploring the Interface

When you first start PowerPoint 2000, you will be prompted by a dialogue box that asks you if you want to create a new presentation or to open an existing presentation. This is not really the standard PowerPoint interface. This dialogue box can be disabled, leaving you with the file commands common to most windows applications. If you have already disabled this dialogue box on your version, click on File and select New. You will then be prompted with a dialogue box that gives you the choice of creating a new blank presentation or using the Auto Content Wizard. This is within the General tab on the dialogue box. There are also two other tabs for design templates and presentations. In order to get the interface pictured in Figure 3.1, click the Design Templates tab and double-click Dad's Tie. You will then be presented with a New Slide dialogue box that allows you to choose from 24 AutoLayouts. The top left AutoLayout is a title slide. Double-click on that and you will have Figure 3.1 on your screen.

Notice that the window is now divided into three separate panes in your work area. The largest pane on the right is the *slide pane*. It gives you a view of what your slide currently looks like. The large pane on the left is the *outline pane*. This pane shows the text elements of your entire presentation without graphics. The outline pane allows you to rearrange your slide show simply by dragging and dropping slides or even bullet points within slides. Notice that right now there is only one slide in the pane with no text elements. This is because nothing has been added to the presentation yet. The lower right side of the

FIGURE 3.1   The PowerPoint 2000 Interface.

screen is the *notes pane.* Here you can add notes to your slides that will not be visible during the slide show.

This is what is called the Normal View in PowerPoint 2000. On the bottom left of the outline pane are view buttons that allow you to change views.

There are five choices on the View menu. The first is the Normal View, which gives you what is shown in Figure 3.1. The Outline View greatly expands the area of the screen occupied by the outline pane, but keeps all three panes visible. The Slide View eliminates the notes area and shrinks the outline pane considerably. The Slide Sorter View shows thumbnails of all of your slides as they currently appear. This view allows you to rearrange your presentation by dragging and dropping individual slides. The Slide Show View simply launches your presentation full screen, which is the way you would want to present it to the audience.

PowerPoint in general works like many other windows applications with a main menu bar with a toolbar underneath at the top of the work area. The main menu bar does change depending on what you are doing at the moment. For most of the time it stays the same. The sole exception is that when you click on a chart in PowerPoint, the menu bar changes to a charting menu bar. Clicking on any portion of the screen outside the chart returns the main menu bar.

Like most windows applications, the menu bar and toolbar can be customized to fit the needs of a particular user. There are a total of twelve different toolbar components that you can customize into your toolbar or access through the View menu on the main menu bar. These include the following:

- Standard
- Formatting
- Clipboard
- Control
- Drawing
- Outlining
- Picture
- Reviewing
- Tables and Borders
- Visual Basic
- Web
- Word Art

The standard toolbar arrangement also includes a Drawing toolbar on the lower left-hand portion of the screen. This is a very standard, if not limited, drawing tool, but also includes the ability to insert "word art" into any PowerPoint slide. Word art is simply colored text with special effects such as sweeps or arcs applied to it. If you click on the Add Wordart button on the drawing toolbar, you will be presented with the thirty different styles of word art that PowerPoint offers. The Word Art toolbar, available from the View menu on the main menu bar, allows manipulation of word art characteristics such as letter spacing and rotation. There is also an Autoshapes button on the Drawing toolbar that allows the addition of flowchart symbols, stars, and banners, and an assortment of other standard and nonstandard drawing elements to your PowerPoint slides.

Features Not Common to Most Windows Applications

In addition to the three window work spaces described previously, there are two other note-worthy features of PowerPoint that are not common to most other windows applications.

Most notably is the Slide Show item on the menu bar. This menu selection controls all aspects of how your computer displays your presentation. It controls all of the elements of navigation for a presentation. It controls slide transition and animation effects. It controls the recording and playback of narration and even controls web broadcasting of your presentation. This item also offers an alternative way to launch the Slide Show view with the command View Show, which allows you to launch the presentation full screen. This is an alternative method to simply selecting the Slide Show view on the View buttons located at the bottom of the outline window on the left side of the work area.

PowerPoint also has a number of printing options that are not available to other windows applications through the Print What? option on the Print command. In addition to printing full-page slides of your presentation, you can select options to print handouts, notes, or the Outline View of your slides. Handouts are smaller copies of your slides with between two and six slides per page. Selecting to print notes, prints half-page slides of your presentation with your notes entries below. Printing an outline prints the information in the outline pane on the left side of your screen. It is all of the text in your presentation with none of the graphics.

The Structure of a Slide Show

Slide shows are almost always linear events. They generally have a beginning, a middle, and an end, and follow each step in between in order. This is not so much a convention forced on humans by the software, but a convention forced on humans by their general time consciousness. If you want to make sure all of your points are covered in the time you have to cover them, you pretty much have to stay linear. After all, it is the shortest distance between two points. In a presentation those points are where the audience is at the beginning of the presentation and where you want them to be when you are finished.

In general, the beginning is about accomplishment. The beginning of a presentation should discuss what you hope to accomplish. This starts with the title slide. The purpose of the title is to let the audience know what the presentation is about. That way, the audience gets to decide if they really want to pay attention to your presentation, or if they are even in the right room. The title should be descriptive of what it is you are talking about. You should avoid using catchy or cute phrases in your title just for the sake of using catchy or cute phrases. They can have the effect of confusing or upsetting audience members or potential audience members. When you have confused or upset audience members, you are running the risk of ruining the entire presentation.

Immediately after the title, you should have a slide that discusses what it is you hope to accomplish with your presentation. This is typically in the form of an objectives slide. This tells the audience exactly what it is you hope they will get out of your presentation. Of course, some of the audience may leave at this time. If they do, it is because they do not want what you have to offer them, and that is all right for them, but good for you as the presenter. Nothing makes a presentation more fun to give than an interested and engaged audience. Telling them what they are getting up front ensures that you will have such an audience. If you let your objectives unfold during your presentation, there is a good chance your audience will think you do not know what you are talking about, because they will not know what you are talking about.

The middle of your presentation is where you accomplish your objectives. You do the things you said you would do at the beginning. A good way to test whether a particular slide or part of your presentation is appropriate is to test it against your objectives. Ask yourself, "Which objective does this accomplish or help accomplish?" If you cannot figure out which objective the point ties back to, leave it out of your presentation.

At the end of your presentation, it is a good idea to summarize. Your summary should sound a lot like your objectives. This lets you explain to your audience that you have accomplished what you told them you would accomplish. This allows the audience to believe that you are a person of your word, that you did exactly what you said you would do. This tends to create a highly satisfied audience—an audience that has every confidence in what you just told them.

Setting up your slides in PowerPoint works exactly like the structure of a presentation in general. Start out by deciding what it is you want to talk about. In many cases this will not be your choice. This will dictate what needs to be on your title slide. Next, generate a list of specific objectives you would like to accomplish during the presentation. This will dictate what needs to be on your objectives slide. As a general rule, you will have to have at least one slide for every objective. You will also need a slide for your summary or conclusion. Once you have these elements in place, you are ready to start generating slides for your live presentation.

Live versus Automated Presentations

Automated presentations can have different structures depending on the nature of the automated presentation. The key to an automated presentation is how much control you want to allow the audience. In a kiosk show, the audience will not and should not have much control. These are typically endless loops of presentation that may or may not have narration. These need to follow the basic structure of a live presentation unless they are very short. These are typically used at trade shows and conventions that draw a large number of audience members to potentially see and hear it. At such shows, individuals typically move around an exhibit hall from booth to booth to view offerings from different vendors. Presentations used at these shows are really advertisements for your product or service and are designed to impact the decisions of potential customers. If you allow the audience control over such a presentation, someone drifting around the conference exhibit hall may not leave the presentation at a point where the next potential customer would benefit most from it. The typical objective of a kiosk-type presentation is promotional, and you are striving for exposure to the message. Keeping it running in an automated fashion will accomplish the maximum exposure for the most potential audience members.

Once the audience is given control of a presentation, the structure of the presentation can change. Here the audience members can look as long as they want, at whatever part of the presentation they want. This is really the introduction of interactivity into the presentation and is appropriate only for small audiences, or virtually small audiences, because in the absence of group consensus, the control of one audience member becomes the enslavement of the others. Virtually small audiences are what are made possible on the Internet. You might reach a large number of people, but as far as they are concerned you are reaching them one at a time. In fact, audience-controlled presentations are characteristic of the Internet, as well as of most training and educational software packages.

When you have audience-controlled software, the structure of the presentation will be the same at the core of the presentation, but you may want to allow for several branches off from the core. You still need to have a title and objectives up front in the presentation. In other words, the way in will be the same for all browsers. Once the browser is into the body of the presentation, the individual may want to learn more about an issue, so you may want to allow for more detail on any subject or point in the body of the presentation. This is where the navigation aspects of the software used to construct the presentation become important. PowerPoint has navigation capabilities, but it is not the software's strongest feature.

Generating Slides: Working with Templates

Templates are in general a good idea. They can give your presentation a consistent look throughout. There are two basic kinds of templates that you may want to use: design templates and content templates. Design templates simply provide a consistent color and graphics scheme that can be utilized as a background on all of your slides to give your presentation a consistent look. They also save on file size if you want to transport your presentation on some sort of portable medium. The color and graphics scheme used in your design template has to be saved only once in your files along with the actual content that you add to your template.

Content templates are useful if you have a set format for a chart or a graph that has to be repeated many times in your presentation. This gives your charts a consistent look during your presentation.

PowerPoint 2000 offers a very large assortment of templates. When you create a file in PowerPoint, you have three choices for creation. You can use a blank presentation with no background colors or graphics, you can select Design Template tab, or you can select Presentation tab. The Design Template tab contains forty-four predesigned color and graphics schemes. The Presentation tab contains twenty-four predesigned entire presentations (ranging from two to twenty slides). Some of the predesigned presentations utilize templates different from the forty-four standard templates offered so there are actually more than forty-four designs you can use. You can also create as many of your own templates as you would like. If you are not particularly artistically inclined, the best choice might be to utilize the standard ones or make small alterations to the standard ones such as adding a logo to them. You can alter the background on any or all of the slides by using the Background selection on the Format menu on the main menu bar.

The predesigned presentations are not set up as presentations, but are really short tutorials on the types of presentations that you might be giving. The presentations have outlines, and each slide includes tips on what information should be contained on the slide.

Once you select a template to use in your presentation, each slide you add will utilize that template. If you use one of the predesigned presentations, you can add or delete as many slides as you like.

Working with AutoLayouts

Once you have selected a template to utilize, you will be prompted with a New Slide dialogue box that includes choices of AutoLayouts. These layout choices are really all that most users will ever require. Although there seems to be twenty-four AutoLayout choices in PowerPoint's New File dialogue box, all are variations of six basic layouts. These six layout varieties are depicted in Figure 3.2.

Layout 1 in Figure 3.2 is a title slide. Title slides are composed of formatting for a title and a subtitle. For some reason, PowerPoint assumes that title slides are different from other slides. Every template in PowerPoint has slightly different layouts for title slides and all other slides. Every presentation that you develop in PowerPoint has two separate master slides: One is called simply the Slide Master, and the other is called the Title Master. If you

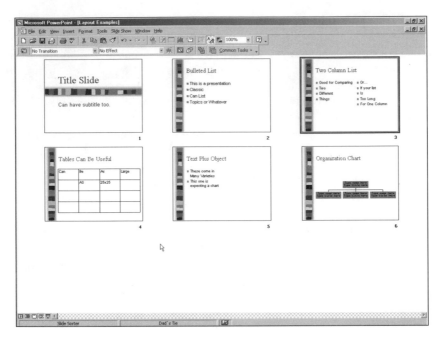

FIGURE 3.2   The Six Basic Layout Options in PowerPoint.

would like to change formatting for an entire PowerPoint presentation and keep it consistent across all slides, you have to alter the formatting on the master slides. The master slides can be accessed through commands on the View menu on the main command bar. There is also a Handout Master and a Notes Master that you can use to alter the appearance of printouts that PowerPoint has available.

Layout 2 in Figure 3.2 is a bullet list slide. This is an interesting convention that seems to be adopted by most of the major presentation packages. In general, you should be discouraged from including text passages in slides in your presentation. Bullet lists are much more common to presentations and keep you from including too many words on your slides.

Layout 3 has two side-by-side bullet lists. These are useful in comparing two different things side by side or are handy if your list is simply too long. The important thing to note about this layout is that it has two text objects in addition to the title of the slide.

Objects are important in PowerPoint because you can apply operations to whole objects, or you can edit objects. For instance, if you had a bullet list slide, you could not apply animation effects to each bullet in the slide. You could apply an animation effect only to the entire bullet list. Objects can include pictures, text boxes, video clips, sound clips, charts, graphs, tables, action buttons, word art, or hyperlinks. You can also insert objects from other programs such as spreadsheets or documents. There are two ways to create objects in PowerPoint. The first method is through the AutoLayout choices in the New Slide dialogue box. The second is with the Insert command on the main menu.

The three other layouts in Figure 3.2 include a table, text with object, and an organization chart. Tables create automatically when you select Layout 4. You will have to enter the dimensions of the table. Keep tables as simple as possible in your presentation. On the text with object choice, layout 5, the object would be on the right of the text, but no object was actually inserted. The AutoLayout could have included a chart or a picture or simply an area for an object. The organization chart, layout 6, was included in the figure because organizational charts are a fairly unique type of chart. Organization charts cannot be inserted through the Insert command; they can come into the presentation only through the Auto-Layout choices.

The other eighteen AutoLayout choices are really variations on these six, although there are no variations on the organization chart. Several other choices are variations on the text with object AutoLayout. In these other choices the elements are merely moved in different configurations, with the object above, below, to the right, or to the left of the text. Some of the other AutoLayouts include an object with a title, only an object, a title with up to four objects, and even a blank slide.

Working with Your Layout

You are not strictly limited to the layouts in the AutoLayout selections of the New Slide dialogue box in PowerPoint. There are several other approaches to changing and enhancing layouts in PowerPoint. Like most windows applications, you can click on any element in a slide to select it and then resize it, or drag and drop to move it.

The Format command on the main menu bar allows you to change layouts once you have chosen them or to apply different design templates to a presentation or individual slide. It also allows you to change the appearance of text characteristics such as alignment or line spacing. It enables you to add symbols to your text, such as math symbols or characters from other languages. This allows you to include formulae or other mathematical notation to slides.

Most types of objects in PowerPoint also have their own myriad of formatting choices. This is particularly true when it comes to charts and graphs, which has always been the strongest point of PowerPoint. In general, right clicking on an object will bring up a menu for editing that object.

You have to be particularly careful when you right click on a chart or a graph because it is not always clear what part of the chart or graph you clicked on, and each portion of the chart or graph typically has its own formatting options. For instance, in a bar chart, there are formatting options for data series, the axes, the grid lines, the titles, the legend, the plot area, and data labels. You can also do three-dimensional manipulations of the chart by rotating it and tilting it in any way desired through the 3-D command on the chart menu in the main chart menu bar. You can even reformat the data table spreadsheet that you type your numbers into. In short, you can manipulate every aspect of a chart or a graph.

Composing Your Slides: Adding Text, Animation, Multimedia, and Effects

Actually composing your slides in PowerPoint is pretty strictly a point-and-click affair. Interestingly enough, text is probably the hardest thing to insert into a PowerPoint slide.

Because PowerPoint treats elements of a slide as objects, you cannot just click on a spot on a slide and start typing. The text has to be part of an object. Most of the AutoLayouts you will be using have sufficient areas for your text, so you can go to those areas and simply click and start typing, but if you want to insert text in other places you must insert a text box object into the slide. Text boxes are inserted directly from the Insert command on the main menu bar. Simply select Insert and then Text Box. You will then have to resize the text box to make sure it can contain the text you type. Inserting videos and sounds works exactly the same. Simply point at the Insert menu and select Movies and Sounds.

Adding animation effects is a little more complicated, but only because there are so many choices. You can add animation effects to two things in PowerPoint. You can animate the entire slide by introducing transition effects from slide to slide, and you can animate any PowerPoint object or any of the elements that are in a slide. Both of these types of animation are introduced through the Slide Show selection of the main menu bar.

PowerPoint offers forty different transition effects from one slide to the next. You can apply transition effects to all of the slides in a show or to any particular slide. Checking random transitions means every slide will transition differently in the slide show. You can also choose from sixteen different sounds to accompany the transition. The slide transition can be set to occur with a mouse click or automatically after a preset amount of time. To introduce transitions for slides, simply click on Slide Show and then Slide Transitions from the main menu bar.

You can also animate each and every object that is in a slide. In order to animate any particular object, select the object and then select Slide Show and then Preset Animations from the main menu bar. There are fourteen preset animations to choose from. If you would like to animate some or all of the objects in a slide, select Slide Show and then Custom Animations from the main menu bar. There are seventeen different custom animation effects that you can do with a slide and fifteen specifically for charts and graphs. If you animate all of the elements of a slide, they will appear on the slide in a designated order one at a time, and they can all use animation effects. You can set them to come in automatically in the prescribed order or in response to a mouse click. If you set them to enter automatically, you can prescribe a set time for them to wait since the last element entered. You can also associate a sound with each effect. You can have text objects come in by word, by letter, or by paragraph.

For charts and graphs, you can have items come in by series, by category, or by element in a series or category. For instance, you can have each bar in a bar chart fly into the slide individually. You can set sounds to play with any of the animation effects.

Navigation between Slides

There are a number of ways to navigate through a PowerPoint presentation and a number of times when navigation becomes an issue. Navigation is different in PowerPoint depending on the View you are using. It also becomes a different issue depending on the type of output you are producing, such as a web presentation or a kiosk show.

In the Normal View, Slide View, or Outline View, navigation from slide to slide is quite simple and there are basically two options. All of these views show you a list of the slides in your presentation. Simply clicking on the slide you would like to go to in your list takes you to that slide. Your other option is to scroll through the presentation using the standard scroll bar or wheel on a wheel mouse. In the Slide Sorter View, navigation is not really an issue because all of your slides are displayed at once. The Slide Sorter View does provide an alternative means of navigating through the Normal, Outline, or Slide Views. In any of these three views, going to the Slide Sorter View and double-clicking on the slide you want to go to returns you to the original view of that particular slide.

Navigation through the Slide Show View is quite different. In general this is the view you will be using to give live presentations. There are a whole host of options to use while navigating through a presentation. In general, if you think something will work, it will. Just about any option that you might think would make sense does. Table 3.1 displays a list of keyboard and mouse options for controlling your slide show. If you have forgotten the keys you wanted to push, pressing F1 on your keyboard (the help key) will give you the list in Table 3.1.

Now that you have been introduced to the operating features of the software, you are ready to begin constructing a presentation. Chapter 4 will walk you through creating a presentation

TABLE 3.1   Slide Show Controls

Press	To
N, ENTER, PAGE DOWN, RIGHT ARROW, DOWN ARROW, or the SPACEBAR (or click the mouse)	Perform the next animation or advance to the next slide
P, PAGE UP, LEFT ARROW, UP ARROW, or BACKSPACE	Perform the previous animation or return to the previous slide
<number>+ENTER	Go to slide *<number>*
B or PERIOD	Display a black screen, or return to the slide show from a black screen
W or COMMA	Display a white screen, or return to the slide show from a white screen
ESC, CTRL+BREAK, or HYPHEN	End a slide show
E	Erase on-screen annotations
H	Go to next hidden slide
Both mouse buttons for 2 seconds	Return to the first slide
CTRL+P	Redisplay hidden pointer and/or change the pointer to a pen
CTRL+A	Redisplay hidden pointer and/or change the pointer to an arrow
CTRL+H	Hide the pointer and button immediately
CTRL+U	Hide the pointer and button in 15 seconds
SHIFT+F10 (or right click)	Display the shortcut menu
TAB	Go to the first or next hyperlink on a slide
SHIFT+TAB	Go to the last or previous hyperlink on a slide

4 A Presentation Project: A Lecture with PowerPoint

Planning the Lecture

Now what kind of lecture would be useful as practice to walk you through some of the major features of a multimedia presentation in PowerPoint? How about a demonstration lecture showing the major multimedia capabilities of PowerPoint? If you organization is like most, you will probably have to deliver the lecture many times. If it is short enough, maybe you can hang it on a web page. That way, you may not have to keep giving it forever. In order to be able to give it both live and over the Internet you will have to make somewhat different versions of the presentation. They will have to at least differ in terms of navigation, so you can add the navigation differences last. An example of the presentation can be found at: http://uhaweb.hartford.edu/katrichis/PowerPoint/Powerpointdemonstration.htm

Deciding on Objectives

The objectives of the presentation indicate exactly what points you would like to get across in the presentation. Be as precise as possible when deciding on the objectives of the presentation. This chapter highlights the kinds of capabilities Microsoft PowerPoint has. The following six features will be covered:

1. Creating Simple Text Charts
2. Creating Graphs and Bar Charts
3. Adding Pictures and Clip Art to Presentations
4. Adding Video Clips and Sounds
5. Adding Animation and Transitions
6. Moving Presentations to the Web

Laying Out the Lecture

Laying out the lecture ahead of time usually means a crisper, more well-thought-out presentation, with a smoother, more logical flow. It also avoids having to rearrange the lecture later, although that is simply a drag-and-drop operation in the Slide Sorter View.

At least nine slides are needed for this presentation. Each of the six objectives requires one, and you will also have to have a title slide, an objectives slide, and a summary slide. So begin the project with the following layout:

Slide 1:   Title
Slide 2:   Objectives
Slide 3:   Creating Simple Text Charts
Slide 4:   Creating Graphs and Bar Charts
Slide 5:   Adding Pictures and Clip Art to Presentations
Slide 6:   Adding Video Clips and Sounds
Slide 7:   Adding Animation and Transitions
Slide 8:   Moving Presentations to the Web
Slide 9:   Summary

Assembling the Elements

In general, assembling the elements can occur on a slide-by-slide basis, or it can be done before the presentation is created. You will always have to have the data that you will want to use for any chart or figure, or table that you would like to construct, but some other elements are available in the clip art library that comes with PowerPoint or other third-party vendors. Typically you will want to assemble your data and any video or audio files that you would like to insert in the presentation. The types of elements that you will have to assemble include data for any of the charts and graphs that you wish to construct, and any video or audio files you would like to insert.

In this case examples from the clip art library will be used. If you would like to make your presentation a little more fun, use a photo of someone from your organization, and download a movie trailer clip from one of the current motion pictures or your favorite sports team's web site.

Creating the Slides: Creating Your Own Template

You can choose from the template library or you could elect to make your own template. Some people tend to like to do both. Those not trained in design often trust the designer's judgment regarding major design elements, yet also like to personalize the templates a little. If you do not like to personalize, you can skip this step and go on to composing the slides.

So the first procedure inside PowerPoint is going to be to create a custom template. The following steps show how.

1. Click on File and New.
2. Select the Design Templates tab and double-click on Dad's Tie.
3. Now you will get the AutoLayout dialogue box. This allows you to choose which layout you would like. Select Blank and click OK.
4. Select View and Master.

The user would typically insert a small graphic such as a logo for a school or simply his or her name in small font or the date in the bottom left or top-right hand corner of the slide to not be obstructive. In general, people will read from left to right and from top to bottom, so your eyes will trail across a slide from the top left corner to the bottom right. Placing elements in either the top right or the bottom left is the least obstructive to the rest of the slide.

1. Select Insert, then Picture, then Clip Art, and make a selection from the clip art gallery.
2. Click on your new picture, and object markers appear around the picture. Use these markers to resize your picture to make it very small, less than 5 percent of the size of the page.
3. Drag and drop your new picture to the lower left-hand corner of the Slide Master so that it will be out of the way of your chart elements.
4. Now click on your graphic to select it. Right click and choose Copy to paste a copy of your graphic in the clipboard.
5. Now select View, then Master, then Title Master. Then right click anywhere in the Title Master and choose Paste. Now drag and drop your new graphic to the same position on the Title Master as you did on the Slide Master.
6. Select View, then Normal. Then select File and Save as. In the Save as File Type section of the box, select Design Template. Type the filename PowerPoint Demo in the filename box and click Save.
7. Select File and Close.
8. Select File and New, and select the General tab. The file PowerPoint Demo now appears on the list.

Every presentation has a Slide Master that dictates the formats for all of the slides in the presentation and a Title Master that dictates the format for title slides. In order to maintain a consistent look throughout your presentation, you must make any changes in slide formatting on these two master slides. Figure 4.1 shows the formatting done to the master slide. You are now ready to begin composing slides.

Creating Slide 1: Title

The title slide is the easiest to construct. First, you will have to choose a title. The title should be as descriptive and yet as short as possible. For this presentation choose Power-Point Demonstration, because it is short and to the point.

You can also elect to have a subtitle. Subtitles are good for further clarification regarding what the presentation will be about. This presentation will include the subtitle Capabilities of Microsoft PowerPoint 2000.

In order to create the title slide, follow these steps:

1. Select File, then New. Select PowerPoint Demo from the General tab. This is the design template you just saved. Notice a standard slide is in the work space, not a title slide. You need to change it to a title slide.
2. Choose Format, then Layout, then Title Slide. You now have a preformatted title slide.
3. Click on Click to Add Title, and type the words "PowerPoint Demonstration."

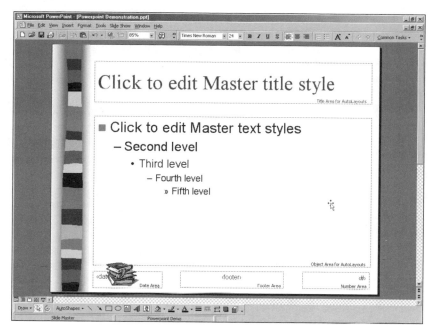

FIGURE 4.1   The Newly Formatted Master Slide.

4. Click on Click to add Subtitle, and type the words "Capabilities of Microsoft Power-Point 2000."
5. Click the notes area and type these words: "A title chart is the simplest of all text charts. To create this chart, follow the following steps." Then copy the steps into the notes area.
6. Choose File from the menu bar, then Save as. Notice that the title is already in the file-name box. Click Save.

Because you used your own template, you were first presented with a blank slide layout rather than being prompted for a layout. Had you taken a standard template rather than your own, you would have been prompted for a slide layout when you first opened the presentation, and step 2 would have been unnecessary. The title slide work area appears as Figure 4.2.

Composing Slide 2: Objectives

For the objectives slide utilize a Bullet List layout. Bullet List slides are also text slides and are also very easy to construct. To construct the objectives slide, follow the following steps:

1. Select Insert, then New Slide. Select Bullet List from the layout options and click OK.
2. Click on Click to Add Title, and type the words "What Will Be Demonstrated."
3. Click on Click to Add Text, and type in the objectives of the presentation. Be sure to hit your return key after each objective in order to get a new bullet.

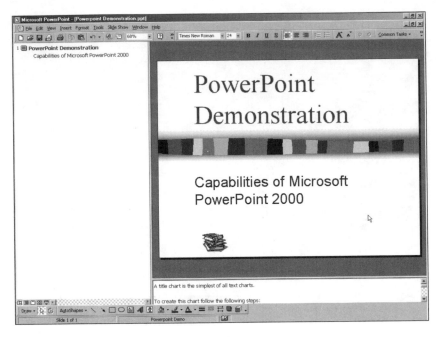

FIGURE 4.2   The Presentation Title Slide.

4. Click the notes area and add the text: "A bullet list is also a simple text slide. To construct this slide follow the following steps." Then copy the steps into the notes area.
5. Select File from the menu bar, then Save.

The bullet list slide appears as Figure 4.3.

Creating Slide 3: Creating Simple Text Charts

You have already constructed two types of text charts when you made the title chart and the objectives chart. Sometimes you may want more free form text in your slides. You may have noticed that PowerPoint does not have a slide layout for free form text. That is easily remedied. For our free form text chart, follow these steps:

1. Select Insert, and New Slide from the menu bar. Choose Title Only from the Auto-Layout selections and click OK.
2. Click on Click to Add Title, and type the words "Simple Text Charts."
3. Choose Insert and Text Box from the menu bar. Click a spot on the slide where you want to begin the text box, and type the words: "The simplest function of Microsoft PowerPoint 2000 is to create simple text charts like this one."
4. Click on your text box to select it. Use the boxes on the outside of the text box to resize your text box and position it where you want it on the slide.

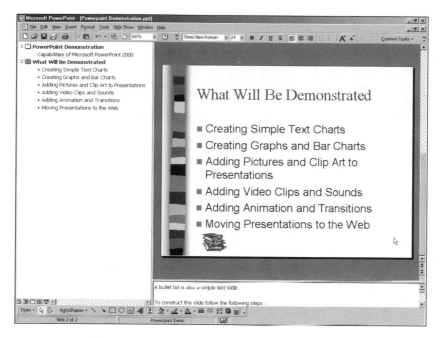

FIGURE 4.3   The Bullet List Slide.

5. Click the notes area and add the text: "Free form text charts can be a little trickier than it would seem. To construct this slide, follow these steps." Then copy the steps into the notes area.
6. Choose File and then Save from the menu bar

The free form text slide appears as Figure 4.4.

Creating Slide 4: Creating Graphs and Bar Charts

Now is the time to make a decision about the layout of the presentation. Do you want to demonstrate both graphs and charts or only one or the other? If you choose to demonstrate both, two slides will be needed here. As it turns out, adding graphs and adding charts are very similar processes. But, both processes are demonstrated so that you can see how similar the processes are.

A summary slide will be included later in the presentation. Summary slides are most likely to be bullet list slides, and how to construct bullet slides has already been demonstrated. So you can save a slide later in the presentation by not having a specific slide for demonstrating animation effects and transitions. You will use the summary slide for that. Here are the steps to construct a simple graph:

1. Choose Insert and then New Slide from the menu bar. Select Chart from the Auto-Layout selections, and click OK.

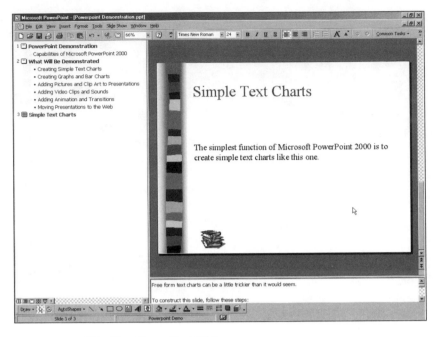

FIGURE 4.4   The Free Form Text Slide.

2. Click on Click to Add Title, and type the words "Creating a Simple Graph."
3. Double-click on Double Click to Add Chart. Notice that a column chart is already selected. The view you have now is the view of a chart object that is Open. There is a picture of your chart and a data table that is open. You can return to this view later by first clicking on the chart to select it and then selecting Edit, then Chart Object, and then edit from the menu bar or simply by double-clicking on the chart.

You can enter your own data in the data table and the chart will automatically adjust. Notice that there is a fairly complicated graph with three separate data series. If you would like to add additional data series, you can simply double-click on the row number in the data table for the additional series. Here you want to simplify the graph so you need to remove some of the data.

1. Notice that PowerPoint is in Chart Edit mode. In this mode you have different menu selections than in Normal View mode. In order to change this column chart into a graph, select Chart, and then Chart Type, from the menu bar. Select Line from the Standard Types tab of the Chart Type dialogue box, and click OK.
2. Click on the number 3 on the left column of the data table, then right click and choose Cut. Do the same for row 2. Notice that the appearance of the graph has already adjusted.
3. With such a simple graph it does not seem sensible to include a legend. To remove the legend, click somewhere in the middle of the graph itself to select it, and right click.

Choose Chart Options from the menu box that appears. Click the Legend tab in the Chart Options box, and click to remove the check in the box marked Show Legend. Click anywhere on the slide outside of the graph to return to Normal View. Notice that the legend box has disappeared, and PowerPoint automatically adjusted the size of the graph.

4. Click on the notes area and add the text: "The greatest strength of PowerPoint is the ability to create charts and graphs. To create this slide follow these steps." Then copy the steps into the notes area.
5. Choose File and then Save from the menu bar.

The simple graph slide appears as Figure 4.5.

Creating Slide 5: Creating a Simple Chart

Creating charts follows the exact same sequence as creating graphs, except you do not have to change the chart type once it is created. To create the simple chart slide, follow these steps:

1. Choose Insert and then New Slide from the menu bar. Select Chart from the Auto-Layout selections and click OK.
2. Click on Click to Add Title, and type the words "Creating a Simple Chart."
3. Double-click on Double Click to Add Chart.

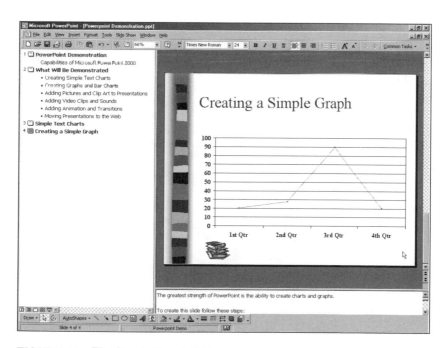

FIGURE 4.5   The Simple Graph Slide.

4. Click on the number 3 on the left column of the data table, then right click and choose Cut. Do the same for row 2. Notice that the appearance of the chart has already adjusted.

5. To remove the legend, click somewhere in the middle of the graph itself to select it, and right click. Choose Chart Options from the menu box that appears. Click the Legend tab in the Chart Options box, and click to remove the check in the box marked Show Legend. Click anywhere on the slide outside of the chart to return to Normal View.

6. Click on the notes area and add the text: "Creating charts is exactly like creating graphs. To create this slide follow these steps." Then copy the steps into the notes area.

7. Choose File and then Save from the menu bar.

The simple chart slide appears as Figure 4.6.

Slide 6: Adding Pictures and Clip Art to Presentations

Creating a slide with pictures and clip art is very simple in PowerPoint. Whether you are using clip art or your own photo, the procedure is the same. In order to create a picture slide, follow these steps:

1. Select Insert and then New Slide from the menu bar. Select Clip Art & Text from the AutoLayout selections in the New Slide dialogue box.

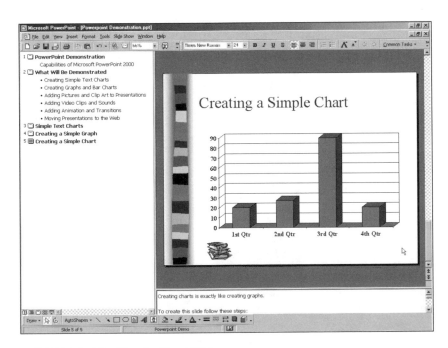

FIGURE 4.6   The Simple Chart Slide.

2. Select Insert, then Picture, then From File from the main menu bar. This will take you to the My Pictures folder located in the My Documents folder on your computer. Selected here is the "Cliff in Clouds" picture supplied with Windows ME. If you have pictures located in a different folder on your computer, the Insert Picture dialogue box allows you to navigate to your own directory. If you have no photographs to insert, insert clip art instead. To do this, select Insert, then Picture, then Clip Art (instead of From File) at the beginning of this step. Select a picture and click Insert.

3. Notice that your picture is pasted in the middle of the slide. Click on it to select it. Then drag and drop it over where the slide indicates Double Click to Add Clip Art. PowerPoint automatically adjusts the formatting to accommodate your picture.

4. Click on Click to Add Title, and type the words, "Adding Pictures and Clip Art."

5. Click on Click to Add Text. Notice that our text box is formatted as a bullet list. Add these bullets: Ease of Adding Pictures and Clip Art, Can Be Added to Any Kind of Slide, and Can Create Slide of Just Picture(s). Be sure to hit your return key after each bullet in order to get a new bullet for the next item.

6. Click on the notes area and add the text: "It is easy to add pictures to any kind of slide. To create this slide, follow these steps." Then copy the steps into the notes area.

7. Choose File and then Save from the menu bar.

Slide 6 appears as Figure 4.7.

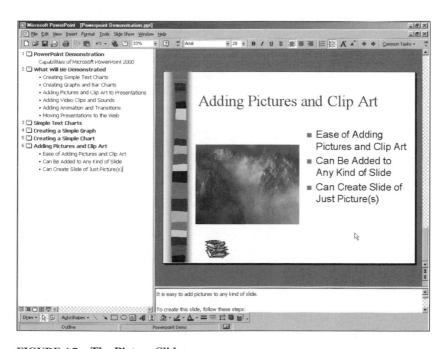

FIGURE 4.7   The Picture Slide.

Creating Slide 7: Adding Video Clips and Sounds

Video clips can be very effective in presentations. They are particularly good at reinforcing points by showing how others have agreed to them. Yet there is a tendency to overdo video, particularly because it is so easy to include in a presentation. In general, limit yourself to one or at most two videos in any particular slide show. In most cases, the slide should have nothing more than the video clip and a title. Cluttering a slide with many elements is always discouraged. In order to add video to the slide show, follow these steps:

1. Choose Insert and then New Slide from the menu bar. Choose the Title Only layout from the AutoLayout selections in the New Slide dialogue box.
2. Choose Insert and then Movies and Sounds and then Movie from File from the main menu bar. Locate your file, select it by clicking, and click OK. A dialogue box appears that offers you the option of playing the movie automatically or having it play after being clicked. Select the No so that it plays after being clicked. You can click on the media clip and resize it if you like, but be careful not to make it too big. Spreading a video clip, especially when you will be projecting it, leaves very poor resolution.
3. Choose Insert and then Movies and Sounds and then Sound from File from the main menu bar. Go to your windows folder and the media folder within that folder. Select a sound and then click OK. Choose Yes when the dialogue box appears asking if the sound should play automatically. Notice that a speaker has appeared in the middle of the slide.
4. Click on the speaker to select it and move it to the middle of your video clip if it is not already there. Right click on the speaker. On the menu that appears, choose Order and then Send to Back. The speaker now disappears. It is still there, but it is simply on a lower graphical layer than the film clip. It is hidden by the video clip.
5. Click on Click to Add Title, and type the words, "Keeping Media Insertions Simple."
6. Click on the notes area and add the text: "It is important not to clutter your presentation with too many media elements. To create this slide follow these steps." Then copy the steps into the notes area.
7. Choose File and then Save from the menu bar.

The video and sound clip slide appears as Figure 4.8.

Creating Slide 8: Moving Presentations to the Web

The next two slides are really both simply bullet lists, but they demonstrate transitions and animation. Transitions make the presentation more interesting in that slides don't simply appear one after another. A transition helps attract the audience's attention by use of motion. On this slide transition effects will be demonstrated. Animation will be added on the summary side. In order to create the web presentation slide, follow these steps:

1. Select Insert and then New Slide from the main menu bar. Select the Bulleted List layout from the AutoLayout selections in the New Slide dialogue box.
2. Click on "Click to Add Title," and type "Moving Presentations to the Web."

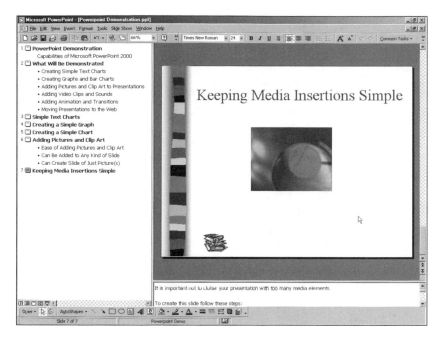

FIGURE 4.8   The Video and Sound Clip File.

3. Click on Click to Add Text and type in these bullets: Add Action Buttons for Naviga-tion, Simply "Save As" a Web Page File, and FTP the File to the Web. Be sure to hit your return key after each bullet to get a new bullet for the next item.
4. Select Slide Show and then Slide Transition from the main menu bar. Select Checker-board Across from the drop-down list, and select Slow for speed. Click Apply.
5. Click on the notes area and add the text: "This is just another bullet list slide, but it includes a transition effect. To create this slide, follow these steps." Then copy the steps into the notes area.
6. Select File and then Save from the menu bar.

The web page slide appears as Figure 4.9.

Creating Slide 9: Summary

For most presentations the last slide is the summary slide. If you want the audience to draw the types of conclusions that you want them to draw, it is always a good idea to tell them what conclusions you expect them to draw.

Animation effects will also be demonstrated in this slide. Animation is attention get-ting because it adds motion. Here you will use the animation effects for a dramatic effect when you draw the conclusions in the summary. Because such effects would be of no use to the web-based presentation, you will be saving a separate file for the web presentation just before adding animation effects.

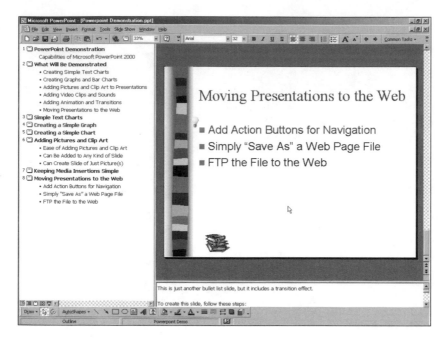

FIGURE 4.9   The Web Page Conversion Slide.

You can animate any object in a slide. Here you will be creating a slide similar to a bullet list, but animating each bullet individually. If you created a standard bullet list, the title would be one object and the list would be a separate one. Instead you will be creating separate text boxes for each point in our list, so that you can animate them individually. To create this slide, follow these steps:

1. Select Insert and then New Slide from the main menu bar. Select the Title Only layout from the AutoLayout selections in the New Slide dialogue box.
2. Click on Click to Add Title, and type "Summary."
3. Select Insert and then Text Box from the main menu bar. Click somewhere in the slide, and type the bullet point PowerPoint Is Extremely Powerful Presentation Software.
4. Repeat step 3 for each of the bullet points: Can Add Pictures, Video, and Audio, Not Just for Charts and Graphs, and Can Move Presentations to the Web.
5. In order to make the presentation look consistent, change the font used in the text boxes. Mark all of the text in the first text box and select the font Arial and 32 from the main menu bar. Repeat this for each of the other three boxes.
6. Click on one of the text boxes to select it. Then select Format and then Bullets and Numbering from the main menu bar. Click the tab marked Bulleted, and select the solid square bullets (upper right-hand corner). Also select the light blue shade from the color drop-down list. Click OK.
7. Repeat step 6 for the other text boxes.
8. You can mark each bullet point box separately now and resize and arrange them on the page.

9. Click on the notes area and add the text: "This looks like a bullet list, but it has separate animation effects for each point. To create this slide follow these steps." Then copy the steps (even the ones not taken yet) into the notes area.
10. Select File and then Save from the main menu bar.
11. Select File and then Save as from the main menu bar. Type PowerPoint Presentation WEB in the filename section. Click Save.
12. Select File and then Close from the menu bar. Select File and then Open from the menu bar. Select PowerPoint Demonstration in the open dialogue box, and click Open.
13. Select Slide Show and then Custom Animation from the main menu bar. Click the check box next to Text 2 in the selection list in the Custom Animation dialogue box. Click Fly and From Bottom from the drop-down lists on the Effects tab.
14. Click the check box next to Text 3 in the selection list. Choose the Checkerboard and Across options on the drop-down lists on the Effects tab.
15. Click the check box next to Text 4 in the selection list. Choose Spiral from the options list.
16. Click the check box next to Text 5 in the selection list. Choose Crawl and From Right from the options drop-down list.
17. Click the Order & Timing tab and then click on Text 2 to select it. Click the Automatically option in the Start Animation option box, and move the timing to 00:02 on the timing scroll bar.
18. Click Text 3 to select it, and check the On Mouse Click option in the Start Animation option box. Do the same for Text 4 and Text 5. Click OK.
19. Select File and then Save from the menu bar.

The animated summary slide appears as Figure 4.10.

Delivering the Live Lecture

Adding Navigation Elements

Adding navigation elements to a slide is quite simple. For the live lecture, it is usually helpful to be able to blank the screen in case you want to direct the audience attention to some other point. This occurs when there is a particularly good question from the audience and you want them to focus on it, or if you are simply done with one slide and not ready for the next one. In order to provide for the blank screen, you will add navigation buttons to the presentation. First you will add a blank slide at the end of the presentation. This slide will need one navigation button to return to the slide that asked for the screen blank. To add the blank slide, follow these steps:

1. Make sure the cursor is at the summary slide in the outline window on the work area. Select Insert and then New Slide from the menu bar. Select Blank from the Auto-Layout choices in the New Slide dialogue box.
2. Select Format and then Background from the menu bar. In the Background dialogue box, check the box Omit Background Graphics from Master, and click Apply. This

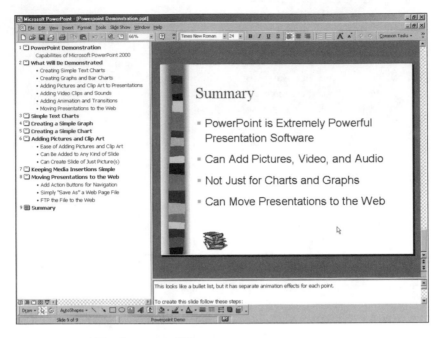

FIGURE 4.10   The Summary Slide.

will give you a completely blank slide without the template graphics on the other slides in the show.

3. Select Slide Show then Action Buttons from the main menu. You will be presented with a set of action buttons to choose from. Select the action button for Return. This will bring you back to whatever slide called for the blank screen. You can click on the button to select it so that you can position it anywhere you want or resize it. A right click will give a menu for changing its properties if you like.

4. Now you have to place a button on slides 2 through 8 in the presentation to call for the blank screen. You will not place a button on the title slide or the last slide. If there is an urgent question at the title slide, you can simply exit the presentation. If a question arises at the summary slide, the blank screen will be the next one anyway, so there is no need to add navigation to get there. Go to slide 2 called What Will Be Demonstrated by clicking on it in the Outline Window of the work area. Select Slide Show and then Action Buttons from the menu bar. Select the Action Button: End, and click somewhere within your slide to place your action button on the slide. Select the action button by clicking on it and reduce its size by about 75 percent. Place the action button in the top right-hand corner of the page.

5. Right click on the action button and select Copy. Go to slide 3 by clicking on it in the Outline Window of the work area. Right click and select Paste. The action button is now on slide 3 and should be in the same position as on slide 2. Repeat this step for slides 4 through 8.

6. Select File and then Save from the menu bar.

Practicing the Lecture

Practicing the lecture at least a few times before giving it is an important step. The practice gives you an idea of how things will go and the timing of the lecture. When delivering the lecture, you will not be speaking in your normal conversational voice. You will be speaking louder than normal in order to project your voice to all members of the audience. You will also be speaking slower than normal. In general you should be speaking about half as fast as in a normal conversation. This is to accommodate different processing speeds of audience members. The best place to practice your presentation is in the room where you will be giving it, using all the equipment you will be using. This allows an opportunity to make sure your equipment is working and that the slide show looks the way you thought it would.

Preparing Notes and Handouts

Notes and handouts are always a very nice touch during a presentation, and PowerPoint makes preparing them easy. First you have to decide what types of handouts you would like your audience to have, and what kinds of notes you would like to have during the presentation. For some speakers, the slides are all the notes they need. If you are a novice presenter, it is a good idea to have prepared notes also. Hopefully, you will not need to use them, but they will give you more confidence in your presentation if you know they are there.

Select Print from the main menu in PowerPoint, and take a look at the choices in the Print What drop-down list of the Print dialog box. The notes pages you have already prepared while creating the slide shows make for excellent speaker notes. Because the presentation is fairly technical in nature, these might make the best handouts as well. In other situations, small copies of the slides make excellent handouts and can be obtained by selecting Handouts in the drop down list.

Keeping Minutes during the Lecture

You can keep minutes during a slide show using two different devices built into PowerPoint. If you right click during your show, a menu box will appear that allows you access to either the speaker notes (which are what you have been entering in the notes area of the work area) or a meeting minder (which allows you to keep minutes and plan action items). You may not want the audience to see your notes during the presentation, so you can use different views with the audience seeing the slide show through the projector, and you can see any other view on your computer. In order to do this, select Slide Show and then Setup Show from the main menu. In the Setup Show dialogue box, select Projector from the Show On dialogue box. Now when you go to the View Show view, only the output on the projector will change.

Moving the Lecture to the Web

Once you have completed a PowerPoint presentation, you can move it to the Web. The next sections explain how to transform your PowerPoint presentation into a web presentation.

Adding Navigation

PowerPoint automatically adds navigation elements to your slide show when you move it to the Web. These allow viewers to navigate back and forth through your presentation, but there is no navigation automatically added that brings viewers out of the presentation. It is a good idea for viewers to be able to move out of the presentation when they would like to, so you will add navigation buttons to all nine slides to do this. This is done exactly like the navigation buttons that you added to the live presentation, except you need to indicate to whoever is accessing the presentation on the Web, exactly what the buttons mean. To add buttons, open the web-based presentation file that you saved before adding animation (this file was named PowerPoint Presentation Web). Follow these steps:

1. From the main menu select Slide Show and then Action Buttons. Then select Custom from the Action Button dialogue box.
2. In the Action Settings dialogue box, check the bubble for Hyperlink to and fill in a URL. Typically you will want the viewers to return to whatever page they accessed the presentation from.
3. Right click on your new button and select Add Text. Type the phrase "Leave Presentation" on the button. Reshape and resize the button to contain the text.
4. Drag the button to the bottom middle of the screen, and place it where it will be out of the way of the other presentation elements, but obvious to the viewer.
5. Right click on the new button and select Copy. Go to all other slides in the presentation, and paste the new button into those pages.
6. Select File and then Save from the main menu bar.

Mechanics of Moving the Lecture to the Web

Moving the lecture to the Web is really quite simple. The easiest way to do it is to select File and Save As Web Page from the main menu bar. This works well if you are actually on the web server when you are doing it.

Another approach is simply to save the file as a web page and use an FTP package to move the file to the server. This approach tends to be the cleanest and easiest method. When you save the file as a web page, it creates a subsidiary directory, which really has most of your presentation in it. Be sure to move both the HTML file created by PowerPoint and the subsidiary directory to the server. Be sure to keep the subsidiary directory as a subsidiary directory with the same name.

One other small issue has to do with the name of the PowerPoint presentation on the Web. You will have to follow naming conventions that are supported by whatever viewers you are supporting. In other words, no blank spaces are allowed in the filename.

CHAPTER

5 Introducing Director

Macromedia Director is a powerful, all-in-one multimedia creation tool providing multimedia developers with a graphical authoring environment. The process of multimedia authoring entails the coordination of various media components into a single presentation or application. With Director, developers are provided with a clean electronic canvas on which to integrate, control, and "direct" motion, sound, images, and text into a single presentation.

Director (Figure 5.1) was initially created in the 1980s as a two-dimensional animation software application. It has evolved over the years to become an industry standard for creating multimedia applications. Part of its success lies in its ability to handle just about any type of media (bitmap images, vector images, digital audio, digital video, two-dimensional and three-dimensional animation).

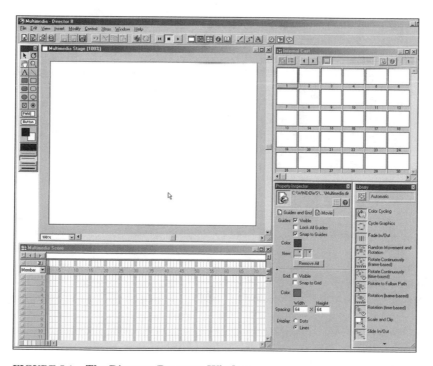

FIGURE 5.1   The Director Program Window.

Similar to the way a spreadsheet program would be used to generate an expense report, Director is a program that can be used to organize media content to generate a final multimedia application. Director works through a graphical user interface, providing drag-and-drop functionality to the multimedia creation process, making it relatively easy to use as well. By storing, organizing, and providing easy access to various media components, Director can be used to assemble these components graphically into a multimedia presentation. Using this graphical drag-and-drop approach, Director simplifies or even eliminates the need to learn complex computer programming structures to create multimedia. Authoring tools such as Director allow the author to worry less about creating and debugging the programming code at the heart of the application and concentrate more on the design and functionality of the application itself.

It should be noted, however, that in order to build truly interactive, quality multimedia applications, users will need to learn and apply Director's built-in programming language, Lingo. Lingo, like JavaScript (described in Chapters 11 to 13), is a scripting language that allows authors to create customized scripts (or behaviors) that perform advanced tasks not available through Director's standard complement of commands and functions. Lingo is a comprehensive language and, therefore, can be intimidating to new users. A complete coverage of this language is beyond the scope of this book; however, some basic features of the language along with simple examples will be explored to enhance some of the applications to be assembled in this unit.

For additional information on Lingo, the authors recommend the following resources:

- *Lingo in a Nutshell*
- *Director 8 and Lingo Bible*
- *Lingo Dictionary*

Director is capable of producing a variety of multimedia applications, including educational CD-ROMs, instructional presentations, games, interactive DVDs, enhanced CD-ROMs, information kiosks, and even interactive web modules using the built-in shockwave export functionality (see Figure 5.2). This diverse list of applications is a testament to the flexibility of this program and the range of creativity that it allows multimedia developers.

When to Use Director and Multimedia

The goal of applying any type of multimedia to a particular project is to enhance the appeal, usability, and interactivity of the application. Multimedia is a powerful tool that can make any application easier to use. Effective multimedia will enable the user to be less reliant on printed instructions because the elements present in the application will have self-evident functionality. However, keep in mind the old adage "more is not necessarily better" is true, especially with new multimedia. One of the pitfalls that new multimedia developers fall into is the tendency to incorporate too many "whizbang" effects into their applications. This can lead to user confusion and decreased usability, effects that are in direct opposition to the intended goal. Remember, if the users must work to figure out what a particular button does or how to get from one area of your application to another, they will quickly become frus-

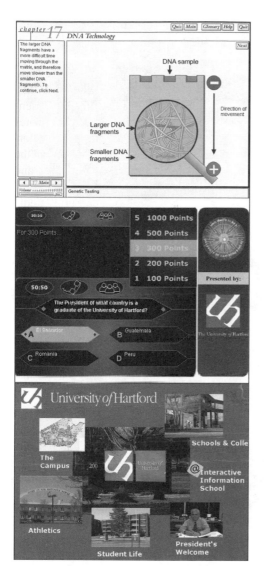

FIGURE 5.2 Director is capable of producing a variety of different multimedia types: educational CD-ROMs (top), games (middle), and promotional CD-ROMs (bottom).

trated with the application, abandoning it for something a little easier to use.

One feature that goes a long way to promote usability of an application is the user interface. The interface of any multimedia application should promote a feeling of "comfort" and "familiarity" for the user. Remember, most end users will have had some experience with previous multimedia titles. As such, developers should stick to common conventions whenever possible to increase the usability of their titles. This begins with the choice of buttons and icons. These graphical elements should convey functionality based on their appearance. In other words, it should be obvious to the users what a particular button does before they actually click on it. Examples of buttons that convey functionality based on appearance are presented in Figure 5.3.

Effective multimedia applications often create an environment that "immerses" the user within the actual application. This is accomplished most easily by having the application completely fill the user's computer screen. The only element visible on the monitor, therefore, is the actual multimedia application with its user interface. By customizing the interface, the user is forced to concentrate on the actual application and is not distracted by other elements such as the operating system, desktop icons, or controls. These elements are still present, but simply work behind the scenes. This promotes the perception that the computer is dedicated to running only the multimedia application and demands the complete attention of the user. By creating this immersive experience, the application becomes more engrossing and usable.

When to Use Director

During the initial planning stage, certain issues should be considered when evaluating the suitability of Director for the project. Does the project require complex animation or interactivity? Does the project rely heavily on graphics or digital video? Does the project need a database storage system or access to network resources? Based on the answers to some of these questions, you may decide whether Director is the program best suited to create your multimedia application. In general, Director is the program of choice for multimedia applications that require graphical animation, interactivity, and digital video.

Advantages of Director

Director has long held a prestigious position within the computer-based training (CBT) field. The reason for this lies in Director's ability to create stand-alone applications that can be used and completed at the user's own pace. It is for this reason that Director is well-suited for creating educational applications, such as educational or training CD-ROMs.

Director applications can be used to encourage students who may become easily "bored" with traditional classroom environments. In a traditional classroom, information is conveyed from instructor to student usually in terms of auditory information supplemented with static diagrams that may be sketched on a blackboard. In this environment, students may be disengaged with the content presented or even tune the entire class out all together. This may occur as a result of information being presented at a rate that is too slow or fast, depending on the individual learning styles of the students. The ability to obtain, process, and assimilate information of a variety of different types and at one's own pace can often make the difference between failure and success for these students.

The key advantage that CBT provides for students in the educational process is the ability to control how fast, and often, information is presented. The users of a multimedia training module can easily spend as little or as much time with a topic as they wish. The computer proves to be an infinitely patient instructor. Individual activities may be repeated as many times as is deemed necessary by the students until they feel they understand the concepts at hand. Students are also afforded the opportunity to actively participate, interact, and explore different media elements presented in the activity. This becomes particularly useful when creating virtual labs in which students may practice manipulating virtual laboratory equipment or reagents while conducting an experiment on the screen.

The obvious advantage of using a multimedia approach for teaching and learning is the ability to provide multiple types of information to the user. An effective mixture of sound, graphics, and animation has a much more profound effect on the learning process and, at the same time, appeals to a wide range of learning styles (auditory, visual, kinesthetic) inherent within a student population. This creates a richer learning experience for all. Studies have demonstrated that effective CBT can actually increase information retention and facilitate the application of gained knowledge. The end result is improved understanding of the content.

By stimulating several senses simultaneously (hearing, sight, coordination), students become immersed in the learning experience. By using this multimode approach, multimedia training applications can work to circumvent the tendency for students to "tune out" when a single presentation mode is applied. An example of an effective use of multimedia for conveying information is the multimedia encyclopedia (see Figure 5.4). If a student were asked to read an encyclopedia from cover to cover, this task would soon become tedious. The student would experience information overload as the sense of sight would become fatigued, resulting in poor retention. By condensing and selecting key elements of text from the encyclopedia, displaying this information along with coordinated narration and digital video or animation for illustration, the presented information would "come alive" to stimulate several senses simultaneously. Using this multimedia approach would lead to faster assimilation of the information and improved learning and retention of the content presented.

🔺 Home
▶ Play
⏹ Stop
⏮ Rewind
⏩ Step Forward
⏪ Step Back
❓ Help

FIGURE 5.3 Examples of Buttons That Convey Functionality Based on Appearance.

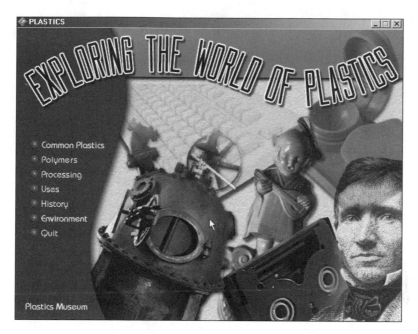

FIGURE 5.4   An Example of a Multimedia Encyclopedia Application: "Exploring the World of Plastics."

Disadvantages of Director

Director is not an ideal choice for creating applications that involve database storage or for projects targeted for delivery over the Internet, including streaming video applications. This is due to the fact that Director application files are often much larger than, for comparison, a Flash movie (see Chapters 8 to 10). Director is also limited when it comes to creating animation that makes use of vector-based graphics. The vector graphic capabilities of Director are quite limited when compared to programs such as Macromedia Flash. This feature has been improved in the later versions of Director (version 8 and later), however.

The creation of simple presentations and slide shows are best left to packages such as Microsoft PowerPoint (see Chapters 2 to 4). PowerPoint is intuitive and easy to use for creating such presentations. Its shorter learning curve, coupled with the built-in easy-to-apply templates, helps novices to create professional-looking presentations in a short period of time.

Applications designed for delivery over the Web might be better suited for an application such as Macromedia Flash (Chapters 8 to 10). Also, JavaScript (see Chapters 11 to 13) can be used to create web-based animation; however, this requires some advanced coding or powerful web site development tools such as Macromedia Dreamweaver, Adobe GoLive, or Microsoft Front Page.

Due to the large file sizes generated by Director, it is also not a good choice for creating multimedia applications designed to deliver video over the Web. Streaming video is a technology that is still in its infancy. Recent advances in technologies from Apple (Quicktime), RealNetworks (RealPlayer), and Microsoft (Media Player) have made huge strides to provide enhanced functionality for presenting multimedia applications involving streaming video. However, Director is still not optimized to make use of these technologies.

If you decide that Director is the tool of choice for your application and it must absolutely be delivered over the Web, Director version 8 (or later) does provide improved capability for exporting applications to be delivered over the Internet. Director applications designed for delivery over the Web are packaged as Shockwave files. Shockwave is a format that compresses file sizes to enable quicker and more efficient downloads over the Internet. Keep in mind that the Shockwave plug-in will be required before the user will be able to play your application in their preferred browser, however. This may create an additional burden on the intended user to download this plug-in.

Despite advances in streaming technology and Shockwave compression technologies, the major drawback for delivering applications via the Web is the large file size associated with Director files. Eventually, connection speeds and equipment may allow for delivery of multimedia at a rate equivalent to CD-ROMs, but until then it is recommended that applications utilizing large images or high-quality audio and video be delivered using the tried-and-true CD-ROM. One of the key advantages of the Director format is that it can produce self-contained executable movie files. These files contain all of the code necessary to play the application on the user's system, eliminating the need to obtain plug-ins or external players or viewers. Because Director "projectors" are often large in size, these are best delivered via CD-ROM (to be discussed later in this chapter).

Delivering the Goods

When planning any multimedia project, several considerations should be made at the beginning of the process. One major consideration must be the mode of delivery for your application to the end user. Will this application be delivered via the Web? Will it be distributed on CD-ROM? Will it be presented as a stand-alone information kiosk? Will it be a combination of all of these? Other considerations would include the sophistication and experience of the intended users (expert computer users? novices?) and the system requirements for running the application (operating system platform, system speed, screen resolution and color, presence of plug-ins, Internet connectivity). Once the target audience is determined and the minimum specifications of the computing system required to run your application are defined, you can then decide on the most appropriate delivery method for your application.

Macromedia Director is best suited for producing applications to be delivered on CD-ROM. CD-ROM delivery of applications provides several distinct advantages and disadvantages. The main advantage CD-ROM delivery provides multimedia developers is large storage capacity and relatively fast data access. Today's CD-ROMs are capable of reading data at a rate of 24X to 40X. The X in the speed rating refers to a transfer rate of 150 kb/second. A CD-ROM capable of transferring data at 24X would, therefore, deliver data at 3.6 MB/second. Compare this rate to a maximum of 56 kb/second available over a typical modem connection. This increased data delivery rate allows the developer to provide richer graphics and higher-quality audio. With expanded data delivery rates, multimedia applications delivered on CD-ROM can also include full-screen and full-frame-rate video.

The main disadvantage of the CD-ROM delivery method for multimedia applications is the reduced flexibility to make changes after the disk has been produced. This requires that the application and its content must be "perfect" prior to production. Therefore, when creating multimedia to be delivered on CD-ROM, applications must be tested and retested thoroughly; the applications must be completely bug-free because once the disk is "burned," it cannot be changed.

Another issue to consider when producing a multimedia application to be delivered on CD-ROM is cross-platform compatibility. Director is capable of producing multimedia applications that can be played on both Macintosh and PC computer platforms. However, in order to accomplish this, the same application must be saved on both types of machines separately. In other words, if an application is created in a PC environment, it would then need to be opened and saved in the Director application on a Macintosh. Although both of these Director file types can share many of the media elements present in the application (such as QuickTime videos), both versions of the program must be present on the CD-ROM in order for it to be cross-platform compatible. The main drawback to this solution is that the amount of available space on the CD-ROM is reduced. In addition, the author must have access to both versions of the program and the equipment to run these applications in order to create these files.

Director Metaphors

For creating multimedia applications, Director uses a "time line" approach, which is analogous to creating an actual animated movie. The final application is designed to display a sequence of frames in sequential order at a predetermined frame rate (frames/second). A basic Director movie will play unimpeded from the first frame to the last frame at the specified frame rate. Obviously, not all multimedia applications play in such a fashion. For this reason, Director also allows for *branching*. During playback, the application can be directed to jump to a different point within the time line of the movie. This allows for user-controlled navigation through the completed application. Branching also allows the developer to organize content in a variety of ways. With so many different options for organizing and navigating through the movie, this necessitates the expenditure of considerable time for planning the structure of the application in advance. The goal is to make navigation as easy and as intuitive as possible, directing users to jump to the area or element that makes a logical "next step" while allowing the flexibility of customized choices. This should be done in a way that is clear and that will keep the user from getting "lost" within the application.

One useful method of planning an effective navigation structure is to generate an overview map or flowchart of the application, highlighting key areas or locations within the application ahead of time (see Figure 5.5). The navigation structure can then be based on this map.

A map will also help define navigation options for users from any particular point in the application. It will also help you to determine at what points various media elements will be required within the application. If you are experienced with web site design, this would be analogous to generating a site map, in which individual pages, their respective content, and the links joining each page are outlined to assist in the navigation process. To further aid the user in navigating the application, the consistent use of menus and buttons will help orient the user no matter where they may find themselves (Figure 5.6).

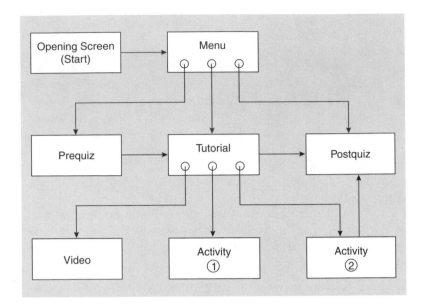

FIGURE 5.5 An Example of a Storyboard Flowchart for a Typical Multimedia Application.

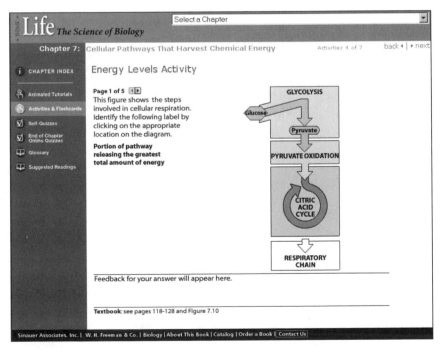

FIGURE 5.6 An Example of an Intuitive Menu and Button System for Navigation through a Multimedia Application.

6 Using Director

Director Basics

Director is one in a family of multimedia development software packages. Other examples of popular software packages include Asymetrix Toolbook, Multimedia Fusion, and Macromedia Authorware. In contrast to these other tools, Director users a time line approach for creating multimedia. As described in Chapter 5, basic multimedia applications created in Director will display a series of frames at a specified frame rate, similar to a motion picture. As the name of the program implies, Director follows a naming convention that uses motion picture terminology. For instance, new Director files are called movies. Understanding this naming convention will assist in learning the basic features of the program interface. Once you have learned the basic features of the program interface and what each panel does, your work will become much easier.

The Interface

The program interface for Director may seem a bit complicated at first. The presence of multiple panels and dialogue boxes contributes to this complexity (see Figure 6.1). Each of the panels visible in the program window are movable, however. This allows users to customize the Director environment to suit their own personal working styles. A nice feature of Director is that it remembers the layout last used by the developer and applies this layout to all new projects.

The key elements of the program interface are: the stage, cast, score, library, and Property Inspector. A detailed discussion of each of these elements follows.

The Stage

The stage is the vast blank area present in the middle of the program window (see Figure 6.1). The stage is where all graphical objects are placed and where the action in the movie takes place. The stage is the location where these objects will appear and interact while the Director movie is played.

The size of the stage will determine the size of the final Director movie. This size can be easily adjusted. For typical multimedia applications, a stage size of at least 640 × 480 is suggested. Whatever stage size is settled on, this would constitute a minimum resolution specification for users of your application. The stage size for Director movies can be modified by selecting the stage (by clicking on it) and then altering the height and width values in the Property Inspector. A series of predefined stage sizes are available by clicking the

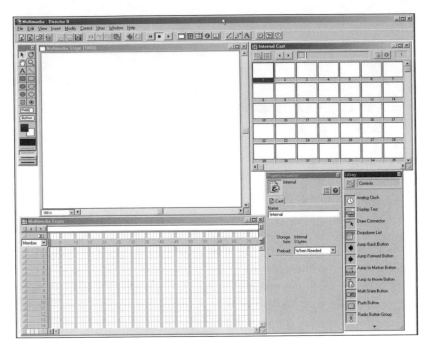

FIGURE 6.1   The Director Interface.

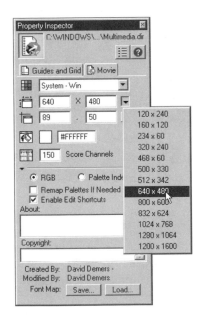

FIGURE 6.2   The properties for the movie can be altered using the Property Inspector.

small arrow next to the width value in the Property Inspector (see Figure 6.2).

Other movie features that can be altered using the Property Inspector include the color palette used by the movie, the background color of the stage, and the number of available channels in the movie. It should be noted that when the background color is specified using the Property Inspector, the color remains for the duration of the movie. The only way to change the background color dynamically during movie playback is to employ Director's scripting language, Lingo.

As mentioned previously, the stage can be positioned within the program window. Moving the stage may be necessary to fit all of Director's palettes and dialogue boxes within the program window. The stage can be positioned by clicking on its title bar and dragging it to the desired location.

The Cast

Whenever media elements (sound, video, graphics, text, etc.) are imported into a Director movie for use, they are stored within the internal *cast*. The cast window is shown in Figure 6.3. The cast is used graphically to organize imported media elements, along with all of the backgrounds, scripts, and customized color palettes used within the project. Each individual element stored in the cast is referred to as a *cast member*. Cast members can be thought of as the "actors" in a Director movie.

Importing cast members into the Director movie can be done in one of several ways. The most common method involves selecting File → Import from the Director menu. This will open a dialogue box labeled Import Files into *"Movie Name"* (see Figure 6.4).

From this dialogue box, you can browse for and select multiple files to import into your movie from your computer. Graphic files imported in this manner will cause Director

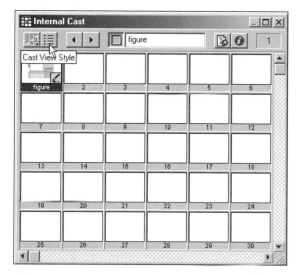

FIGURE 6.3 The Cast Window. The cast window can be toggled to display either thumbnail icons for each cast member or the members as a list.

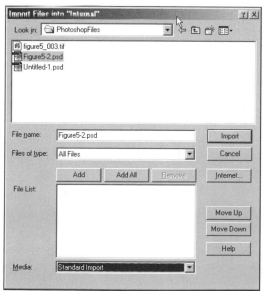

FIGURE 6.4 The Import Files dialogue box allows you to search for media files on your local computer for import into your current project.

to ask about the type of graphic file being imported. The options are Animated GIF or Bitmap Image. A second method of importing media elements into the cast is by selecting Insert → Media Element from the Director menu. Using this option will present options specific for each type of media element displayed in the list. The types of media elements that can be imported using this method include bitmap images, QuickTime movies, Shockwave audio, Flash movies, and animated GIFs. Inserting bitmap images with this technique will open up Director's built-in Paint window. From here, you will be able to paste images from the clipboard and edit them directly with this simple bitmap editor. Perhaps the easiest method of importing media elements into the cast involves dragging the intended element from the computer's desktop or folder directly onto the movie's cast.

The display of cast members within the cast can be readily altered. Cast members can be viewed as icons (default) or as a list. In the icon view, small thumbnail representations of the cast members are displayed. This is useful for browsing for a particular graphic cast member. This display can be toggled by clicking on the Cast View Style button present at the top of the cast window (see Figure 6.3). In order to assist in the organization of cast members within your movies, each cast member can be given its own unique name. This is highly recommended, especially for movies with several dozen cast members or more. Naming cast members is done by entering a name in the Cast Member Name field at the top of the cast window with the cast member selected, as shown in Figure 6.5.

Viewing the cast window can be controlled in several ways. The view of the cast window can be toggled by selecting Window → Cast from the Director menu. This may be useful when screen real estate is at a premium, especially when working on a smaller monitor. The size of the cast window can also be adjusted by dragging the bottom-right corner of the window.

In the default icon view of the cast, each variety of cast member present will be depicted with a small icon present in the lower right-hand corner of the cast member's thumbnail (see Figure 6.6).

Cast members with the small *paintbrush* icon are bitmap graphics that can be edited using Director's built-in Paint window. Members represented with an *A* icon are text mem-

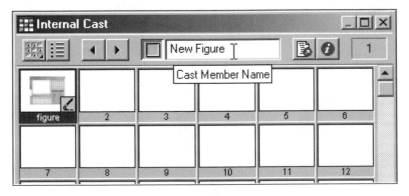

FIGURE 6.5   Naming cast members can be done by entering the name into the Cast Member Name field of the cast window with the desired cast member highlighted.

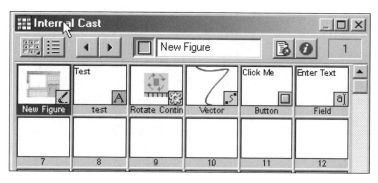

FIGURE 6.6   Identifying Cast Member Type. The type of each cast member is denoted with a small icon that appears in the lower right-hand corner of the cast member's thumbnail in the cast window.

bers, which can be edited in Director's Text window. Members with a *gear* icon indicate "behaviors" or Lingo scripts, which will be explored later in this chapter. The *dots connected with a line* icon indicates the cast member is a vector graphic that can be edited with Director 8's Vector Editing window. The *square* icon represents button cast members, whereas the *a[* icon represents a text field cast member, which can display or collect dynamic text data. Each of these cast member types will be described in detail in this chapter and the next as they are used to assemble simple Director movies.

When ready for use, cast members are placed onto the stage. This is most easily done by dragging the cast member from the cast and placing it directly onto the stage. Each occurrence of the cast member on the stage is referred to as a *sprite*. When sprites are placed onto the stage, Director provides basic information about the sprite through its implementation of *overlays* (see Figure 6.7).

When the sprite is selected on the stage, the sprite overlay displays information such as cast member name, sprite size and location, "ink" effect, opacity, and behaviors attached to the sprite.

Because a single cast member may be used several times throughout the movie, each copy of the cast member present on the stage is a unique sprite. The properties of an individual sprite—such as its size, transparency, and rotation—can be altered without affecting the original cast member. These properties can be altered through the Property Inspector while the sprite is currently selected (see Figure 6.8). These options will be discussed in more detail later in this chapter.

Although sprites can be altered independent of the cast member, please note that if the properties of a cast member are changed, all occurrences (sprites) of that cast member in your movie will be updated to reflect these changes. To alter the properties of a cast member, click the small circle with the *i* in the center at the top of the cast window (see Figure 6.6). This will take you to the Cast Member Properties section of the Property

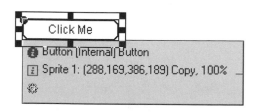

FIGURE 6.7   Sprite Overlays. Sprite overlays are useful for obtaining quick information about the sprite on the stage "at-a-glance."

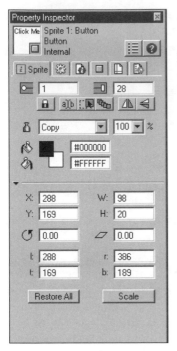

FIGURE 6.8   Altering Sprite Properties. Sprite properties can be easily altered by using the context-sensitive Property Inspector.

Inspector, which will display options specific for that cast member type that can be changed. The small icon to the left of the cast member properties icon (paper page with small circle and arrow in front of it) is the Cast Member Script icon. This icon will take you directly to the Lingo script editing window; there, behaviors may be assigned to the cast member. Remember, any behavior associated with a cast member will also be associated with each occurrence (sprite) within the movie.

To assist in organizing casts of large size, Director allows developers to *sort* cast members. This is done by selecting or highlighting all of the cast members you wish to sort, and then selecting Modify → Sort from the Director menu. This will open a dialogue box that presents several options for sorting the cast (see Figure 6.9).

From this dialogue box, you can select to have cast members sorted by their Usage in Score (order of appearance in the movie), Media Type, Name, or Size. A final option, Empty at End, will simply compress all the cast members into sequential slots within the cast. This will eliminate empty member slots within the cast window.

Additional Cast Options

When cast members are imported into your movie using one of the methods described in this chapter, they are considered to be embedded within your movie. This means that when your movie is complete and you produce the final Director file for delivery, the cast members are embedded within this Director file. An additional option for cast members is to import *linked* cast members. Linked cast members are just as the name implies—they are linked to an external file outside of the Director movie. The main advantage to using external cast members in this manner is the ability to update or change the linked file. Any changes made to the linked member will then be reflected in the Director movie. In order for Director to make use of linked cast members, however, the actual files for these members must be located in the same directory as the Director movie. The main disadvantage of using linked cast members is convenience. Embedded cast members are always accessible through the cast window while working on your project.

Another option available to developers is the *external* cast. Using the methods described in this chapter will result in cast members being imported into the *internal* cast. Internal casts, as the name implies, are an integral part of the Director movie. When the final movie is compiled (or produced), the internal cast is packaged along with the movie. This is in contrast to an external cast. Cast members in an external cast can be used within a Director movie, just like an internal cast; however, they are present in an external file and are not compiled within the completed movie. The main advantage to using an external cast is that the same cast members can be used in several different movies.

FIGURE 6.9   Sorting the Cast. The members of the cast can be sorted in several ways.

This is useful when producing a series of movies that will become part of a larger production. An external cast allows you to use the same cast members (buttons, graphics, icons, etc.) to maintain a consistent look between your movies. In addition, when a cast member needs to be updated across several movies, an external cast allows you to make the necessary changes once to the cast member. The changes will then be reflected in all of the movies that utilize this external cast. In order to make use of external casts, click on the Choose Cast icon present in the upper left-hand corner of the cast window (see Figure 6.10).

On the menu, select the New Cast option. This will open a dialogue box that will allow you to create and name a new external cast. Be sure to select the External storage option in the dialogue box. When you click Create, a blank external cast will be ready and available for you to use in your current movie. The next time you save your project, you will then be asked to name and save your external cast. Just as with linked cast members, this new external cast must be present in the same directory as the completed Director movie in order to make use of any of the external cast members.

The Score

The score is a table-type box that is used to direct what happens in each frame of your Director movie. The score can be thought of as the "screenplay" of the movie. The cast is simply the collection of actors waiting to take part in the scenes of the movie. Until the actors are given direction, they are simply a group of individuals waiting to be used. The score is the tool that arranges and organizes the action that occurs in each scene (or frame) of the movie.

The score is divided up into a series of numbered columns, which represent individual frames in the movie (see Figure 6.11). As mentioned previously, a Director movie starts at frame 1 and continues until it reaches the last frame with content associated with it. This means a Director movie can be 10 frames in duration or 10,000 frames, depending on how

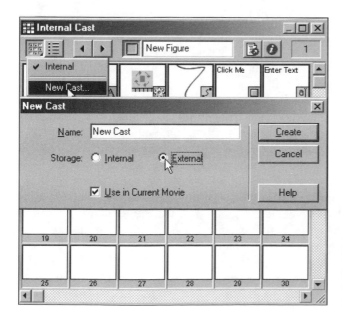

FIGURE 6.10   Using External Casts. External casts are convenient for utilizing the same cast members in multiple projects or movies.

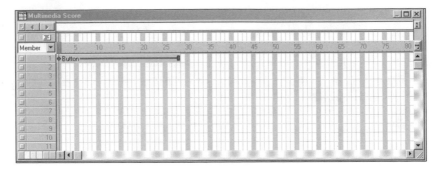

FIGURE 6.11   The Score. The score is a matrix representation of the various frames and channels available in the current movie.

you decide to arrange the content. The rows present in the score represent *channels*. The intersection of the numbered frames and channels are called *cells*. Each cell can contain only a single sprite, and each sprite present on the stage will occupy at least one cell. When a sprite is placed onto the stage, it will be present in the score starting at channel 1/frame 1 and continue for the default duration of the sprite (usually 28 frames). The duration of the sprite as indicated in the score will determine the duration of its appearance on the stage.

The red rectangle with vertical red lines found on the numbered line in the score window (see Figure 6.11), is the *playback head* for the movie. The playback head indicates the frame currently displayed on the stage. This playback head will move through the score one frame at a time when the Director movie is played or previewed. In addition, the playback head can be dragged back and forth through the movie to allow developers to preview content visible in a particular frame or over a series of frames.

As cast members are placed onto the stage, their associated sprites are placed in subsequent channels in the score. The channel number associated with the sprite becomes its Sprite Number. There are up to a total of 1,000 channels available in Director. The number available in the score can be altered by selecting Modify → Movie Properties from the Director menu, and changing the number in the Score Channels box present in the Property Inspector. The default is 150 channels. The sprite number for an individual sprite can be altered by dragging the sprite within the score to a different channel. Another feature of channels that is important for controlling your movies is that the channel numbers indicate the order of layering that occurs on the stage. Sprites present in channels with higher numbers appear in front of sprites present in lower numbered channels. For example, if you wish to have a button icon appear on the stage in front of a background image, you would need to make sure the button icon is placed in a channel that has a higher number than the background image.

Sprites can be altered directly in the score window. Each sprite present in the score has an associated Sprite Indicator Bar, which appears as an elongated purple rectangle within the associated channel (see Figure 6.11). The Sprite Indicator Bar spans the duration of the sprite (in frames) in the time line. The Sprite Indicator Bar can be cut and pasted or dragged within the score to move the sprite to a different channel. This can be done to alter the layering of the sprites within your movie. Other sprite parameters that can be changed in the score include sprite duration and appearance of the sprite in the time line. To change the duration of the sprite in the score, simply click and drag the small rectangle present at the end of the Sprite Indicator Bar to another cell in the channel. To change the frame in which the sprite first appears on the stage, you can click and drag the small circle on the left of the Sprite Indicator Bar to the desired frame. This procedure will also alter the duration of the sprite, however. If you simply wish to shift the appearance of the entire sprite without altering its duration, simply click and drag the Sprite Indicator Bar horizontally in its respective channel.

Additional options available in the score include viewing or hiding additional non-sprite movie effects channels. This can be accessed by clicking on the Hide/Show Effects Channels button, present on the upper-right corner of the score (see Figure 6.12).

The effects channels are reserved to handle nongraphical sprites such as tempo settings, color palettes, scene transitions, sound, and frame-associated Lingo scripts/behaviors. These channels are not numbered, but rather denoted with representative icons. For instance, the tempo channel can be used to alter the frame rate of the movie once the playback head hits a particular frame. To associate a tempo setting to a frame, simply double-click the desired cell in the tempo channel (denoted with small stopwatch icon). This will open the Frame Properties: Tempo dialogue box, which will present the developer with several options (see Figure 6.13).

These options include adjusting the frame rate (tempo) and holding the playback head on the frame for a specified duration (in seconds) or until a particular action occurs (mouse click). Another effects channel that warrants mention is the transitions channel

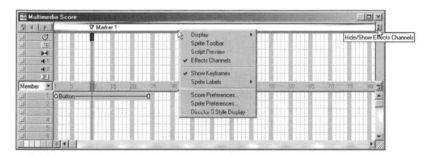

FIGURE 6.12   The Effects Channels. Additional channels present in the score can be used to control various effects such as scene transitions, sound, and frame-based scripts.

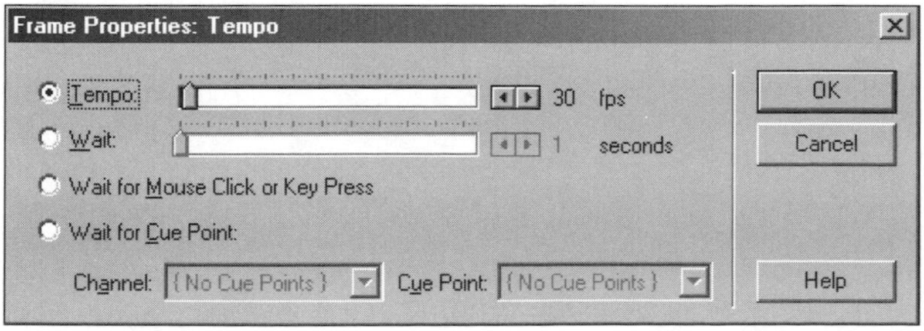

FIGURE 6.13   Tempo Settings. The tempo channel provides an easy mechanism for changing the frame rate of a movie.

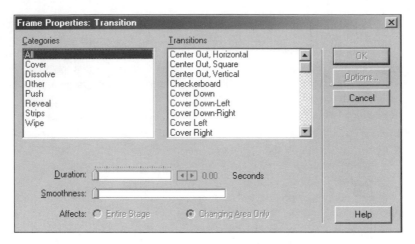

FIGURE 6.14   Transitions. The transition channel can be used to apply a wide array of special scene transition effects to individual frames in your movie.

(denoted with double triangle icon see Figure 6.12). The transition channel allows the developer to add some interesting frame transition effects to the movie. When a transition is added to a particular frame (by double-clicking the appropriate cell in the transition channel), the Frame Properties: Transition dialogue box is presented (see Figure 6.14).

From this dialogue box, you can select from an extensive list of prebuilt transition effects including Dissolve, Wipe, Cover, and Reveal. When a transition is applied to a frame and the Director movie enters the associated frame during playback, the transition will occur, blending the contents from the previous frame and the current frame using the selected effect. Altering the transition is simply a matter of double-clicking the transition sprite in the appropriate cell in the score. You will make use of some of the other effects available in these channels in the upcoming activities.

Above the effects channels is a white margin called the marker channel. The marker channel is the area in which internal "markers" are placed. These internal markers can be named and act as "street signs" within your movie (see Figure 6.12). Each marker is associated with a single frame in the movie. This allows for easy navigation to a particular frame within the movie, by simply associating an action to locate and go to a particular marker.

Additional view options for the score can be accessed by right clicking (PC) on the score window (see Figure 6.12). From this dialogue box, you can specify to include a Sprite Toolbar in the score display. This may be useful for altering the properties of a sprite directly in the score; however, the additional space required reduces the number of channels that can be viewed at once in the score.

The Library

As noted already, much of the power of Director lies in its ability to apply behaviors to individual objects on the stage. Director provides a series of "behaviors," which are essentially prewritten Lingo programming scripts, that allow users to make sprites or frames interactive without having to learn the elements of Lingo programming. These behaviors are available to the developer in the Library (see Figure 6.15).

Behaviors can be assigned to individual sprites, cast members, or even frames. Behaviors provide the author with the ability to interact with the user and can be customized; however, this is not necessary. The behaviors available in the palette can be used as is, providing novice users with the basic tools to create simple multimedia applications without having to learn or modify a single line of Lingo code. The behaviors available in the Library can be applied to sprites simply by dragging them from the Library onto a sprite present on the stage.

You can view a detailed description of each behavior by moving your mouse over the behavior's icon, which will display the corresponding tool tip (see Figure 6.15). A list of available libraries is accessible by clicking on the Library List icon at the top left-hand corner of the Library. The list of available behaviors is extensive, ranging from animation-specific behaviors to Internet-specific behaviors. Please note that several behaviors may be attached to a single sprite; however, only a single behavior may be attached to any frame.

The Property Inspector

One new feature available in Director 8 is the Property Inspector (see Figure 6.16).

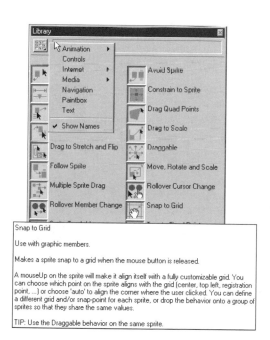

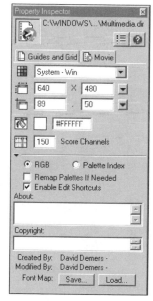

FIGURE 6.15   The Library. The Library contains many prewritten behaviors that can be applied to sprites, cast members, or frames.

FIGURE 6.16   The Property Inspector. The Property Inspector is a context-sensitive dialogue box that presents changeable parameters for a selected element in your movie.

We have already seen how useful the Property Inspector is for changing the properties of cast members, sprites, or the entire Director movie itself. Previous versions of Director made use of individual dialogue boxes for different Director elements. The new Property Inspector is a single, tabbed, context-sensitive dialogue box. The tabs available in the Property Inspector change according to which element in the Director environment is currently selected. Each corresponding tab contains information specific for that element that can be changed directly in the Property Inspector. This convenient new tool also allows you to change the properties of multiple selected objects in your movie simultaneously, a process previously unavailable in Director. The Property Inspector can also be customized to display more or less information. This is done by clicking the Expander arrow at the bottom of the Property Inspector (see Figure 6.16). The Property Inspector will be used extensively in the exercises that follow.

Getting Started: Basic Animation with Director

In this example, you will use Director to explore some of the animation capabilities of the program. To work through this example, make sure the Director program is currently running. If it is not, please start the program now.

Keyframe-based Animation

1. Start a new Director file by selecting File → New → Movie from the Director menu.

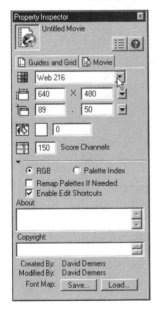

FIGURE 6.17   Changing movie properties using the Property Inspector.

2. For this project, start by entering movie settings for the project. Access the Movie Properties by clicking on the stage and making sure the Property Inspector is visible. If it is not, select Window → Inspectors → Property from the Director menu. In the Property Inspector, set a stage size of 640 × 480 and set the color palette to Web 216. This will ensure that the colors used in the project will display correctly on all machines (see Figure 6.17).

3. For this simple example, you will create a single cast member, which will be an oval. To create this cast member, select the Filled Ellipse icon from the toolbar (see Figure 6.18), and draw an ellipse on the stage by clicking and dragging your mouse. This will automatically and simultaneously create a new cast member, which is now present in the cast, and a new sprite, which is visible in both the stage and the score.

4. The next step is to change the duration of the sprite to 50 frames. This can be done in one of two ways (discussed previously). The sprite duration can be altered directly in the Property Inspector or by dragging the small rectangle present on the Sprite Indicator Bar in the score to the desired frame (see Figure 6.19).

5. Animation in Director is based on *keyframes*. Keyframes are single frames of a sprite that hold frame-specific information, such as a change in

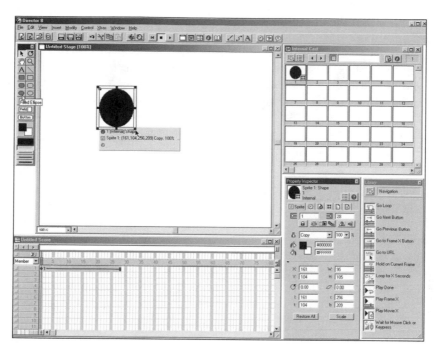

FIGURE 6.18   Creating a New Cast Member. By selecting the Filled Ellipse tool from the toolbar and dragging it onto the stage, a new sprite is created on the stage.

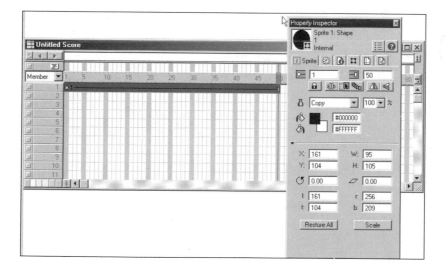

FIGURE 6.19   Altering the Duration of a Sprite. The duration of a particular sprite is represented numerically in the Property Inspector and graphically by the Sprite Indicator Bar in the score.

location, size, rotation, or opacity. Keyframes for a sprite are indicated in the score by the presence of a small circle in the Sprite Indicator Bar. Each sprite will have at least one keyframe—at the beginning of the sprite. This keyframe defines the initial settings, including position, for the sprite on the stage. To create a simple animation, such as movement from one location to another location on the stage, a new keyframe must be added to the sprite's occurrence in the score. For this example, we will add a keyframe to the last frame of the sprite using the Sprite Indicator Bar. To do this, click on the small rectangle at the end of the Sprite Indicator Bar and select Insert → Keyframe from the menu (see Figure 6.20). Keyframes can be inserted anywhere within the Sprite Indicator Bar using this method. (Note: A shortcut sequence for inserting keyframes is to press the <Ctrl>-<Alt> and <K> keys simultaneously.)

6. With the new keyframe selected, click and drag the object to a new location on the stage. Notice the appearance of the path-tracking line as you drag the sprite to its new location. This line contains numerous dots on it, indicating the position of the sprite during each frame in the time line (see Figure 6.21). This method of animation is called *tweening*. Director automatically calculates the position of the sprite between the first keyframe and last keyframe in the time line to create the illusion of animation. Test it out! This can be done by clicking the Play button at the top of the Director window (see Figure 6.21). During playback, you will see the sprite move from the position indicated on the first keyframe toward the position indicated on the last keyframe. This type of animation is referred to as *keyframe-based animation.*

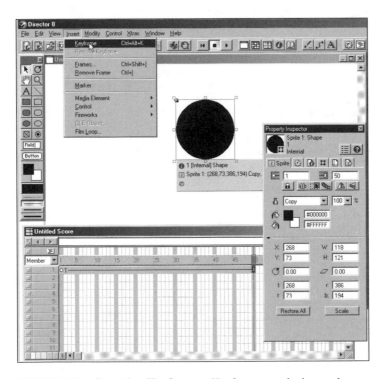

FIGURE 6.20   Inserting Keyframes. Keyframes can be inserted directly into the Sprite Indicator Bar in the score.

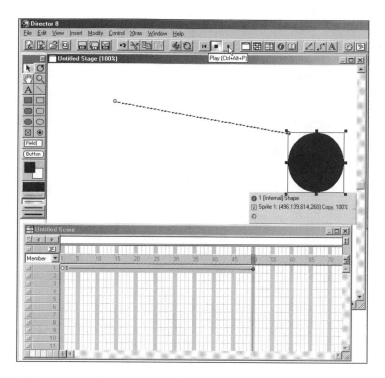

FIGURE 6.21   Creating a Motion Path. A motion path can be created by dragging a sprite to a new location with a keyframe selected.

7. Keyframes can also be added to an existing path to alter the route the sprite takes during its animation. This is handy because the majority of animation you create will probably not follow a simple linear path as you created in step 6. To add a keyframe to the path, click on frame 25 within the sprite's Sprite Indicator Bar and select Insert → Keyframe from the Director menu. This will insert a keyframe in the middle of the current path (see Figure 6.22). With this keyframe selected, click and drag the sprite to a different location. Notice that the path changes to reflect the new location of the sprite at this keyframe. This technique provides the developer with more direct control over the path of animation that a sprite takes.

Real-Time Recording

1. Another animation option available in Director is Real-Time Recording. To test this method, delete the sprite currently present on the stage (Don't worry! The cast member is still present in the cast) by clicking on it and hitting the Delete button.

2. Drag the oval cast member from the cast onto the stage. Select the newly positioned sprite by clicking the sprite on the stage. The entire Sprite Indicator Bar should be highlighted. To mark the start point for the recording, make sure the playback head is located on the desired frame; in this case, the playback head should be located on frame 1. Select Control → Real-Time Recording from the Director menu. You will notice that the sprite

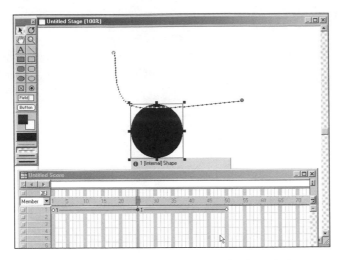

FIGURE 6.22   Altering the Path. The path of a sprite's animation can be adjusted by adding keyframes to the sprite's Sprite Indicator Bar. The sprite can then be positioned precisely on the stage with the new keyframe selected.

appears to be bounded by a red box (see Figure 6.23). This indicates the sprite's motion is ready to be recorded.

3. When you are ready to record this motion, click and drag the sprite on the stage following the desired path. You will notice that Director automatically records the path as you move the sprite, adding keyframes to indicate changes in direction (see Figure 6.24).

Lingo-Based Animation

1. A final method of creating motion in Director is through its built-in scripting language, Lingo. This method is a little more involved than the other methods, but provides the developer with an unprecedented level of control over the movement of sprites on the stage.

2. Remember, by default, Director movies operate on a time line. This implies that the movie progresses from start to finish in a continuous fashion. You exploited this property when you created keyframe-based and recorded animations. The positions of the sprites were based on differences in location between keyframes. Director displayed each frame in the time line, calculating the new position of the sprite as the playback head progressed from keyframe to keyframe. In Lingo-based animation, you must exhibit some control over the playback head's progression through the time line.

3. To begin, clear the stage of all sprites. Drag the oval cast member from the cast onto the center of the stage. The goal of this exercise is to provide controls that will make the oval move and change directions while the playback head remains on the same frame. Therefore, keyframes will not be used in this example. In the process, you will explore some basics of the Lingo scripting language, along with some of the built-in behaviors available through Director.

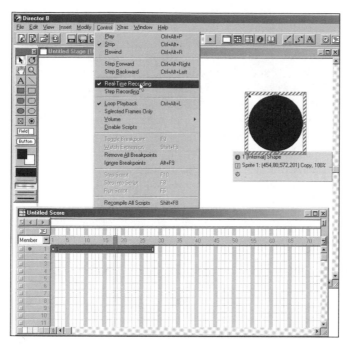

FIGURE 6.23   Real-Time Recording. Turning on Real-Time Recording alters the appearance of the sprite on the stage.

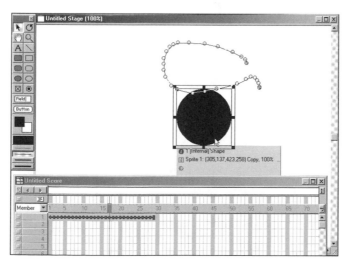

FIGURE 6.24   Recording the Path. With Real-Time Recording turned on, the sprite can be dragged on the stage. Director automatically records the exact path along which the sprite was dragged in real time.

4. Set the duration of the newly placed sprite to 2 frames.

5. What needs to happen in this example is the playback head must stop on the last frame of the movie and stay there. In this case, you want the playback head to stop on frame 2. This can be accomplished in one of two ways. The first method involves making use of Director's built-in behaviors (available in the Library Palette). If the Library is not visible, open it by selecting Window → Library Palette from the Director menu. Click the Library List icon at the top left of the library, and select Navigation from the drop-down list. This will present a list of all of the navigation behaviors available in the Library. From this list, select Hold on Current Frame and drag this behavior onto frame 2 of the script channel in the score located just above the numbered time line. The script channel is denoted with a small icon that resembles a page with printed text on it (see Figure 6.25).

6. The Hold on Current Frame behavior does just what its name implies: It holds the playback head on the current frame, displaying the contents of only this one frame. For illus-

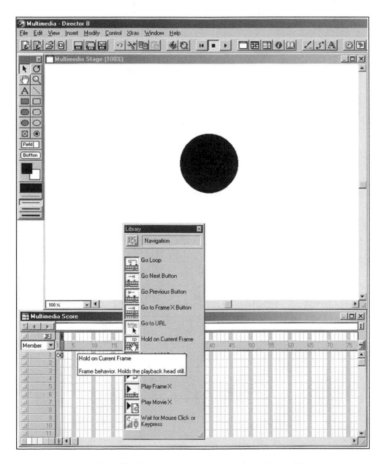

FIGURE 6.25   The Script Channel. The script channel is present above the numbered time line in the score.

tration, you can examine the code of this behavior. To open up the behavior's script, simply double-click on the script in frame 2 of the script channel. This will open the script window, which will display the actual Lingo code that makes this behavior work (see Figure 6.26). Most of the code present in this behavior is descriptive and has no real function. The piece of the code that does all the work is found in the series of lines that read:

```
on exitFrame me
  go the frame
end exitFrame
```

7. The first line [on exitFrame me] starts a new *function* and tells Director to carry out whatever instructions follow this statement whenever the playback head goes to exit the current frame. The *me* in the statement refers to whatever object or frame the behavior is attached to, in this case, frame 2.

8. The second line [go the frame] instructs the playback head to return to the current frame while the third line [end exitFrame] closes the function. Therefore, when the playback head attempts to exit this frame (frame 2), it will be directed to jump back to the start of the frame. The end result is that the playback head remains on the current frame and will stay there until it is instructed to do differently.

9. The second method of pausing the playback head entails creating a new behavior script from scratch. This can be done by double-clicking the cell in the script channel associated with the frame to which you wish to attach the new behavior. In this case, you would double-click frame 2 in the script channel. This will open up a New Behavior Script window. Notice that Director already knows that you are, in this case, creating a new frame-based script, and

FIGURE 6.26   The Hold on Current Frame Behavior.

as a result automatically enters the [on exitFrame me] and [end] lines to the script. All you must do is add the code that appears between these two lines. In this case, the command would be:

```
go the frame
```

In this window, you can also enter a name for your new behavior directly in the Cast Member Name field at the top of the window (see Figure 6.27). Enter the name My New Behavior in this field. This simplified version of the behavior works just as well as the longer version used in step 6.

10. When the movie is played, notice that the playback head moves to frame 2 and stays there. Congratulations! You have just created your first Lingo script! But you are not done yet. Now that the playback head remains on frame 2, you must provide the controls that will cause the oval sprite to move.

FIGURE 6.27   A New Behavior. A revised, streamlined version of the Hold on Current Frame behavior.

11. Next you will create a series of four buttons that will control the direction of movement for the oval. These four buttons will be labeled Down, Right; Up, Right; Down, Left; and Up, Left. To create the buttons, select the Push Button tool from the toolbar on the left side of the Director window. Click and drag on the stage to create a new push button. When you release the button, you should be able to type a label for the button, in this case Down, Right. This label will appear within the boundaries of the button. Repeat this process for the remaining three buttons. The stage should appear as shown in Figure 6.28.

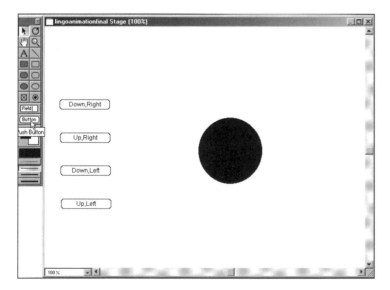

FIGURE 6.28   The Basic Activity. The layout of the buttons and the movable sprite for the Lingo-based animation activity.

12. Now that the buttons are labeled, they should be given names in the cast. For simplicity sake, name the Down, Right button *dr,* the Up, Right button *ur,* the Down, Left button *dl,* and the Up, Left button *ul.* These names will be used to track which button the user is currently pushing.

13. Adjust the duration of the four button sprites in the score, if necessary.

14. To keep track of which button the user pushes, you will need to make use of a variable. Lingo allows for both global and local variables. The main difference between the two is that a global variable can be defined or changed anywhere within the movie. This means several behaviors can make use of a single global variable. In order to define a global variable within a script, the variable name must first be declared within the script. This is done using the [global] command. For this activity, you will need a variable to track the direction of movement for your movable sprite. In this case, you will define the variable name *direction* to keep track of this information. The best place to define this variable will be right at the beginning of the movie. Therefore, create a new frame script by double-clicking on frame 1 in the script channel in the score. Name your new script OpenFrame. In the script window, type in the following code:

```
global direction
on exitFrame me
 direction = ""
end
```

Your script should look like Figure 6.29. The first line of this script [global direction] tells Director that you wish to define a global variable named *direction.* The next three lines set up a function that will define this variable (direction) when the playback head exits the current frame (frame 1). In this case, it sets the value of direction to a null value. This is done by setting the variable equal to "": [direction = ""]. When finished, simply close the script window.

15. Now that your variable is defined, the next step is to change the value of the variable depending on which button the user clicks. For this purpose, you will make use of the unique cast member names for each of the four buttons: *dr, ur, dl,* and *ul.* When the user clicks on the Down, Right button, for instance, you want to create a script that will set the value of the variable *direction* to *dr.* Based on the value of this variable, you can then program the oval to move in the appropriate direction on the stage. This could easily be done by creating four different scripts for each of the four buttons that will set the value of the variable depending on which button is clicked. However, you will be a little more resourceful in this example and create a single behavior script that can be used with all four buttons. The name of this script will be GetName. To create this script, click on the Down, Right button on the stage. With this sprite highlighted, click on the Behavior tab

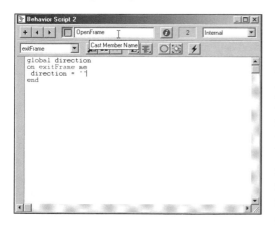

FIGURE 6.29   The OpenFrame Script.

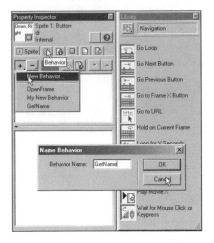

FIGURE 6.30 The GetName Script. When new scripts are created, they can be named in the Name Behavior dialogue box.

of the Property Inspector (see Figure 6.30). With the Behavior tab displayed in the Property Inspector, click on the small + button at the top of the window. This will display a drop-down list. From the list, select New Behavior and type GetName in the Name Behavior dialogue box as shown in Figure 6.30.

16. Your new behavior, which is associated with the *dr* button, will now be listed in the Property Inspector. Select the behavior (GetName) from the list, and click the Script Window icon located above the script list in the Property Inspector (see Figure 6.31). This will open a new script window in which you can compose the script.

17. In this new script window, you will want to make use of the global variable *direction,* so you must first declare this by typing:

```
global direction
```

at the top of the script window. You want this behavior to extract the name of the button that is currently pressed. Therefore, you must assign a function that will register this name when the user clicks the button with his or her mouse. The command that will execute when the mouse button is clicked is called the mouseUp command. The mouseUp command will execute when the user clicks and then releases the mouse button. To add this command to set up your function, you will need to add the following lines to the script:

```
on mouseUp me
end mouseUp
```

This will set up a function that will execute when the user clicks and releases the mouse.

FIGURE 6.31 Editing the New Behavior. Opening the script editing window is done by clicking the Script Window icon in the Property Inspector.

18. But what will this function do? The goal is to set a value to the variable *direction,* which has been declared as a global variable in this script. As mentioned previously, you will utilize the cast member names for each of the buttons (*dr, ur, dl,* and *ul*) to set the value of your variable. The code that will accomplish this goal is:

```
direction = sprite(the currentSpriteNum).member.name
```

You can dissect this line of code. The segment of code [`direction =`] is used to define the global variable *direction.* The segment [`sprite(the currentSpriteNum)`] tells Director to determine which sprite is currently selected. The term *currentSpriteNum* is generic Lingo used to identify the sprite number of the object to which the script is attached. If the Down, Right button happens to be in channel 2 in the score, the value of [`sprite(the currentSpriteNum)`] will be 2. To use this same script for all four buttons, you need to determine the sprite number of the button selected dynamically in this fashion. The remainder of the line [`.member.name`] is considered

FIGURE 6.32   The Magic Script. This script extracts the name of the button that is clicked on the stage and assigns the name to the global variable *direction*. This script can then be used for each of the four buttons on the stage.

dot syntax, which is shorthand for extracting particular properties of an object. In this object-oriented approach, [.member.name] will extract the name of the cast member associated with the currently selected sprite (or button). In this case, the script will determine that sprite 2 is a representation of the cast member named *dr* and will assign the value *dr* to the global variable *direction*. This accomplishes the goal of this script. Your script should resemble Figure 6.32. Notice that this script now appears in your cast as well. Drag this behavior to each of the remaining three buttons present on the stage.

19. Test the movie by clicking the Play button at the top of the Director window. Click each of the buttons. Nothing happens! Why? Well, all of the pieces are in place to make the oval move, but you still need to provide directions for which direction and how fast the oval will move based on the button that is clicked. These definitions can be added to the frame script currently found on frame 2 (named My New Behavior in step 9). Open this script by double-clicking the script in frame 2 of the script channel. The first piece of information that must be added to the script is the declaration that we would like to use the global variable *direction* in this script. Therefore, at the top of the script, add the line:

```
global direction
```

Within the function on exitFrame, you will add code that will provide the desired functionality. First, define what you would like to happen when a button is pushed. For example, when the Down, Right button is pushed (as indicated by the variable *direction* being set equal to *dr* by the button's script), you would like the oval sprite to move down and toward the right from its current location. Locations on the stage in Director are indicated in pixels from the top left corner of the stage. The top left corner is defined as (0,0). The bottom right corner of the stage is defined by the stage size, in this case 640 horizontal pixels and 480 vertical pixels (640,480). Therefore, first define the location of the oval sprite, then, depending on which button is pushed, change the location of the sprite by adding or subtracting pixels to its horizontal and vertical location. The code that will accomplish this is shown below. We will dissect this code line by line in the next step.

```
global direction
on exitframe
  case direction of
    "dr":
      sprite(6).locH = sprite(6).locH + 1
      sprite(6).locV = sprite(6).locV + 1
    "ur":
      sprite(6).locH = sprite(6).locH + 1
```

```
              sprite(6).locV = sprite(6).locV - 1
          "dl":
              sprite(6).locH = sprite(6).locH - 1
              sprite(6).locV = sprite(6).locV + 1
          "ul":
              sprite(6).locH = sprite(6).locH - 1
              sprite(6).locV = sprite(6).locV - 1
        end case
       go to the frame
     end exitframe
```

20. The first line in the function on (exitFrame) sets up a conditional statement. In this conditional statement [`case direction of`], what you are asking Director to do is match the value of the variable *direction* to one of several "cases" or possibilities. The cases are shown below this line. There are four possible cases for the value of *direction*: *dr, ur, dl,* and *ul.* When the playback head exits the current frame, it will compare the value of the variable *direction* to these possible values. When a match is found, the code associated with that particular case is then executed. For example, let's assume that the value of *direction* is *dr.* In this case, the lines below the *dr* case will be executed:

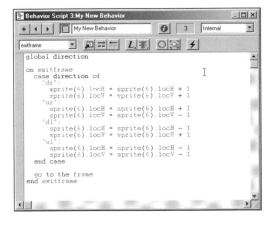

FIGURE 6.33 The Entire Script. The script responsible for generating the movement of the sprite is shown.

```
sprite(6).locH = sprite(6).locH + 1
sprite(6).locV = sprite(6).locV + 1
```

These commands will change the horizontal location [`.locH`] and vertical location [`.locV`] for the identified sprite [`sprite(6)`] by the defined amount. In this case the horizontal location of sprite (6) will be shifted 1 pixel to the right, and the vertical location of sprite (6) will be shifted 1 pixel down, resulting in an overall sprite movement that is down and to the right. Using the same logic, the direction of movement for the remaining three cases is also defined based on the value of the variable *direction.* An example of the completed behavior is shown in Figure 6.33. Close the script window and test the movie now. When each of the four buttons are clicked, the sprite begins to move in the appropriate direction! All of this is done without using multiple keyframes in the movie.

Where to Now?

In this chapter, you have explored the basics of the Director interface and learned how to utilize various features to create basic animation. Three different types of animation techniques were explored: keyframe-based animation, real-time recording, and Lingo-based animation. In the process, you have also learned how to apply some simple Lingo scripting and worked with Director variables. In Chapter 7, you will build on these tools to assemble an actual interactive activity.

7

The Director Project

A Recap

In the previous chapter, you saw how some of the built-in elements of the Director working environment could be used to assemble a simple multimedia application. You also began to work with some simple Lingo scripting to provide interactivity to the application. In this chapter, you will build on these skills to produce a fully interactive educational game.

When working with Lingo, it should be noted that Macromedia provides with every copy of Director a Lingo Dictionary, which contains descriptions and examples of each Lingo command and describes some of the syntax used for this versatile programming language. In addition, within the program's help system, an electronic version of the Lingo Dictionary is available (see Figure 7.1). This online system provides quick access to all of the Lingo commands with in-context examples for each. The Lingo Dictionary is accessible by selecting Help → Lingo Dictionary from the Director menu.

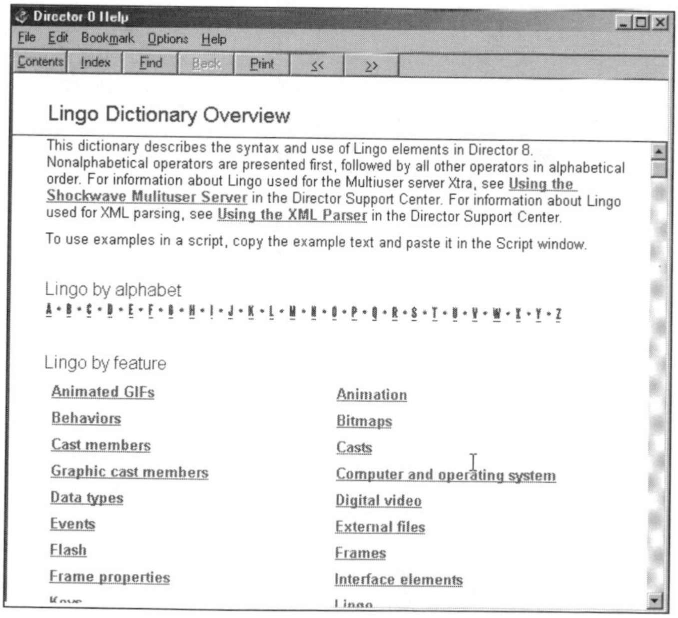

FIGURE 7.1   The Built-in Lingo Dictionary.

For further help with Lingo scripting, an additional feature is available within the script window interface. In the script window, Director also provides quick access to prewritten "snippets" of Lingo code written in the appropriate syntax. To access these small pieces of code, simply click on the Alphabetical Lingo or Categorized Lingo icon present at the top of the script window (see Figure 7.2).

Each of these icons will open a drop-down list that provides access to Lingo code organized either alphabetically or by category. When a selection is made using these tools, Director automatically inserts the appropriate code into the script window, highlighting the variables that must be specified by the developer (see Figure 7.3). These methods of constructing Lingo scripts are effective ways to become familiar with proper Lingo syntax.

Planning the Application

Planning is the single most important step in the process of creating multimedia applications. Careful and effective planning is the hallmark of creating quality multimedia. Because multimedia often involves the fusion of graphics, video, sound, text, as well as computer programming, the process of planning is an imperative first step. For a typical

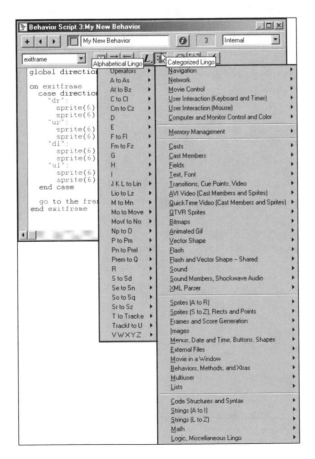

FIGURE 7.2   Accessing Prewritten Lingo from the Script Window. Clicking the Alphabetical Lingo or Categorized Lingo icon at the top of the script window will provide quick access to prewritten Lingo "modules."

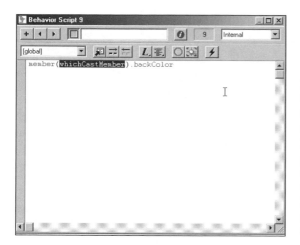

FIGURE 7.3   A Lingo Module Inserted from the Categorized Lingo Option. This simple Lingo script was placed into the script window from the Categorized Lingo section for cast member options. It is designed to obtain the background color of a particular cast member. In this example, Director automatically placed the code shown in the script window. The developer would then replace the highlighted segment [`whichCastMember`,] specifying the cast member for which he or she wanted to obtain the background color information.

professional multimedia application, it is the job of the project coordinator to make sure that all of the video is recorded and edited to specifications, all of the audio is recorded and error free, all of the graphics are in place and ready to go, and all of the programming is complete and tested. Unless all of the key players are on the same page, the project will not come together to create the harmonious final project, and quality will suffer.

Some key questions and guidelines that should be determined before a project is started include the following:

- What is the purpose of this project? What will it actually "do," and how will it actually "do it"?
- Who is the target audience? Will this application be used by students? If so, what age group?
- What is the deadline for this project? When does it absolutely need to be done by?
- Who will do what in the development process? Are all of the key tasks assigned to the proper individual(s)?
- In order to complete the project on time, what are the key milestones that must be achieved and by what date? When does the video need to be ready? When does the audio need to be recorded by?
- Will there be any plug-ins or external software applications required to run this application? If video is used, should a licensed copy of QuickTime be provided on the CD-ROM?
- How will this project be delivered to the user?
- Some of these questions were addressed in Chapter 5; however, before a project is started, answers to each of these should be readily at hand.

This chapter walks through the process of creating an actual multimedia application. The application that will be created is a simple puzzle. The final interface for the application is shown in Figure 7.4. In the process of building this application, you will concentrate on "how" the project is started, assembled, and completed. Through this example, you will build on some of the skills presented in Chapter 6.

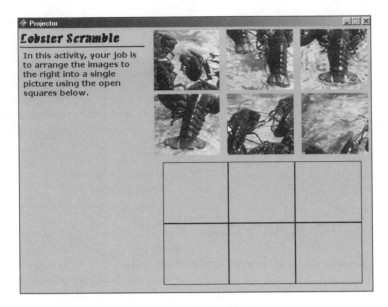

FIGURE 7.4   The Finished Sample Application.

Getting Started

As discussed in Chapter 5, a recommended starting point for a multimedia project is to create a storyboard, or an outline of the application. This outline should include the various "scenes" within the application and the navigational logic. For the puzzle example, a storyboard was created as a flowchart prior to beginning the project. This sample storyboard is shown in Figure 7.5.

In this example, the activity will have an introduction screen that presents directions for users. When users choose to continue the application, they will be taken to the actual puzzle screen; there they can interact with the activity to assemble the puzzle pieces into

FIGURE 7.5   A Sample Flowchart Outlining the Key Elements and Navigational Logic of the Application to Be Built.

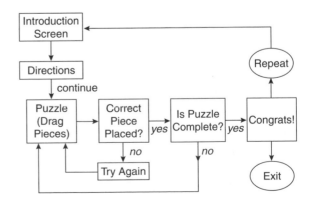

their correct positions by dragging and dropping them onto the grid provided on the stage. Once a puzzle piece is dropped, you will need to use Lingo to decipher whether it has been placed in the right location. If it has not been placed correctly, the user will be told to "try again" and returned to the puzzle interface. If it has been placed correctly, the user will be told that he or she was correct. In this case, we will also need to decipher whether the puzzle is complete (all pieces placed correctly). A Lingo variable will be employed to track the number of puzzle pieces that have been placed correctly. If all of the puzzle pieces have been placed correctly, then the user will be taken to a "closing" screen, told "congratulations," and offered a chance to repeat the puzzle or to exit the program. Much of the logic in this simple puzzle will be constructed using Lingo. Some of the other features of this activity, such as the ability to drag sprites on the stage, will utilize built-in Director Behaviors available in the Behavior palette discussed in Chapter 6.

1. Start a new Director movie.

2. The first step will be to make sure the movie settings are correct. For this activity, a stage size of 640 × 480 pixels and a light green background are needed. To ensure that the colors will display correctly on the widest array of computers, the color palette will also be set to Web 216. These properties can be changed using the Property Inspector, as discussed in Chapter 6.

3. Next, you will want to import your cast members. For this activity, a simple JPEG image was "sliced" into six equal parts using an image editing package. The slices were then saved as separate JPEG images. To import all of these images, select File → Import from the Director menu. This will open the Import Files dialogue box. From this box, you can browse the computer for the correct files and click the Add button to add them to the list of files to be imported, followed by the Import button to bring them into the movie's cast (see Figure 7.6).

4. When importing bitmap images into Director using this method, you will need to specify the settings for the images. This can be done with the Image Options dialogue box that appears during the import of these images (see Figure 7.7). In this dialogue box, you can specify the color depth of the images and the color palette to use. In this case, to have the images match the color depth and palette used in the movie, select the Stage (24 bits) option in the dialogue box. (Note: When importing multiple images at once, if you do not specify Same Settings for Remaining Images, you will need to specify the color depth for each imported image separately.) After the images have been imported into the cast, you will rename each of them. In this case, the slices will be named sequentially as Lob one, Lob two, Lob three, and so forth. The reason for this naming convention will become apparent later.

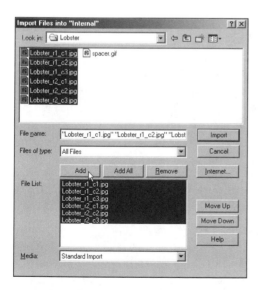

FIGURE 7.6 The Import Files Dialogue Box. The image "slices" for the project are selected for import into the Director cast.

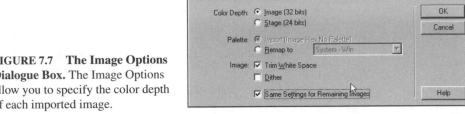

FIGURE 7.7 The Image Options Dialogue Box. The Image Options allow you to specify the color depth of each imported image.

5. The next step will be to create the introductory screen for the activity. When the movie is started, the playback head will remain on this screen. The introduction screen will contain a brief text description of the activity, an image of the completed puzzle, and a button that will allow the user to continue on to the next scene containing the puzzle.

6. Using the Text tool from the Tool palette, add text to the stage as shown in Figure 7.8. To change the font or size of the text, highlight the text and select Modify → Font from the Director menu. Using the Font dialogue box, you can select different fonts, styles, and sizes to be applied to the text.

7. If you have selected a background color other than white, you will notice that the text appears to stand out from the background (see Figure 7.8). To remove the white background from the text, select the text and open the sprite tab in the Property Inspector. The ink setting for the text is currently set to Copy. In order to apply a transparent background to the text, click the small arrow next to the ink bottle icon. This will display a drop-down list of all the available inks that can be applied to the selected sprite. In this case, you want the

FIGURE 7.8 The Introductory Screen.

FIGURE 7.9 The Sprite Property Inspector. The ink of the sprite can be changed using this inspector. To remove the background from the sprite, the Background Transparent ink is applied.

background to blend with the background, so you will select Background Transparent from the list to apply this ink to your text (see Figure 7.9). Repeat this for all of the text boxes on the stage.

8. To finish the layout of the opening screen, a button is added. This is done by selecting the Push Button tool from the Tool Palette and dragging on the stage to create the button. Once placed on the stage, enter the text Forward to the button, as shown in Figure 7.10.

9. To begin building the navigation structure of the activity, the next step is to alter the score. First, set the duration of each of the sprites present on the opening screen to 15 frames. As discussed in Chapter 6, this can be done either with the Property Inspector or by dragging the end handle on each individual Sprite Indicator Bar in the score. Next, add a "marker" to frame 1 of the score. The marker can be added by clicking above frame 1 in the white space above the script channel (refer to Figure 7.11). When you click in this space, an inverted triangle will be placed on the specified frame (indicating that this is the frame the marker will be associated with), and you will need to supply the Marker Name. For frame 1, name the marker Opening. Add a second marker named Puzzle to frame 20, as shown in Figure 7.11. Finally, when the movie is played, you want the playback head to stop on frame 15 to wait for the user to click the Forward button present on the stage. Add a Stop Frame script to frame 15, as shown in Figure 7.11. As discussed in Chapter 6, the simplest script that will achieve this function is:

```
on exitFrame me
  go the frame
end
```

Name the script StopFrame, as shown in Figure 7.11.

10. The next step will be to program the Forward button on the opening screen. For this purpose, you will make use of one of Director's built-in behaviors. Make sure the Forward button is visible on the stage (you may need to move the playback head). In the Behavior palette, open the Navigation behaviors by clicking the Library List button in the palette and selecting Navigation from the drop-down list (see Figure 7.12). From the list of Navigation behaviors, drag the Go Next behavior onto the Forward button. As the description for the behavior states, this function will cause the playback head to jump to the next marker in the score when the button is clicked. This is exactly what you want this button to do—to move forward to the next marker in the score, in this case, the Puzzle marker.

11. The next step will involve setting up the Puzzle screen. Several elements will need to be added to the movie to set up this screen. First, text will be added to the top right-hand corner of the stage, providing a title ("Lobster Scramble") and directions for the activity (refer to Figure 7.4) for this layout. The actual puzzle pieces will be arranged in random fashion at the top of the screen. In addition, six small bitmap boxes will be drawn on the stage. These graphics will be the drop targets for the puzzle pieces. Each square should match the dimensions of the puzzle pieces. These squares can be drawn using the Paint window in Director.

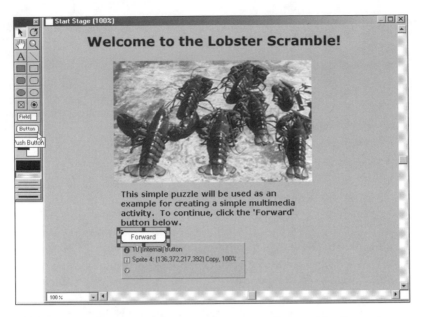

FIGURE 7.10   The Final Layout for the Opening Screen. The Forward button is added to the stage to allow the user to proceed to the puzzle.

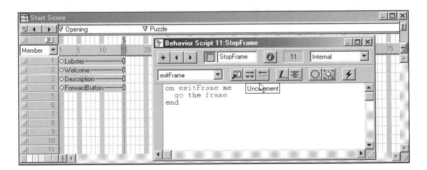

FIGURE 7.11   Changing the Score. The score must be adjusted to accommodate the function of the opening screen.

The dimensions of the actual puzzle pieces for this exercise are 120×110 pixels. When the rectangles are drawn on the screen, their size can be adjusted precisely using the Property Inspector (see Figure 7.13). Be sure to name each rectangle in the cast. To correspond with the puzzle pieces, name the squares sequentially as "one," "two," "three," and so forth.

12. The final element of the puzzle screen will be an "invisible" feedback box, which will provide feedback to users based on their actions. This feedback box will essentially be a "holding bin" for text in the activity. To create this feedback box, select the Text tool from the Tool palette and draw a text box on the stage, as shown in Figure 7.14. Do not enter any text in the box. Be sure to set the ink for the text to Background Transparent, as demonstrated previously.

FIGURE 7.12 **Attaching a Behavior.** By selecting the Navigation option in the Behavior Library, you can assign the Go Next behavior to the Forward button.

13. For organizational purposes, you will now adjust the score a bit. Set the duration of each element on the Puzzle screen to 10 frames (each sprite should span from frame 20 to frame 30 in its respective channel). Place your StopFrame behavior on frame 30 to stop the playback head on this frame. The stage and score should resemble Figure 7.15.

14. The next step in the process is to program the actual puzzle pieces so they can (a) be dragged on the stage by the user, (b) be tested for correct placement, and (c) based upon placement, remain on the drop target or be returned to the original location. As you can imagine, this will entail some detailed Lingo programming. All three of these functions will be accomplished by a single Lingo script containing several subroutines. To begin, select one of the puzzle pieces on the stage, and attach a new behavior to it (as outlined in Chapter 6). Name this new script PuzzleDrag.

15. This script will need to keep track of several different parameters for each puzzle piece during the activity. For instance, you want the puzzle pieces to be "draggable" on the stage until they have been correctly placed onto the corresponding drop target, in which case they will no longer be draggable. You also need to know how many puzzle pieces have been correctly placed onto the drop targets; in other words, you must know when the activity has been completed. In order to keep track of these and other properties, you must define these parameters as "properties" in the actual script.

16. With the script window open for your new script, type in the following code:

```
global gNumberCorrect
property SpriteNum
property pDrag
property pOffset
property pLocked
property pOrigLoc
```

17. The global variable *gNumberCorrect* will be used to track the number of correctly placed puzzle pieces during the course of the activity. The SpriteNum property will be used to identify which puzzle piece is currently being dragged. The pDrag and pLocked properties will be used to track whether the puzzle piece has been placed correctly onto its drop target, and if so, made no longer draggable. The pOffset and pOrigLoc properties will track the difference between the position of the puzzle piece on the stage and where the mouse "grabs" it, and the original location of the puzzle piece, respectively.

18. Continuing with the new script, the initial parameters for the puzzle piece must be defined. This is done by adding the code:

```
on beginSprite Me
  pOrigLoc = sprite(me.spriteNum).loc
  pDrag = false
```

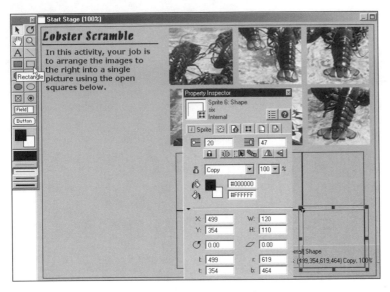

FIGURE 7.13   Adding the Drop Targets. Bitmap boxes are added to the stage to represent the drop targets for the puzzle pieces. The exact dimensions of these targets can be controlled in the Property Inspector by entering values directly in the width and height (W: and H:) fields.

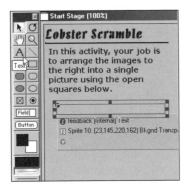

FIGURE 7.14   Creating a Feedback Box on the Stage.

```
        pLocked = false
    end
```

19. The beginSprite routine will record the original location of the puzzle piece into the variable pOrigLoc. The sprite's location is obtained with the code [sprite(me.spriteNum).loc]. Referring to the associated sprite by me.spriteNum, as opposed to the actual number of the sprite, will allow you to use the same script on all of the puzzle pieces (sprites). The pDrag and pLocked properties are set to false to indicate that the sprite should not be draggable and it should not be locked into place at this time.

20. Being able to drag a sprite on the stage is a bit tricky because it involves constantly updating its position relative to where the cursor is currently placed. In order to do this constant updating, you must provide a function that constantly updates while the current frame is displayed. The following code will accomplish this:

```
on prepareFrame me
  if pDrag then
    sprite(me.spriteNum).loc = the mouseLoc + pOffset
  end if
end
```

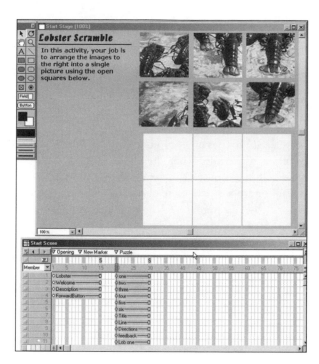

FIGURE 7.15 Completed Layout and Score of the Puzzle Screen.

21. In the prepareFrame subroutine, you are basically asking whether pDrag has been set to "true" for the current sprite. If it has, then the location of the current sprite [sprite(me.spriteNum).loc] is set to the current location of the mouse [mouseLoc] plus the variable pOffset, which will be defined in the next segment. This small subroutine is responsible for updating the sprite's location as it follows the mouse's movement on the stage.

22. Continuing with the script, you must define how the puzzle piece sprites will interact with the mouse. For this, the following code is added to the script next:

```
on mouseWithin me
  cursor 280
end

on mouseLeave me
  cursor -1
end

on mouseDown me
  if pLocked = true then exit
  sprite(me.spriteNum).locZ = sprite(me.spriteNum).locZ + 20
  pDrag = true
  pOffset = sprite(me.spriteNum).loc - the mouseLoc
end
```

```
on mouseUp me
  cursor -1
  if pLocked = true then exit
  pDrag = false
  sprite(me.spriteNum).locZ = sprite(me.spriteNum).locZ - 20
  checkLock(me)
end
```

23. The first two subroutines in this segment of code (mouseWithin and mouseLeave) simply change the appearance of the cursor when the user moves the mouse "within" the sprite or "leaves" the sprite with the mouse. The [`cursor 280`] command line simply changes the cursor to a "pointing finger" when the user moves the mouse within the puzzle piece, whereas the [`cursor -1`] command line simply returns the cursor to its original state (pointer). The mouseDown routine defines the action when the user presses the mouse button while over the attached sprite. In this case, the first line of this subroutine determines whether the sprite has been locked. The sprite should be locked only if it has been placed onto the correct drop target. So, initially, the query [`if pLocked`] should return "false." If pLocked were set to "true," then the subroutine would stop (determined by the [`then exit`] statement) and not execute any more of the code. Assuming pLocked is false, the routine would continue to the next line [`sprite(me.spriteNum).locZ = sprite(me.spriteNum).locZ + 20`], which simply moves the attached sprite in front of the other sprites on the stage. This command is not required to make the activity run, but it does add aesthetic appeal to the activity because without it, puzzle pieces in lower-numbered channels would be dragged behind the other puzzle pieces when assembling the puzzle. The next two lines perform the bulk of the work in this routine. [`pDrag = true`] enables the attached sprite to be dragged on the stage while the mouse is down. In order to drag a sprite on the stage, we must keep track of the position of the cursor relative to the point within the sprite where the user clicked. This is done with the next line in the subroutine: [`pOffset = sprite(me.spriteNum).loc - the mouseLoc`]. This command line calculates the difference between the location of the mouse (mouseLoc) and the puzzle piece (sprite(me.spriteNum)) and assigns this value to the property pOffset, which you can utilize later in the script. The mouseUp routine essentially reverses everything that was done with the mouseDown routine with one major exception: It also triggers a new subroutine—checkLock(me). The checkLock routine will compare the sprite currently being dragged to its drop target and determine if they match.

24. The checkLock routine is the meat of the script. The actual code looks like this:

```
on checkLock me
  correctBox = sprite(me.spriteNum).member.name.word[2]
  repeat with i = 1 to the lastChannel
    if sprite(i).member.name = correctBox then
      if closeEnough(me, sprite(i).loc,
        sprite(me.spriteNum).loc) then
        sprite(me.spriteNum).locH = sprite(i).locH
        sprite(me.spriteNum).locV = sprite(i).locV
        pLocked = true
        puppetsound 3, "correct"
```

```
        gNumberCorrect = gNumberCorrect + 1
        member("feedback").text = "Good Job! Keep
        Going . . . "
        if gNumberCorrect = 6 then
          member("feedback").text = "Excellent job! To repeat
          this activity, click Reset."
          sprite(17).visibility = true
          exit
        end if
      end if
    end if
  end repeat
  if pLocked = false then
    sprite(me.spriteNum).loc = pOrigLoc
    member("feedback").text = "That is not correct. Try again"
    puppetsound 3, "incorrect"
  end if
end
```

25. The first line of the checkLock routine will assign the second word in the name of the current sprite [`sprite(me.spriteNum).member.name.word[2]`] to the variable correctBox. Remember, when the bitmap images for the puzzle pieces were imported into the cast, you named them Lob one, Lob two, and so on. What this command does is extracts the second word in the cast member name (e.g., *one*) and assigns it to the correctBox variable. As you might guess, the correctBox variable will be used to compare whether the sprite is being dropped onto the correct box. The next segment of this subroutine starts a program loop, which will simply cycle through all of the sprites currently on the stage. This is accomplished with the [`repeat with i = 1 to the lastChannel`] command line. While the routine cycles through the values of *i*, it will carry out the subsequent lines of code. The following line [`if sprite(i).member.name = correctBox then`] compares the name of each sprite on the stage to the value of the variable correctBox. When a match is found, the remainder of the code is executed: [`if closeEnough(me, sprite(i).loc, sprite(me.spriteNum).loc) then`]. This segment of code branches to a new subroutine: closeEnough. This subroutine will determine whether the sprite has been dragged close enough to the drop target sprite on the stage. This subroutine will be covered in detail later; for now, let's assume that the sprite is indeed close enough and the subroutine closeEnough returns true. This means the next lines of code will be executed:

```
sprite(me.spriteNum).locH = sprite(i).locH
sprite(me.spriteNum).locV = sprite(i).locV
pLocked = true
puppetsound 3, "correct"
gNumberCorrect = gNumberCorrect + 1
member("feedback:").text = "Good Job! Keep Going . . . "
```

26. Here, the location of the puzzle piece sprite will be set to be equal to the drop target (`sprite(i).loc`). This will make the puzzle piece "snap" into position. Once in correct position, the following line [`pLocked = true`] "locks" the puzzle piece into place (it will no longer be draggable). This also causes a small WAV sound file, named *correct,* to be played and increments the value of gNumberCorrect by one. In addition, you place a new message in your Feedback text field with the line [`member("feedback").text = "Good Job! Keep Going . . . "`]. The next segment of the checkLock subroutine is designed to test whether the puzzle has been completed:

```
if gNumberCorrect = 6 then
  member("feedback").text = "Excellent job! To repeat this
  activity, click Reset."
  sprite(17).visibility = true
exit
end if
end if
end if
end repeat
```

27. Because the value of gNumberCorrect is incremented each time a puzzle piece is placed correctly onto a drop target, and there are a total of 6 puzzle pieces to be placed, when gNumberCorrect reaches 6, the feedback field is updated to reflect the successful completion of the activity. The [`sprite(17).visibility = true`] will be explained in a subsequent step. For each *if* and *repeat* statement used in the subroutine, there must be a corresponding *end if* and *end repeat* statement, which make up the remainder of this segment of the subroutine. The next segment of the checkLock subroutine executes only if the puzzle piece was not placed correctly onto a drop target (correctBox did not match the drop target used by the user):

```
if pLocked = false then
  sprite(me.spriteNum).loc = pOrigLoc
  member("feedback").text = "That is not correct. Try again"
  puppetsound 3, "incorrect"
end if
end
```

28. In this case, pLocked remains false and the following lines of code execute. The command [`sprite(me.spriteNum).loc = pOrigLoc`] works to return the current sprite (puzzle piece) to its original location (initially stored in the property pOrigLoc). The feedback text field is updated to reflect that the puzzle piece was not placed correctly onto the drop target, and an incorrect WAV sound file is played. The subroutine is then closed with the end command.

29. This leaves the final segment of the PuzzleDrag script: the closeEnough subroutine. This subroutine checks the location of the puzzle piece when the user releases the mouse relative to the location of the drop target. The code looks like this:

```
on closeEnough me, loc1, loc2
  maxdistance = 100
  if abs(loc1.locH—loc2.locH) < maxdistance then
  if abs(loc1.locV—loc2.locV) < maxdistance then
```

```
      return true
    end if
    end if
    return false
end
```

30. Remember, the checkLock subroutine contained the code [if closeEnough (me, sprite(i).loc, sprite(me.spriteNum).loc) then]. This line of code executes the closeEnough subroutine, passing two location parameters to the routine, in this case the location of the drop target [sprite(i).loc] and the location where the user actually drops the puzzle piece [sprite(me.spriteNum).loc]. The closeEnough subroutine compares these two values, comparing them to a maximum allowable difference [maxdistance = 100], which can be easily altered by the developer. If the horizontal positions of the two sprites are within 100 pixels [if abs(loc1.locH - loc2.locH) < maxdistance] and the vertical locations of the two sprites are also within 100 pixels [if abs(loc1.locV - loc2.locV) < maxdistance], then the closeEnough subroutine returns the value of true to the checkLock subroutine. Otherwise, it returns the value of false and closes the script.

31. The entire PuzzleDrag behavior is now complete. When entered into the script window, it should resemble the following:

```
global gNumberCorrect
property SpriteNum
property pDrag
property pOffset
property pLocked
property pOrigLoc

on beginSprite Me
  pOrigLoc = sprite(me.spriteNum).loc
  pDrag = false
  pLocked = false
end

on prepareFrame me
  if pDrag then
    sprite(me.spriteNum).loc = the mouseLoc + pOffset
  end if
end

on mouseWithin me
  cursor 280
end

on mouseLeave me
  cursor -1
end
```

```
on mouseDown me
  if pLocked = true then exit
  sprite(me.spriteNum).locZ = sprite(me.spriteNum).locZ + 20
  pDrag = true
  pOffset = sprite(me.spriteNum).loc—the mouseLoc
end

on mouseUp me
  cursor -1
  if pLocked = true then exit
  pDrag = false
  sprite(me.spriteNum).locZ = sprite(me.spriteNum).locZ—20
  checkLock(me)
end

on checkLock me
  correctBox = sprite(me.spriteNum).member.name.word[2]
  repeat with i = 1 to the lastChannel
    if sprite(i).member.name = correctBox then
      if closeEnough(me, sprite(i).loc,
      sprite(me.spriteNum).loc) then
        sprite(me.spriteNum).locH = sprite(i).locH
        sprite(me.spriteNum).locV = sprite(i).locV
        pLocked = true
        puppetsound 3, "correct"
        gNumberCorrect = gNumberCorrect + 1
        member("feedback").text = "Good Job! Keep Going . . . "
        if gNumberCorrect = 6 then
          member("feedback").text = "Excellent job! To repeat
          this activity, click Reset."
          sprite(17).visibility = true
          exit
        end if
      end if
    end if
  end repeat
  if pLocked = false then
    sprite(me.spriteNum).loc = pOrigLoc
    member("feedback").text = "That is not correct. Try again"
    puppetsound 3, "incorrect"
  end if
end

on closeEnough me, loc1, loc2
  maxdistance = 100
  if abs(loc1.locH - loc2.locH) < maxdistance then
    if abs(loc1.locV - loc2.locV) < maxdistance then
```

```
        return true
      end if
    end if
    return false
end
```

32. Drag the PuzzleDrag behavior from the Cast onto each of the 5 remaining puzzle pieces on the stage. This will automatically attach the behavior to these sprites.

33. You are almost done with the activity. A bit of "housekeeping" must be done first, however. Because you are using variables to track the number of correctly placed puzzle pieces in the PuzzleDrag behavior and the Feedback text field to convey information to the user, these values should be reset at the beginning of the activity. It is also important to provide users with the opportunity to repeat the activity once they have completed the puzzle. These elements can be easily added to the activity. First, to reset the gNumberCorrect variable and the Feedback text field, you can create a frame script that executes at the beginning of the Puzzle screen. Do this by double-clicking frame 21 in the script channel to create a script named ClearData. Enter the code as shown in Figure 7.16. This frame-based script must declare that it will use the global variable *gNumberCorrect* at the top of the script. When the script executes, it will set the text of the field Feedback to " " (blank) and reset gNumberCorrect to 0.

34. The final piece of this activity lies in the mysterious sprite(17) seen in the PuzzleDrag behavior and the ClearData script. Sprite(17) is nothing more than a Reset button that you would like to hide from the user until the puzzle has been completed. The actual location and appearance of the button are shown in Figure 7.17.

35. To control the appearance of the Reset button, you must utilize the visibility property of the sprite. In the ClearData frame script, you set the visibility of this sprite to false [sprite(17).visibility = false] (see Figure 7.16). The Reset button, therefore, remains hidden from the user until the visibility is turned back on. This is done in the PuzzleDrag behavior within the checkLock subroutine. The [sprite(17).visibility = true] line appears within the [if gNumberCorrect = 6 then] segment. Therefore, when all of the pieces have been correctly placed into the puzzle (gNumberCorrect = 6), the Reset button will magically appear.

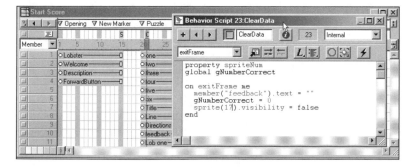

FIGURE 7.16   The ClearData Frame Script. This script is placed at the beginning of the puzzle screen to reset the data used during the activity.

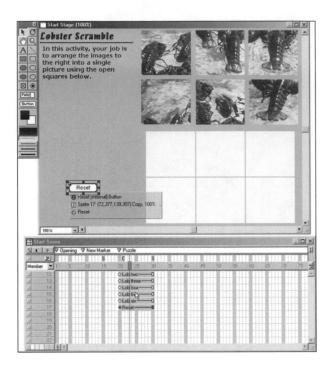

FIGURE 7.17   Sprite(17).
The Reset button.

36. The only piece that remains is actually to program the Reset button. You would like this button to return the user to the Puzzle marker on clicking it. This can easily be done by selecting the sprite and adding a new behavior to the button (discussed previously). The code that will accomplish this task is:

```
on MouseUp me
  go marker ("Puzzle")
end
```

37. In this script, the MouseUp function will execute the go marker command. In this case, the playback head will be directed to go to the marker named Puzzle, performing the desired function.

38. When tested, the movie will now behave as originally scripted in your storyboard (see Figure 7.18). Try it out.

Delivering the Goods

Once your project is complete, the final step is to package the project for delivery to the users. Director provides the ability to package all of the media elements and programming structure into a self-contained executable file. This is done by selecting File → Create Projector from the Director menu (see Figure 7.19).

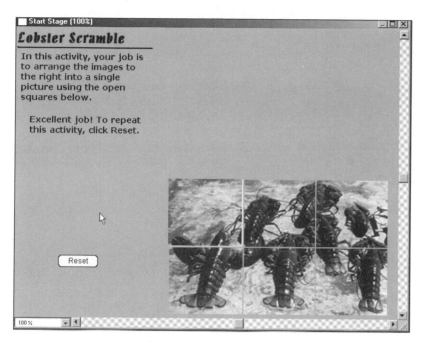

FIGURE 7.18   The Finished Product!

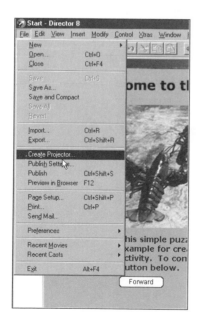

When creating a Projector, you actually have the option of packaging as many Director movies or casts as you would like into the executable file. Select the Director file that you wish to create a Projector from in the Create Projector dialogue box and click the Add button (see Figure 7.20). When all of the files have been added, click the Create button. Director will automatically create an executable file that will contain all of the information necessary to run your application on a remote user's computer. This executable file is ready for delivery to the end user. Depending on the size of the file, you may need to burn a copy of the file onto a CD-ROM to get it into the hands of your users.

Conclusion

FIGURE 7.19   Creating a Projector.

As has been evident in these last few chapters, Director is a powerful multimedia authoring tool. The capabilities of Director are limited only by your own imagination, patience, and commitment. Learning to program Director using Lingo can take quite a bit of time. However, once you have a few basics down, the learning process becomes much easier. The best way to learn a complex

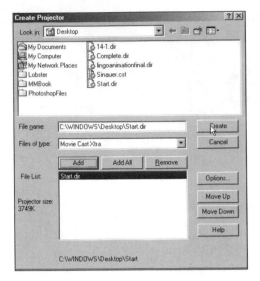

FIGURE 7.20   The Create Projector Dialogue Box.

package such as this is simply to "play" with it as much as possible. Start with small, easy projects and build your skills from there. Another convenient way to learn this tool is to "dissect" movies that have been created by professionals. Discover how they created those interesting animation effects. Look to see how variables are used in interactive exercises. Examine the Lingo scripts used in the activities to try and figure out how the different commands are used in context. With time, the rewards will be great.

8 An Introduction to Flash

Macromedia Flash is software that gives authors the power to produce visually compelling drawings, smooth animations, and complete interactivity. Even better, Flash Player movies, the final product that an author publishes to the Web, are extraordinarily small and have correspondingly lightning-fast download times.

Because of all of these benefits, both educational and advertising media now make extensive use of Flash in web-based presentations. More and more textbook publishers are including Flash-based media either on disk or online, and many major corporations incorporate Flash presentations in their web presences.

This chapter and the next two provide the reader with an introduction to using Macromedia Flash. This chapter gives the reader a quick tour of almost everything Flash has to offer in terms of drawing and animation. Chapter 9 provides a strong initial orientation to the drawing tools available in Flash. Chapter 10 provides details about animation and interactivity and ends with a project: producing an interactive online set of study flashcards.

Although these three chapters are designed to be read in sequence, it may be useful for you to refer to later chapters while working through the example in this chapter. In any case, Flash is an extremely flexible tool for producing incredible online material, and exploring its capabilities is likely to provide immediate rewards.

The Flash Work Environment

Figure 8.1 shows the Flash work environment as you would see it when you first open Flash. To begin, here is a description of the main parts of the Flash work environment, working down from the top of the screen.

The time line looks like several strips of movie film, stacked on top of one another. Each of the strips of movie film is called a layer. Any object you place in a Flash presentation is stored in a layer. Layers superimpose themselves over layers below them and are blocked out by layers above them.

Following the movie film analogy, each layer is divided into tiny rectangles called frames. If you click on a frame, the stage below will show what the Flash presentation looks like at that point.

The playhead is an orange rectangle that appears above the top layer. A vertical orange line extends from the bottom of the playhead and passes through the center of the frames that are active, being shown on the stage, below. Dragging the playhead allows you to view different frames on the stage.

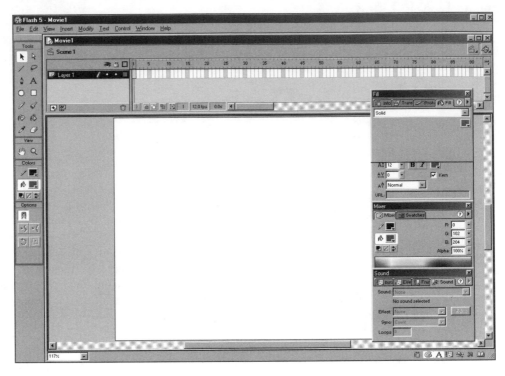

FIGURE 8.1   The Flash Work Environment.

Keyframes are special frames that begin or end events in the Flash presentation. They are indicated by a black border around the frame in which the keyframe is inserted.

The stage is a rectangular box under the time line. Anything contained in the current keyframes appears on the stage and will appear in the Flash presentation. You also generally work with objects, creating them and moving them, on the stage. The borders of the stage are the borders of the final Flash presentation you produce.

Around the stage is a light gray section called the *work area.* Objects that are in the work area will not appear in the Flash presentation. If you want an object to move onto the stage eventually, you can keep it in the work area and move it onto the stage later.

New versions of Flash provide a wide range of *tools,* which are shown in the column on the left. Many of these tools may be modified by the *panels* that are shown in a column on the right. For example, the Fill panel on the right may be used to change the color created by the Paintbrush tool.

Flash Drawing and Animation Quick Start

To get a quick idea of how to draw objects and animate them using Flash, begin with the following project. You will draw a simple boat and animate it so that it moves back and forth across a banner-sized background.

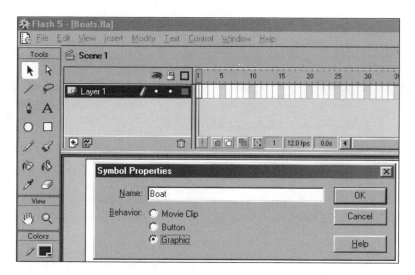

FIGURE 8.2   Inserting the Boat Symbol.

First save a blank Flash movie as Boats. Do this by clicking on File>Save As>Boats. Make sure that you are saving it as a Flash Movie file type.

Set the size of the movie by choosing Modify>Movie and, under Dimensions, selecting a width of 550 and a height of 300, and clicking OK.

Creating a Symbol

Next, create a symbol. Symbols are objects that you can use repeatedly in Flash. In this example, the symbol will be the boat that you will later animate.

To create a symbol, click on Insert>New Symbol. The Symbol Properties box will appear, as shown in Figure 8.2. In this box, type in a Name for the symbol. In this case it will be Boat. Indicate the Behavior that the symbol will be able to perform. In this case, it will be a Graphic. Finally, click OK to finish this step.

Once you have clicked OK, you will notice that you have moved out of Scene 1 and into the graphic symbol Boat. This is shown on your screen through the highlighted Boat sign that appears next to the Scene 1 sign, as shown in Figure 8.3.

Click on the Circle drawing tool, and move your pointer onto the stage, near the crosshairs at the center of the stage. Hold down the left mouse button and move the mouse down. You will begin to draw a circle. Hold down the Shift key to keep the circle perfectly round.

All you will see at this point is the outline of the circle. By moving the mouse around, you can change the size of the circle. Release the mouse button, and a

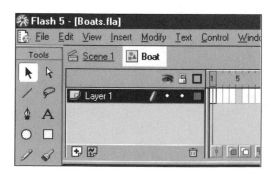

FIGURE 8.3   The Boat Symbol Work Area.

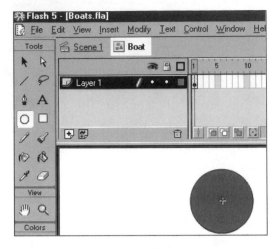

FIGURE 8.4   Drawing a Circle.

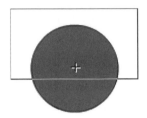

FIGURE 8.5   Selecting an Area for Editing.

**FIGURE 8.6
Top Two-Thirds
of Circle
Highlighted for
Editing.**

filled-in circle will appear on the stage, as shown in Figure 8.4.

Now you will turn the circle into a boat. Start by clicking on the Arrow tool. Next, point the arrow to the left of the circle, slightly above the circle, and click the left mouse button. Drag your mouse to move the arrow down and to the right. The top half of the circle will begin to be surrounded by a rectangle, as shown in Figure 8.5. This indicates that this area is selected for some editing action.

Once you have covered the top two-thirds of the circle, release the mouse button. You have now selected the top two-thirds of the circle. That part of the circle will be highlighted, as shown in Figure 8.6.

Now click on the Scale button, at the lower right-hand corner of the drawing tools. The Scale button changes the size of the object. You should see a set of small squares appear around the selected part of the circle, as shown in Figure 8.7.

Clicking on any of these squares allows you to resize the object from the direction of the square. Shrink the top half of the circle by clicking on the top right square and dragging down and to the left.

Then move the arrow to the middle of the resized top part of the circle and click on it. Then drag it to the middle of the bottom half of the circle and release it. See the boat? Figure 8.8 shows how it should look.

Now use the ink bottle to give the boat a dark border. The ink bottle draws lines around the edges of objects you have created. First, while the Arrow tool is still active, click anywhere on the stage to deselect the top of the boat. The boxes around the top of the boat should disappear.

Next, click on the Ink Bottle in the drawing tools section, as shown in Figure 8.9. Then activate the Stroke panel by choosing Window>Panels>Stroke, or clicking on the Stroke tab if it is visible. Select solid for the type of line and 2.0 for line thickness. The Stroke panel appears in Figure 8.9.

FIGURE 8.7   The Scale Button.

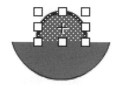

FIGURE 8.8 Reducing Selection Size with the Scale Tool.

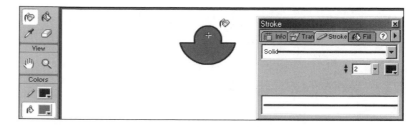

FIGURE 8.9 Using the Ink Bottle and Stroke Panel.

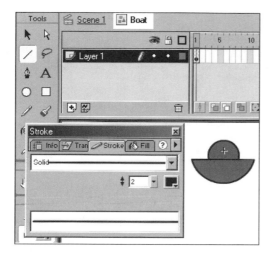

FIGURE 8.10 Using the Line Tool and Stroke Panel.

Finally, move the ink bottle to the edge of the drawing of the boat. Click on the edge with the ink bottle. Repeat as necessary, working your way around the boat, until it has a thick black outline all around it.

To separate the top of the boat from the bottom of the boat, use the Line tool. Click on the Line tool, and make sure that the Stroke panel is set to a line type of solid and thickness of 2, as shown in Figure 8.10. You will notice that if you move the pointer over the stage, it now turns into an X.

Start the line by moving the pointer to the spot that you want the line to begin. Click on the beginning spot and then drag with the mouse until you have finished the line. Release the mouse button.

Now use the paint bucket to make the top of the boat a lighter color. First click on the Paint Bucket. You will notice that if you move the pointer over the stage, it now turns into a bucket, as shown in Figure 8.11.

Activate the Fill panel by selecting Window>Panels>Fill or clicking on the Fill tab if it is visible. Select a color by clicking on the Fill Color box on the right of the Fill area. A choice of colors will appear on a grid. Click on light gray.

Finally, move the paint bucket to the middle of the top of the boat and click. The top of the boat will now be filled with gray, as shown in Figure 8.11.

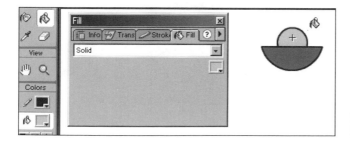

FIGURE 8.11 Using the Paint Bucket and Fill Panel.

Now use the Pencil tool to create a flagpole for your boat. First, click on the Pencil tool. The pointer will now look like a pencil when it is over the work area.

On the Options panel, click on the Line Straighten button, which is shown active in Figure 8.12. This will make the line you draw perfectly straight, regardless of how you actually draw it. On the Stroke panel, give the flagpole a thickness of 1.5. Now, using the pencil, draw a vertical flagpole on your boat, as shown in Figure 8.12.

To add a flag, use the Paintbrush tool. Click on the Paintbrush tool, as shown in Figure 8.13. Under the Options area, make the paintbrush fairly small by clicking on the fourth smallest circle on the Brush Size menu. Change the shape of the paintbrush to an oval by selecting the oval shape in the Brush Shape menu. The pointer will now look like an oval when it is over the work area.

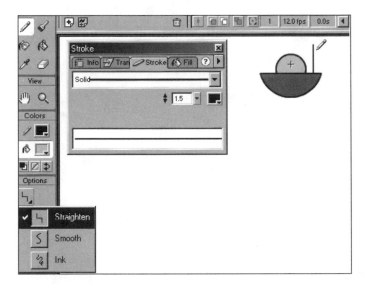

FIGURE 8.12   Using the Pencil Tool and Stroke Panel.

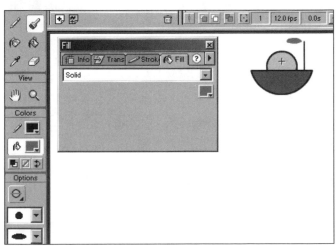

FIGURE 8.13   Using the Paintbrush Tool and Fill Panel.

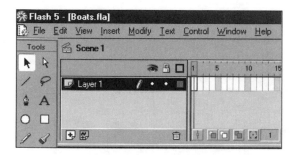

FIGURE 8.14   Returning to Scene 1.

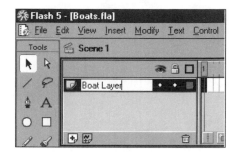

FIGURE 8.15   Renaming Layer 1.

Select the color that the paintbrush will produce by choosing the Fill panel, and selecting your color of choice from the color choice menu. Draw a flag at the top of the flag-pole, as seen in Figure 8.13.

Now that you have created a boat symbol, you can insert it into the Flash movie. To do that, click on Scene 1 above the layers, as shown in Figure 8.14. The boat will disappear, and Scene 1 of the movie will appear. Right now it is blank, with nothing appearing on the stage or the time line.

Layer 1 will be the layer that the boat goes in. First rename Layer 1 by double-clicking on Layer 1.

That area will become highlighted, as shown in Figure 8.15. Type in Boat Layer to indicate that the Boat symbol will be in that layer.

Using the Library

Next, you have to retrieve your symbol, the boat, from the movie's library. First click on Window > Library. Doing so will display all of the symbols in your library, on a box to the right. The only symbol in your library right now will be Boat, as shown in Figure 8.16. Click on Boat and you will see it appear in the top of the Library box.

To put an instance of the symbol Boat into the Boat Layer, click on the image of the boat in the Library and drag it onto the stage. Place it near the top of the stage, as shown in Figure 8.17.

Using Keyframes

At this point, the boat is in a keyframe. It is at the beginning of the movie, in a keyframe at Frame 1, on the Boat Layer. You will notice that the keyframe at the beginning of the Boat Layer now has a black dot in it. This indicates that an object is now placed in that keyframe.

Next, you will add another keyframe at a later point in the Boat Layer that will indi-cate where the end of the animation will be. Because the boat will move back and forth across the screen in this animation, the end of the animation will be exactly the same as the beginning of the animation. The default speed for Flash is 12 frames per second; so to make a fairly long animation, you will use 120 frames.

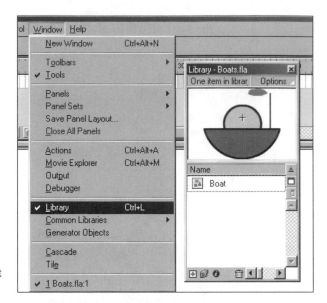

FIGURE 8.16   Finding the Boat in the Library.

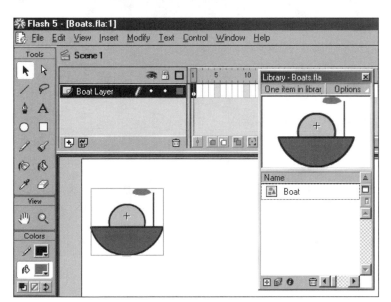

FIGURE 8.17 Positioning the Boat on the Stage.

Insert a keyframe at Frame 120 through the following steps. Under the Boat Layer there is a drag bar. Pull this drag bar to the right until Frame 120 is visible. Click on Frame 120. It will turn black and the orange playhead will appear over it. On the menu, click Insert>Keyframe, or press F6 (see Figure 8.18). A black dot will appear in Frame 120, indicating that a keyframe exists at Frame 120 and that an image appears in that keyframe. The image is the boat, located at the far left of the stage.

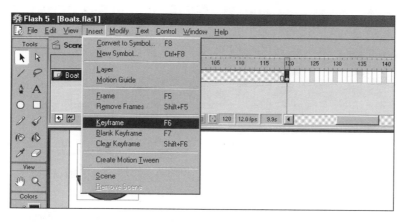

FIGURE 8.18   Inserting a Keyframe at Frame 120.

Creating Animation

Now it is time to animate the boat. Animations in Flash are done by inserting keyframes at different points along the time line in a layer, and then moving the object in that layer to different locations on the stage at different keyframes.

With the boat banner, we want the boat to travel to the right of the stage, turn around, and move back. The first step is to insert a keyframe about halfway through the animation. At this point, the boat will have reached the far right end of the stage.

Click on Frame 60 and insert a keyframe, following the same steps used when inserting a keyframe at Frame 120 (see Figure 8.19). Make sure that you are still located on the keyframe you have inserted at Frame 60 by clicking on that keyframe again. The orange playhead should be located on that keyframe.

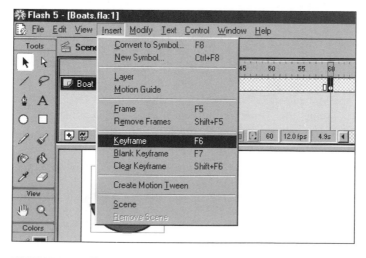

FIGURE 8.19   Inserting a Keyframe at Frame 60.

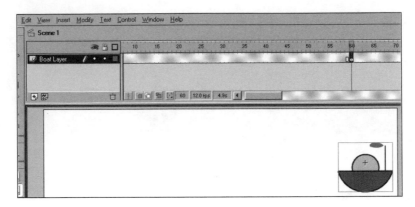

FIGURE 8.20   Changing the Boat Position at the Keyframe at Frame 60.

Then click on the Boat symbol you inserted into the Boat Layer. Drag it all the way to the right, as shown in Figure 8.20. You can now see what the animation would look like as a Flash movie.

Previewing the Movie

Previewing can be done in two ways. The first way is to click on the orange rectangle of the playhead and move it back and forth. If you do that, you will see that the boat jumps from the left of the stage to the right of the stage at Frame 60 and then jumps back to the left at Frame 120.

The second way to see what the animation would look like as a Flash movie is to click on Control>Test Movie. A Flash movie will appear on your screen. At about five seconds, the boat will jump to the left. At about ten seconds, the boat will jump back to the right. To stop the Flash movie, click on the X in the upper-right hand corner of the movie that just appeared on your screen.

Creating a Tween

The next step is to create a smooth motion for the boat, so that it appears to move across the screen instead of jumping back and forth. In Flash, this is done with a motion tween.

Tweening is a procedure in Flash in which Flash automatically creates smooth animations between keyframes that you have created on the stage. Motion tweening works to move symbols smoothly across the stage. Shape tweening (discussed in Chapter 10 on flash animation) changes objects' shapes.

To make the boat move back and forth, you will add some more keyframes to change the direction of the boat and then create motion tweens to make the boat move smoothly. These steps make the boat turn around at Frame 61. First, add a keyframe at Frame 61, by clicking on Frame 61 and either selecting Insert>Keyframe or pressing F6. That will be the point where the boat will turn around.

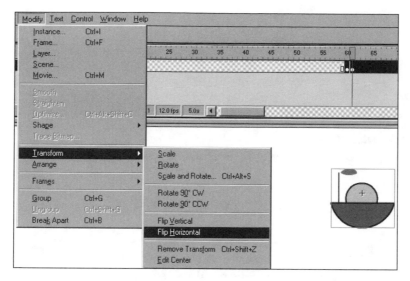

FIGURE 8.21   Flipping the Boat Horizontally.

Next, turn the Boat symbol around. To do this, click on the boat to select it, and then click on Modify>Transform>Flip Horizontal, as shown in Figure 8.21. The boat will flip so that the flag is now pointing to the left at Frame 61.

To make the boat appear to move back to the left of the stage while pointing in that direction, click on the keyframe in Frame 120, and click on Modify>Transform>Flip Horizontal. Now at Frame 120, the boat will be pointing to the left, as it was in Frame 61.

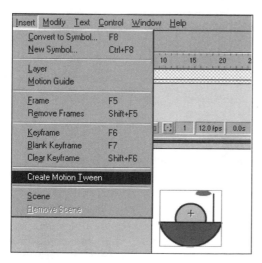

FIGURE 8.22   Adding a Motion Tween between Frames 1 and 60.

Check the movie by dragging the playhead back and forth or by clicking Control>Test Movie. The boat should appear to jump to the right of the stage, quickly turn around, and then jump back to the left of the stage.

To add smooth animation to the film, use the Motion Tween function, as shown in Figure 8.22. First, click on the keyframe in Frame 1. A blue rectangle should appear around the boat, which should be at the left end of the stage, with the flag on the right side of the boat. Next, click on Insert>Create Motion Tween. The frames to the right of Frame 1 will now turn blue, and an arrow will point to the right from Frame 1, continuing to Frame 60. Use the playhead or Control>Test Movie to see the result of creating the motion tween. The ship should now move smoothly from the left to right, then turn around, and jump back to the left of the stage.

To finish the animation process, add another motion tween between Frame 61 and the end of the

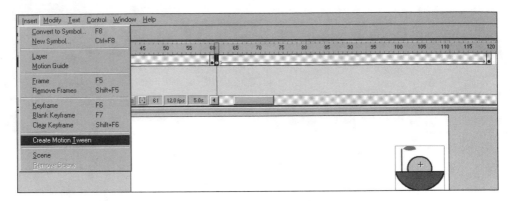

FIGURE 8.23   Adding a Motion Tween between Frames 61 and 120.

animation. Do this by clicking on Frame 61 and then clicking on Insert>Create Motion Tween. The frames to the right of Frame 61 will now turn blue, and an arrow will appear, pointing to Frame 120, as shown in Figure 8.23.

This completes the basic animation of the boat banner. Moving the playhead or clicking Control>Test Movie will now show the boat moving smoothly from the left to the right of the stage, turning around, moving back to the left of the stage, and turning around again. This will repeat over and over, in a process called Looping.

Adding New Layers

To make the animation more interesting, you can add a blue sky background and a green ocean foreground for the boat to sail in. At first, this could seem like a complicated process, because the sky has to be behind the ship, while the ocean, for the ship to appear to move inside it, has to be in front of the ship.

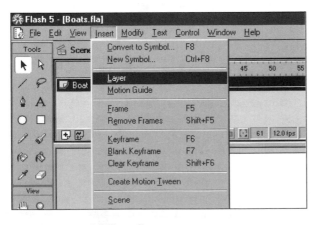

FIGURE 8.24   Adding a Layer.

Putting the sky behind the ship and the ocean in front of the ship is accomplished in Flash by using layers. First, you will create a background layer for the sky. To do this, click on the Boat Layer so that it is highlighted. Then, click on Insert>Layer, as shown in Figure 8.24. A new layer will appear above the Boat Layer. It will initially be labeled Layer 2. Click on Layer 2 and rename it as Sky Layer, as shown in Figure 8.25.

The next step is to move the Sky Layer so that it is under the Boat Layer. That way, the sky will appear behind the boat in the Flash animation. Do this by clicking on

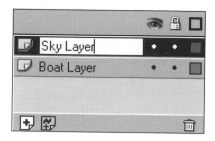

FIGURE 8.25   Renaming Layer 2.

FIGURE 8.26   Moving the Sky Layer and Locking the Boat Layer.

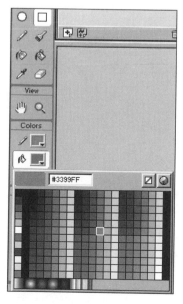

FIGURE 8.27   Selecting Colors for a Rectangle.

the Boat Layer with the left mouse button and dragging the Boat Layer up until it overlaps the Sky Layer. Releasing the mouse button now will move the Boat Layer above the Sky Layer, as shown in Figure 8.26.

Because you will now be working with the Sky Layer, make sure that the Sky Layer is active, by clicking on it. A pencil will appear next to the Sky Layer label, indicating that that layer is active. One mistake people using Flash for the first time often make is to add objects to the wrong layer, which makes animation very difficult. One way to avoid this is to "lock" layers you are not using, by clicking under the Lock image on any layer you are not working with. A lock will appear on that layer. Then that layer cannot be modified until you click on the lock again, to unlock the layer. In Figure 8.26, the Boat Layer is locked.

It is also possible to hide inactive layers (layers you are not currently working on) altogether, by clicking under the Eye image on those layers. A red X will appear, indicating that that layer is now invisible to you while you are working on it (although it will still appear in any Flash animations you make). Clicking on the red X will make the layer appear again.

To create the blue sky background, draw a blue rectangle that fills up the Sky Layer. First, click on the Rectangle tool in the Tools column, and then click on the Pencil Color box under the Colors section. As shown in Figure 8.27, a grid of different colors will appear under the Fill Color box, and the pointer will turn into an eyedropper. Select a shade of blue to create a blue outline for the rectangle you are about to draw.

Next, click on the Fill Color box directly underneath the Pencil Color box. It is indicated by an image of a bucket next to the box. Click on the same shade of blue to select a blue fill for the rectangle.

Now draw the rectangle. Make sure that the Sky Layer is the active layer by checking to see that the pencil in the Sky Layer is visible. Next, making sure the Rectangle tool is selected, move the pointer to the upper left corner of the stage, click, and begin to drag down and to the right. As shown in Figure 8.28, a rectangle will begin to appear across the stage. Once you have created a rectangle the size of the stage, release the mouse button. A blue rectangle the size of the stage will appear, with the boat in front of it, as shown in Figure 8.29.

Test the Flash animation by moving the playhead or using Control>Test Movie. You will see the boat moving back and forth in front of a blue sky.

Now you can add a layer for the sea. First, click on the label for the Boat Layer. Then click Insert>Add Layer.

Another layer will appear above the Boat Layer. Because this layer will contain the sea, which will partly block out your view of the boat, this layer should be above the Boat Layer. Label this layer Sea Layer.

Click on the Sea Layer to make it active, as shown in Figure 8.30. You might want to make sure that the Boat and Sky Layers are locked to avoid accidentally modifying them. Now draw another rectangle filled with a green color that reaches from the middle of the boat down to the bottom of the stage, as shown in Figure 8.31.

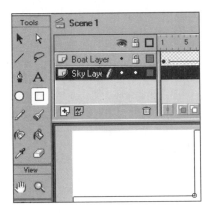

FIGURE 8.28   Using the Rectangle Tool.

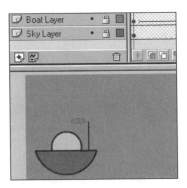

FIGURE 8.29   The Boat on a Blue Background.

FIGURE 8.30   Inserting the Sea Layer with the Boat and Sky Layers Locked.

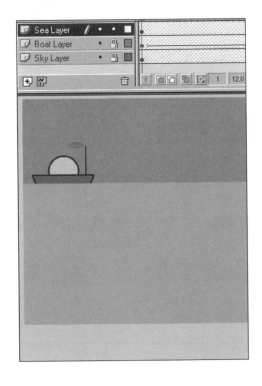

FIGURE 8.31   The Sea, Boat, and Sky Layers.

Adding Text

Text is added to Flash animations using the Text tool on the Tools column. Text can be modified by using the Text panel.

Start by clicking on the Sky Layer and then click Insert>Layer to insert a layer above the Sky Layer. Label this layer Text Layer, as shown in Figure 8.32.

Next, click on the Text button on the Tools column, as shown in Figure 8.33. Move the pointer to where you want the text to appear on the stage, somewhere in the sea. It can be easily moved about the stage once it has been created, so do not try to align it perfectly before you have typed the text.

Next, type Bob's Boatyard, the text that will appear on the animation. The text will look more appealing if it is in a large and attractive font.

To make these changes, first activate the Character panel by selecting Window> Panels>Character. The Character panel will appear, as shown in Figure 8.34. Highlight all of

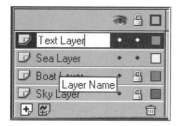

FIGURE 8.32   Adding the Text Layer.

FIGURE 8.33 Inserting Text.

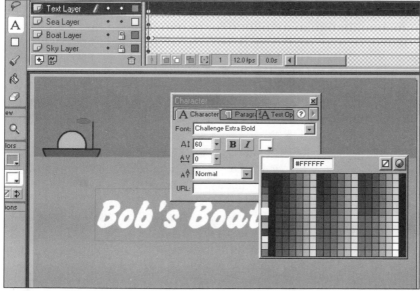

FIGURE 8.34 Modifying Text with the Character Panel.

the text by clicking on the *d* in *Boatyard* and dragging the mouse to the left until all of the text is highlighted. Then, on the Text panel, click the Down arrow in the Fonts box and select Challenge Extra Bold. To make the text larger, click on the Down arrow next to the Font Size box under the Font box, and drag the bar that appears upward until the number 60 appears (or any other size you prefer), as shown in Figure 8.34. To change the color of the font, click on the Font Color box and select White. Finally, to move the new text box to exactly where you want it, click on the Arrow tool in the Tools column and then click on the text box. A blue rectangle will appear around it, indicating that the text box is selected. Move the text box around the stage until it is situated where you want it.

If you want to change the text, simply use the Arrow tool to double-click on the text box. The background of the text box will become white. Then you can change the text and any of its characteristics, such as font or color.

Adding Sound

It is possible to add sound at any point in a Flash animation. One of the big benefits of Flash is that sound files, which often are very large, can be reduced to a very small size in a Flash animation. Also, sounds in Flash will play in any browser that plays Flash animations, so viewers do not have to have any other plug-ins.

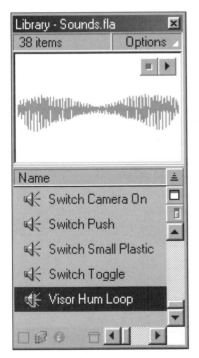

FIGURE 8.35   The Sounds Library.

You can add a sound that will play every time the boat moves across the center of the stage, both from left to right and from right to left. For this example, we will use a sound that already is available in the Flash library.

First, add a layer and label it Sounds Layer. It does not matter where this layer is located in the stack of layers, because nothing visible will be inserted into it.

Next, use the playhead to move through the animation until the boat has moved almost halfway across the screen, from left to right. You want the sound to begin just before the boat reaches the center.

Add a keyframe in the Sounds Layer at the point where the boat has almost reached the middle. In this example, it will be around Frame 22.

To find a sound that Flash already contains, look in the Flash library of sounds. To do this, click on Window>Common Libraries>Sounds. A library will appear that looks the same as the library that contains the Boat symbol you created. This library contains the sounds that Flash provides. You can test different sounds by clicking on the name of the sound in the library and then pressing the Play button in the upper right corner of the library, as shown in Figure 8.35.

Click on different sounds available in the library until you find one you like. In this example, the sound Visor Hum Loop is selected. Clicking on the arrow in the upper right corner of the box that shows the image of Visor Hum Loop will play the sound.

To insert the sound into the Flash animation when the boat is almost at the middle of the screen, click on the keyframe you inserted into the Sounds Layer. Make sure that the Sounds Layer is the active layer by checking to see that the pencil next to the Sounds Layer label is visible. Now click on the sound you selected, and drag the sound onto the stage. Release the sound anywhere on the stage.

As shown in Figure 8.36, you will see a blue image of the sound wave appear on the Sounds Layer, beginning at the keyframe you inserted on that layer. The length of the wave that appears on the layer indicates how long the sound will play in your animation. Now use Control>Test Movie to hear the sound play as the boat passes the center of the screen, as it moves from left to right.

Now insert another copy of the sound as the boat crosses the center of the stage, moving from right to left. First, use the playhead to locate the point on the time line at which the boat is moving from right to left and has almost reached the center of the screen.

Insert a keyframe on the Sounds Layer at this point, at Frame 85. Drag Visor Hum Loop from the library again, and drop it onto the stage. A blue sound wave symbolizing that sound should now begin at the keyframe you inserted. Test the movie again. The sound should now play each time the boat passes the center of the screen, moving in either direction. Figure 8.37 shows the final Flash Player movie.

FIGURE 8.36   Inserting a Sound into the Keyframe at Frame 22.

FIGURE 8.37   Boats.swf.

Saving the Flash Player Movie

Finally, to save the Flash Player movie so it can be uploaded, select File>Export Movie, name the film, and select Save. Chapter 10 on animation and interactivity contains a section on different options for exporting Flash Player movies for the Web and other purposes.

Conclusion

This quick introduction to Macromedia Flash introduced the basics of drawing and animation with this exciting software. The following two chapters go deeper into the mechanics of using Flash and show more of its potential for animation and interactivity.

CHAPTER

9

Flash Drawing Tools

One of the most useful elements of Flash is the complete set of drawing tools it provides. Although it is simple to import graphics from other programs, the drawing tools Flash contains allow one to create compelling, low-bandwidth images that perfectly complement the Flash animation process. This chapter covers Flash drawing tools in detail.

The Arrow Tool

The Arrow tool allows you to select and move instances of objects on the Flash workspace. Clicking on the Arrow tool turns the pointer into an Arrow with a rectangular box to the right of the arrow.

Selecting with the Arrow Tool

If you are working with a drawing (as opposed to an instance of a symbol), you can select all or part of the drawing. For example, if you draw a circle with a red fill and a black outline,

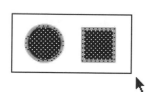

and you click on the red fill, only the red fill will be selected. You can then delete, change, or move the red fill, without affecting the black outline.

There are two ways to use the Arrow tool to select more than one item, such as selecting the fill and the outline. The first way is to draw a rectangle, or marquee, around the items.

Select multiple items by clicking somewhere outside the items and then using the mouse to drag the pointer over the items. A rectangle, the marquee, will appear around the items.

Selecting multiple items with the arrow tool.

When you release the mouse button, everything within the marquee is selected. Flash shows you that the items are selected by highlighting them, changing their color slightly to make them lighter.

The second way to select more than one item is to click on the first item using the Arrow tool. That item will now be highlighted. Next, hold down the Control and Shift keys and use the mouse to click on another item. Now both items will be highlighted. Repeat this process until all intended items are highlighted.

Finally, you may also use the Arrow tool to select parts of items on the workspace. Clicking the Arrow tool somewhere outside of an object, line, or fill, dragging the resulting marquee over part of the item, and then releasing the mouse button, will select only the part of the item that was included by the marquee.

Note: You cannot select parts of instances of symbols that you have included in a movie. To change a symbol, you must edit the symbol itself, and not an instance of it in a movie.

Moving with the Arrow Tool

The Arrow tool also serves to move objects around the work area. To move an object or objects with the Arrow tool, first select the objects to be moved (see the previous section). When the Arrow tool is over a selected object or objects that can be moved, the Arrow tool will change to an arrow next to a cross with pointed ends. Click with the left mouse button and drag the object or objects to their new locations on the workspace.

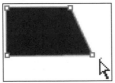

Reshaping a circle with the arrow tool.

Reshaping Objects with the Arrow Tool

The Arrow tool also allows you to reshape objects that you have already drawn. For example, if you draw a circle, you can use the Arrow tool to stretch one end of the circle to give it a pear shape.

To reshape an object, point the Arrow tool over the outline of the object. The pointer for the Arrow tool will turn into an arrow to the left of an arc. If you now click and drag the mouse, the shape of the object will change, stretching in the direction that the pointer moves.

The Subselect Tool

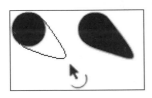

Changing an object's shape with the subselect tool.

The Subselect tool also allows you to change the shapes of objects. The Subselect tool converts the outline of an object into a series of line segments, which you can then modify, to change the shape of the object.

For example, to change a rectangle into a trapezoid using the Subselect tool, first click on the Subselect Tool button. The pointer will turn into a small white arrow. If you move the pointer over the edge of the rectangle and click, you will notice that the outline of the rectangle turns blue, and the corners of the rectangle become blue squares, called points. To change the shape of the rectangle, click on one of the points and drag the point in the appropriate direction. The rectangle will begin to stretch in that direction. You can further reshape the object by clicking and dragging these points.

The Line Tool

The Line tool draws straight lines on the work area. Flash allows you to change many characteristics of a line you draw, including its color, thickness, and solidity.

Drawing a Line

To use the Line tool, first click on the Line Tool button. The mouse pointer will turn into a large crosshairs.

- Place the pointer where you want to begin the line, and left click the mouse. Start dragging the mouse. The line will begin to appear.
- When the line is the correct length, release the mouse button to stop drawing the line.

Drawing a line with the line tool.

Specifying the Characteristics of a Line

The Stroke panel allows you to specify the characteristics of a line, either before or after you draw the line. See the Stroke panel section to find out how to change the characteristics of a line.

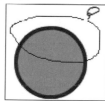

The Lasso Tool

The Lasso tool is used to select a part of an object or objects on the work area. Use the Lasso tool when you want to cut out or otherwise modify a small part of a drawing.

Selecting part of a circle with the lasso tool.

- To use the Lasso tool, first click on the Lasso Tool button.
- The mouse pointer will turn into a lasso.
- Drag the lasso on the work area, drawing a line through or around objects you want to select.
- When you release the lasso, the area enclosed in the line will be selected.

The Pen Tool

The Pen tool is similar to the Subselect tool. The Pen tool is used to draw lines, to change the lines to very smooth curves, and to reshape the outlines of objects. Points (which appear as blue boxes on lines worked on with the Pen tool) may be dragged to reshape the line, making the line a curve.

Reshaping a circle with the pen tool.

The Text Tool

The Text tool inserts text into the Flash work area. A wide range of fonts and an unlimited range of font sizes and colors are available in Flash.

Inserting Text

To insert text into the Flash work area, first click on the Text Tool button. When the mouse pointer is placed over the workspace, it will turn into a crosshairs with a capital letter *A* next to it. Click on the work area, about where you want to insert your text. A rectangular box will appear on the work area, with a blinking cursor in it.

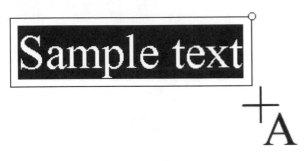

Inserting text with the text tool.

You will notice there is an empty circle in the upper-right corner of the rectangle. In the text box, type in the text you want to appear in the work area. As you type, the text box will become wider and wider. If you continue typing, eventually the text box will extend past the end of the stage. Text that extends past the end of the stage will not appear in the final Flash movie, so you should set the width of the text box.

To set the width of the text box, stop typing and move the pointer over the empty circle in the upper-right corner of the text box. The pointer will turn into a horizontal line with arrows on both ends. Click with the left mouse button, and drag the right side of the text box until the text box is the width you want.

The empty circle now becomes a square. This indicates that the width of the text box will now remain the same as you type. When the text box fills up with type, it will automatically insert another line at the bottom and continue your text in the next line. You can always adjust the width of the text box by clicking on the square in the corner again and dragging the right side of the box.

Flash also allows you to modify the font, color, size, and style of any text you insert. Text is modified using the Character panel, discussed later.

The Oval Tool

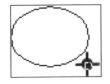

Drawing an oval with the oval tool.

The Oval tool draws ovals and circles. To draw an oval or circle, first click on the Oval Tool button. When you move the mouse pointer over the work area, it will turn into a crosshairs. Click the left mouse button and drag the crosshairs; an oval will begin to appear on the work area.

- As you drag the pointer more, the oval will become larger. Moving the pointer around will change the shape of the object, from a circle to a rounded oval to a broad flat oval.
- To draw a perfect circle, hold down the Shift key while you drag the pointer. This will limit the shape of the object you create to that of a circle.

In Flash, ovals and circles have two special characteristics, stroke and fill. Stroke involves the characteristics of the outer edge of the circle, such as whether the circle has an outer edge of a certain color, a certain pattern (e.g., solid or dashed), or a certain thickness. Fill is the color or pattern that fills the circle. You can modify the stroke and fill of any oval or circle you draw by using the Ink Bottle tool, Paint Bucket tool, and the Stroke and Fill panels, discussed later.

The Rectangle Tool

The Rectangle tool draws rectangles and squares and also allows you to control the sharpness of the edges of the rectangle or square you draw. To draw a rectangle or square, first click on the Rectangle Tool button. When you move the mouse pointer over the work area, it will turn into a crosshairs.

Click the left mouse button and drag the crosshairs. A rectangle will begin to appear on the work area. Moving the pointer around will change the height and width of the rectangle or square. To draw a perfect square, hold down the Shift key while you drag the pointer. This will limit the shape of the object you create to that of a square.

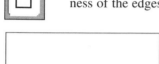

Drawing a rectangle with the rectangle tool.

In Flash, rectangles and squares have two special characteristics, stroke and fill. Stroke involves the characteristics of the outer edge of the object, such as whether it has an outer edge of a certain color, a certain pattern (e.g., solid or dashed), or a certain thickness. Fill is the color or pattern that fills the object. You can modify the stroke and fill of any rectangle or square you draw by using the Ink Bottle tool, Paint Bucket tool, and the Stroke and Fill panels, discussed later.

The Round Rectangle Radius Option

The Round Rectangle Radius button appears in the Options box when you use the Rectangle tool. The Round Rectangle Radius option allows you to make the corners of a rectangle or square more or less rounded. If you click on the Round Rectangle Radius option after clicking on the Rectangle Tool button, a box titled Rectangle Settings will appear on the screen. You can type in a number from 0 to 999 into the Corner Radius input box.

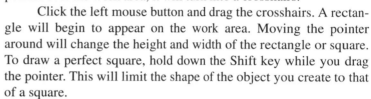

Entering 0, the default number, will cause any rectangle or square that you draw to have completely sharp, 90-degree angle corners. Entering a larger number will cause the rectangle or square to have more rounded corners. The same effect can be accomplished by using the Up and Down Arrow keys while you drag the pointer. Pressing the Up Arrow key while dragging the pointer will make the corners more sharp, whereas pressing the Down Arrow key while dragging will make the corners more rounded.

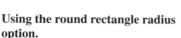

Using the round rectangle radius option.

The Pencil Tool

The Pencil tool allows you to draw straight and curved lines. Flash also provides some excellent options for the Pencil tool that improve your drawing by straightening or smoothing lines you draw.

Drawing with the pencil tool.

To draw with the Pencil tool, first click on the Pencil Tool icon. Now when the mouse pointer is over the stage or work area, it will appear as a small pencil. To begin drawing, click with the left mouse button where you want the line to begin. Drag the mouse, and a line will appear; release the mouse button, and the line will end where the mouse pointer now rests.

Changing Pencil Stroke Colors

There are two ways to change the color of the line you create with the Pencil tool. First, under the Pencil tool in the Colors column, you can click on the Stroke Color box, which is to the left of a Pencil icon. Once you have clicked on the Stroke Color box, a panel with a selection of colors appears, and the pointer becomes an eyedropper. You can now select a color for the line.

The other way to change the color of lines you draw with the Pencil tool involves using the Stroke panel, discussed later. The Stroke panel also can be used to change the thickness and other characteristics of the line.

Pencil Mode Options

Three pencil modes are available: Straighten, Smooth, and Ink. These modes change the shape or path of the line you draw.

Pencil mode options.

The Straighten and Smooth modes in Flash are very useful tools for drawing, because they clean up the lines drawn with a mouse and create more attractive images. To select a pencil mode, click on the Pencil Mode button. A menu will appear that includes the three modes available.

The Straighten mode makes lines you draw straighter than the mouse movements you make. For example, if you draw a roughly rectangular form using the Pencil tool with the mouse, and if you are in Straighten mode, the figure will become a perfect rectangle once you finish drawing. Similarly, if you draw a roughly straight line, and if you are in Straighten mode, it will appear as a very straight line.

In Smooth mode, lines you draw will become smoother. For example, if you draw a somewhat curved line with a few bumps in it, Smooth mode will make the line into a smooth arc. Similarly, rough circles or ovals drawn in smooth mode will become closer to perfect circles or ovals.

Finally, in Ink mode, lines will appear exactly as you create them with the mouse. Lines may later be edited using the Arrow tool, the Pen tool, and the stroke of a line may always be changed with the Stroke panel.

The Brush Tool

The Brush tool is used to create relatively thick brush strokes in Flash. Many options are available with the Brush tool, including the size, shape, and color of the brush, and the type of area the brush will paint.

To use the Brush tool, first click on the Brush Tool button on the Tools column. When you move the mouse pointer over the stage or work area, it will now turn into the shape and color you have selected for the brush. To being painting with the brush, position the pointer where you want to begin painting. Click the left mouse button and begin to drag the mouse. The paintbrush will continue to paint until you release the left mouse button.

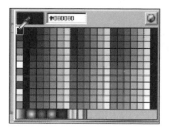

Selecting a color with the eyedropper tool.

Changing Brush Colors

In Flash the color of images you create with the Brush tool is called a Fill, as opposed to the Stroke, which is associated with lines drawn with pencils and other tools such as the Rectangle and Circle tools. Changing the color you produce with the Brush tools is done with either the Fill Color box in the Tools column or with the Fill panel. To change the color of the brush using the Fill Color box in the Tools column, first select the Brush tool and then click on the Fill Color box. If you hold the mouse button down for a moment, a color palette will appear, and the mouse pointer will become an eyedropper.

You may now select a new color from the color palette. You may also change the color using the Fill panel, discussed later.

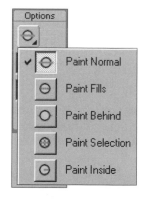

Brush mode options.

Paint normal, paint fills, paint behind, paint selection, and paint inside options.

Brush Mode Options

Five different brush modes are available in the Options panel. The different modes may be selected by clicking on the Brush Mode button and then selecting from the different modes presented.

Paint Normal allows you to use the brush as it normally would work if you were using an ordinary paintbrush. Anything on the layer you are working with will be covered up if you paint over it in the Paint Normal mode.

Paint Fills allows you to paint over and around objects on the active layer without affecting the lines that form the edge of an object. For example, if you select Paint Fills and then drag the paintbrush over a circle you have drawn, the brush will affect the space around the circle and will affect the inside of the circle, but will not affect the lines that form its outline.

Paint Behind causes the paintbrush to paint only behind any already-existing objects on the active layer. For example, if you select Paint Behind and then drag the paintbrush over a circle you have drawn, the brush will paint only on empty space around the circle. It will appear to go behind the circle when you pass over the circle with the brush.

Note: You are not actually painting behind strokes or fills when using the Paint Behind option. If you paint behind another stroke or fill using the Paint Behind option, and then delete that stroke or fill, you will not see the new paint behind that object.

Choosing the Paint Selection brush mode causes the paintbrush to paint only in selected areas of objects already on the layer. For example, if you have drawn a circle and you select half of it (using the Arrow tool, the Lasso tool, or another selection tool), and then drag the paintbrush over the entire circle while in Paint Selection mode, only the selected part will be affected. If the brush is in Paint Select mode, it also will not affect empty spaces on the work area or stage, where nothing yet has been drawn. The paintbrush in Paint Select mode affects only selected parts of already existing objects.

Choosing the Paint Inside brush mode causes the paintbrush to paint only inside the lines of an object you have drawn. For example, say you draw a circle with the Circle tool, and then begin painting inside the circle with the brush in Paint Inside mode. If you move the brush from inside the circle to outside the circle, the paint will only "stick" inside the circle. Paint Inside works like a crayon in a coloring book, if the crayon only drew "inside the lines" and could not cross over them.

Brush Size Options

The size of the brush stroke may be changed using the Brush Size box in the Tools column. Larger brush sizes allow you to fill larger areas more quickly and to create smooth, broad strokes. Smaller brush sizes allow you to create greater detail in a painting. Clicking on the Down arrow to the right of the Brush Size box shows a range of possible brush sizes. Clicking on a specific brush size selects that size.

Brush Shape Options

The shape of the brush stroke may be changed using the Brush Shape box in the Tools column. Several shapes are available, including circles, ovals, rectangles, and lines. Using the circle and oval shapes allows you to paint smooth, rounded objects. Using the rectangle and line shapes allows you to paint straight objects. In addition, using oval, rectangle, and line shapes allows you to create a calligraphy effect while painting. To select a specific brush shape, click on the Down arrow to the right of the Brush Shape box. The possible brush shapes will appear in a column. Clicking on a specific brush shape selects that shape.

Brush size options.

Brush shape options.

The Ink Bottle Tool

The Ink Bottle tool changes the characteristics of lines and outlines of objects. For example, if you have drawn a circle with a thick black outline, the Ink Bottle tool could be used to give the circle a thick blue outline.

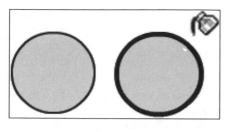

Using the ink bottle tool.

- To use the Ink Bottle tool, first click on the Ink Bottle button.
- When you move the mouse pointer over the work area or stage, the pointer will now turn into an ink bottle.
- Touching the ink bottle to the edge of an object, or touching the Ink Bottle tool to a line, and clicking the left mouse button will give the edge or line the characteristics you have chosen for the Ink Bottle tool.

Characteristics for the Ink Bottle tool are set using the Stroke controls that are also used with the Line tool. To set the color that the Ink Bottle tool will produce, either click on the Stroke Color button in the Tools column, or use the Stroke Color button in the Stroke panel. All of the styles and other attributes that can be set for the Line tool can be used with the Ink Bottle tool and applied to existing lines and outlines of objects. Refer to the Stroke panel description, below, for details on changing the attributes of lines and strokes.

The Paint Bucket Tool

The Paint Bucket tool changes a shape's fill, the color or pattern inside the shape. The Paint Bucket tool provides several options, including the option to fill shapes that have gaps in their outlines and to adjust the color gradient of a fill to make the shape look three-dimensional.

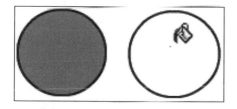

Using the paint bucket tool.

- To use the Paint Bucket tool, first click on the Paint Bucket button.
- When the mouse pointer is over the work area, the pointer will now turn into a bucket that is tipped to the left.
- Moving the bucket over the inside of a shape and clicking the left mouse button will change the fill of the shape to the color or other attribute you have selected.

The color of an object's fill can be selected in two ways. The first method involves using the Fill Color button in the Tools column. Click on the small arrow on the right of the Fill Color box. A grid of color swatches will appear, and the mouse pointer will turn into an eyedropper. Passing the eyedropper over the color swatches allows you to select a new fill color. If you apply the paint bucket to an object now, the fill will become that color.

Notice that at the bottom of the grid of color swatches, there are more complex color patterns called gradients. Using gradients as fills for an object gives the object visually interesting characteristics such as three-dimensional effects. The second method for changing the color of a fill involves using the Fill panel, described later.

Paint Bucket Options

The options associated with the Paint Bucket tool are the Gap Size, Lock Fill, and Transform Fill tools.

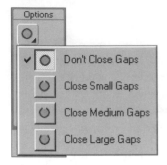

The gap size option.

The lock fill option.

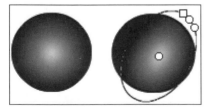

Two circles without lock fill (top) and two circles with lock fill (bottom).

The transform fill option.

Using the transform fill option.

The Gap Size option changes the amount of gap in the outline of a shape that can exist and still have the Fill tool fill the shape. For example, if you draw a circle with the Circle tool, there will be no gaps in the outline of the circle. However, if you draw a circle fairly quickly with the Pencil tool, you may leave a gap somewhere in the circle, such as where the beginning and end of the line almost meet, but do not meet perfectly. The Gap Size tool allows you to select whether the Paint Bucket will fill an object with a gap in it. To use the Gap Size tool, first click on the Gap Size button under Options. A panel will appear with a series of Gap Size options, ranging from Don't Close Gaps to Close Large Gaps. Select the Gap Size option you want, and then use the Paint Bucket tool to fill the object.

Note: Make sure when you are using the Paint Bucket tool that the layer containing the object you want to work with is active. Otherwise you will end up modifying some other object, or nothing at all.

The Lock Fill option is used when you are filling objects with a gradient or a bitmap. When the Lock Fill option is selected, Flash will treat the active layer on the entire stage as though it were filled entirely with that gradient or bitmap. As you draw and fill objects, every fill of every object you draw on that layer will correspond to the point on the gradient or bitmap you have locked. For example, if you select a radial gradient that runs from bright green in the center to black on the outside without Lock Fill, each object that you fill will have a bright green center and dark edges. With Lock Fill, the gradient will be spread across filled objects. The same process holds true for bitmap fills.

The Transform Fill option is also used when you fill objects with a gradient or a bitmap. The Transform Fill option allows you to change the characteristics of the gradient or bitmap that fills an object. For example, you may have drawn a circle with a Radial Gradient Fill, which gives the circle a three-dimensional effect. You can use the Transform Fill option to change the center of the Radial Fill. That will change the appearance of light and shadow on the circle.

To use the Transform Fill option, first click on the Paint Bucket tool, and then click on the Transform Fill button.

- Next, select an object that has a gradient or bitmap fill. You will notice that a square and a set of circles will appear.
- One circle is at the middle of the gradient. Moving this circle changes the midpoint of the gradient, which changes the appearance of the source of light and shadow on an object.
- Dragging the square squeezes or stretches the gradient or bitmap, making it appear wider or narrower without affecting the height.
- The circle next to the square changes the size of the gradient.
- Finally, dragging the last circle rotates the bitmap or gradient.

The Eyedropper Tool

The Eyedropper tool copies the fill or outline of one object, so that you can apply that fill or outline to other objects you create. For example, if you have a red circle with a green outline, you can transform any other object you draw into the same color scheme using the Eyedropper tool. The Eyedropper tool also works with bitmap and gradient fills, as well.

To use the Eyedropper tool, first click on the Eyedropper button. When you move the pointer over the work area, it will turn into an eyedropper.

If you want to copy the stroke (or outline) of an object for use with other objects, place the eyedropper over the object's outline and click.

Immediately, the Ink Bottle tool (which controls outlines) will be selected, and it will show the attributes (e.g., color and thickness) of the outline you selected. You may now copy these line attributes onto other objects.

Similarly, if you want to copy the fill of an object for use with other fills, place the eyedropper over the object's fill and click. Immediately, the Paint Bucket tool (which contains fills) will be selected, and it will show the attributes of that fill (e.g., color, transparency, gradient, or bitmap). Now you may use the Paint Bucket tool to apply these fill attributes to other objects.

The Eraser Tool

The Eraser tool removes all or part of a stroke or fill. Several options are available with the Eraser tool, including the size of the eraser, the specific things it will erase (e.g., only fills or only strokes or lines), and whether it erases by dragging or by erasing entire parts of an object. The Eraser tool shares many properties with the Paintbrush tool.

To use the Eraser tool, click on the Eraser button in the Tools column to the left. When you move the mouse pointer over the stage or work area, it will now turn into the shape you have selected for the eraser.

To being erasing, position the pointer where you want to begin. Click the left mouse button and begin to drag the mouse. The erase will continue to erase until you release the left mouse button.

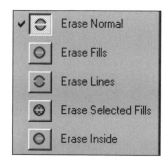

Eraser modes.

Eraser Mode Options

Five different eraser modes are available in the Options panel. The different modes may be selected by clicking on the Eraser Mode button and then selecting from the different modes presented.

1. Erase Normal allows you to use the eraser as it normally would work if you were using an ordinary eraser. Anything on the layer you are working with will be erased if you drag the pointer over it in the Erase Normal mode.

2. Erase Fills allows you to erase fills in an object without affecting the stroke (or lines) that forms the edge of an object. For example, if you select Erase Fills and then drag the eraser over a rectangle you have drawn, the erase will affect the fill of the rectangle, but will not affect the lines that form the outline of the rectangle.

3. Choosing the Erase Lines selection causes the eraser to erase only the lines the eraser is dragged over, without affecting any fills it passes over.

4. The Erase Selected Fills selection allows you to erase only selected fills or parts of fills you have already selected using one of the selection tools (such as the Arrow tool or the Lasso tool). For example, if you selected half of the fill of a circle using the Lasso tool, dragging the eraser over the circle in this mode would erase only within the selected half and would not affect the unselected half.

5. Choosing the Erase Inside brush mode causes the eraser to erase only inside the fill of an object. For example, if you draw a circle with the Circle tool, and then begin erasing inside the circle with the eraser in Erase Inside mode, if you move the eraser from inside the circle to outside the circle, the eraser will erase only inside the circle.

The Faucet option makes the eraser remove all of a fill or line, when you click on that fill or line. Using the Faucet eliminates the process of dragging the mouse pointer to erase. For example, if you select the Faucet while erasing and then click on the outline of a circle, the entire outline will be erased. Similarly, if you click on the circle's fill, the entire fill will be erased.

Eraser Shape

The size and shape of the eraser stroke may be changed using the Eraser Shape box in the tools column. Larger eraser sizes allow you to erase larger areas more quickly. Smaller eraser sizes allow you to exercise more control in erasing. Clicking on the Down arrow to the right of the Eraser Size box shows a range of possible eraser sizes. Clicking on a specific Eraser Size selects that size.

Eraser shape.

The Fill Panel

The Fill panel allows you to specify an object's fill—the color, pattern, or image that is inside the object. An object may have no fill, giving it a transparent interior, or a solid fill, with a single color. An object may also have linear or gradient fills, whereby the fill is multiple colors that blend together following a pattern you specify. Finally, an object may be filled with a bitmap, such as a photograph you import into Flash.

The None selection gives an object a transparent fill. An object with a transparent fill will have only the outline (or Stroke) that you gave it, and other objects behind it will be visible.

Note: The None selection works only with new objects. Once you give an object a fill other than None, you cannot change the Fill to None using the Fill panel. Instead, use the Arrow tool to select the fill and then delete the fill using the delete button.

The Solid selection gives an object a solid color fill. To select a solid color fill using the Fill panel, first click on Solid in the Fill Style box (see Figure 9.1). Then click on the Fill Color box. The Color Swatches panel will appear, as shown in Figure 9.2, and the pointer will turn into an eyedropper. Clicking on a color will select that color for the fill. You may also enter a color's hexadecimal code directly into the Color Code box that appears over the color swatch.

The Linear Gradient selection allows you to create a fill that changes from one color to other colors in a straight line. The Linear Gradient panel contains the Gradient Preview, which shows what the gradient will look like, and the Gradient Definition bar, which you use to create the Gradient, as shown in Figure 9.3. This panel also contains Pointers, which specify what color appears at a certain point in the Gradient and how wide the color is on the Gradient. Finally, there is a Pointer Color box for defining the color of each pointer.

The Radial Gradient selection produces a fill that changes colors following a circular pattern, much like a target with a bull's eye and rings of different colors around it. The procedure for creating a Radial Gradient Fill is the same as the procedure for a Linear Gradient Fill.

The Bitmap selection allows you to fill an object with an image you have imported from outside Flash, such as a scanned image, a digital photograph, or any other standard digital image. Although this option is called Bitmap, most digital images can be used, including .gif, .bmp, and .jpg files. These files are all converted to bitmap format when they are imported into Flash.

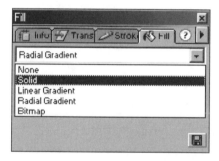

FIGURE 9.1   The Fill Panel.

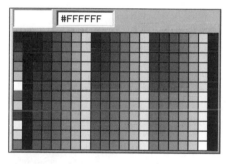

FIGURE 9.2   Color Swatches Panel.

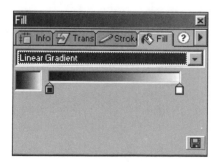

FIGURE 9.3   Linear Gradient Selection.

The Stroke Panel

The Stroke panel changes the width, size, and color of lines and outlines around objects (also known as Stroke, in Flash). Near the top of the panel is the Stroke Style box, as shown in Figure 9.4. This box allows you to change the style of lines and other strokes you draw. Different styles include solid lines, dashed lines, lines made of dots, and broken lines. Clicking on the Down arrow to the right of the Stroke Style box allows you to select a style.

FIGURE 9.4   The Stroke Panel.

Line thickness is also changed in the Stroke panel, through the Stroke Height box. Click on the Down arrow to the right of the Stroke Height box and a slider will appear. Dragging the slider up increases the stroke height, which is the same as line thickness. Dragging the slider down decreases thickness. You will notice that the number in the Stroke Height box changes as you drag the slider. This number corresponds to the thickness of the line. You may also change the line thickness directly by entering a number into this box.

Use the Line Color box in the Stroke panel to change the color of the line. Clicking on the box displays the Standard Swatch panel, from which colors can be selected. The Stroke Preview box at the bottom of the Stroke panel displays the appearance of the line.

The Transform Panel

The Transform panel allows you to rotate selected objects and change their size and shape. Activate the Transform panel by clicking on its tab or by using the main menu and selecting Windows>Panels>Transform, as shown in Figure 9.5.

To change the size of an object, first select the object using the Arrow or other selection tool. Next, enter a percentage size (under 100% to shrink the object; over 100% to expand the object) in the width and height boxes. Checking the Constrain box links the height and width together, so that if you decrease height to 50%, width decreases by 50% as well.

To rotate an object, click on the Rotate box and enter the number of degrees you want to rotate it. Entering a negative number rotates the object counterclockwise, and entering a positive number rotates the object clockwise.

Skewing an object changes it by moving it along either the horizontal or vertical axis, such as changing a rectangle to a trapezoid. To skew an object, click on the Skew button, and enter the number of degrees you want to skew it horizontally or vertically. Figure 9.6 shows examples of rotation and skew.

The Align Panel

The Align panel aligns selected objects according to their location or size. Activate the Align panel by selecting Window>Panels>Align, as shown in Figure 9.7. To align a group

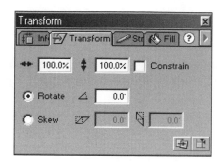

FIGURE 9.5   **The Transform Panel.**

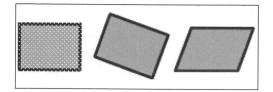

FIGURE 9.6   **An Untransformed Rectangle and Examples of Rotation and Skew.**

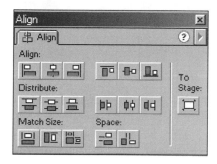

FIGURE 9.7   **The Align Panel.**

of objects, first select the objects using the Arrow or other selection tool. The To Stage option determines whether the selected objects will be aligned according to the boundaries of the stage of your Flash movie or to an average value of their own locations. Usually the Stage option is selected.

Several alignment options are available.

- Align Left Edge aligns the objects to the left edge of the stage, if the Stage option is selected, or to the left edge of the leftmost object, if the Stage option is not selected.
- Align Horizontal Center aligns the objects to the horizontal center of the stage, if the Stage option is selected, or to the center of all of the objects, if the Stage option is not selected.
- Align Right Edge aligns the objects to the right edge of the stage, if the Stage option is selected, or to the right edge of the rightmost object, if the Stage option is not selected.
- Align Top Edge aligns the objects to the top of the stage, if the Stage option is selected, or to the top edge of the topmost object, if the Stage option is not selected.
- Align Vertical Center centers the objects to each other and aligns them to the top of the stage, if the Stage option is selected, or to the average center of the objects, if the Stage option is not selected.
- Align Bottom Edge aligns the objects to the bottom of the stage, if the Stage option is selected, or to the bottom edge of the bottommost object, if the Stage option is not selected.

The Align panel also allows you to distribute objects, evenly spacing a group of objects' centers or edges. Distribute Top Edge evenly spaces the top edge of selected objects. Distribute Vertical Center evenly spaces the vertical centers. Options are available for distributing according to horizontal and vertical centers and left, right, top, and bottom edges.

The Align panel also allows you to match the sizes of selected objects. Three options are available.

1. Match Width equalizes the width of all selected objects. All objects become the width of the stage if the Stage option is selected, or the width of the initially widest object, if the Stage option is not selected.
2. Match Height equalizes the height of all selected objects. All objects become the height of stage if the Stage option is selected, or the height of the initially tallest object, if the Stage option is not selected.
3. Match Width and Height equalizes the width and height of all selected objects. All objects become the width and height of the stage if the Stage option is selected, or the height and width of the initially widest and tallest object, if the Stage option is not selected.

The Align panel allows you to space objects evenly in two ways.

1. Space Evenly Vertically moves the objects so that they are an equal distance apart vertically. If the Stage option is selected, the highest and lowest objects move to the top and bottom of the stage, respectively, and the remaining selected objects are separated equally in between. If the Stage option is not selected, the highest and lowest objects remain in the same position, and the remaining objects are separated equally in between.
2. Space Evenly Horizontally moves the objects so that they are an equal distance apart horizontally. If the Stage option is selected, the leftmost and rightmost objects move to the left and right of the stage, respectively, and the remaining selected objects are separated equally in between. If the Stage option is not selected, the leftmost and rightmost objects remain in the same position, and the remaining objects are separated equally in between.

The Info Panel

The Info panel provides size, shape, location, and other information about a selected object. You can also change the size, shape, and location of an object using the Info panel.

Activate the Info panel by clicking on its tab or by selecting Window>Panels>Info, as shown in Figure 9.8. Beneath the Info tab, a symbol indicates the properties of the object (i.e., whether it is an object, a symbol, a movie, or some other object). The Width (W) and Height (H) boxes provide that information about the selected object. Entering a new number in the corresponding box will change its width or height. The object's location, relative to the upper left corner, is shown by the X-axis and Y-axis boxes. You can move an object to an exact location by typing in specific values into these boxes.

The bottom half of the Info panel provides information about the exact area the mouse pointer is located on, on the work area. The color levels are shown in the RGB area, and the transparency or Alpha (A) level also appears. The exact location of the mouse pointer appears on the *XY*-axis.

The Swatches Panel

The Swatches panel provides a range of colors and gradients for Fills and Strokes, as shown in Figure 9.9. Choose a color from the grid of swatches or the line of gradients, and the fill or stroke you have highlighted will match that color.

The Mixer Panel

The Mixer panel allows you to select a very precise color mix for fills and lines, instead of limiting you to the color swatches available in the Swatches panel. To use the Mixer panel, first click on the Mixer tab. The Mixer panel will appear, as shown in Figure 9.10. On the left of the Mixer panel are the Stroke Color and Fill Color selection boxes.

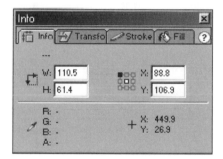

FIGURE 9.8   The Info Panel.

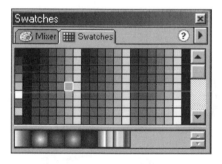

FIGURE 9.9   The Swatches Panel.

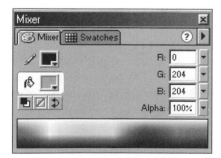

FIGURE 9.10   The Mixer Panel.

Below these boxes are the Black/White button and the Swap Colors button. At the bottom of the Mixer panel is the Color Selection area.

At the top right of the Mixer panel is a selection arrow for precise color selections. Below that are the R (Red), G (Green), and B (Blue) Color Value Indicator boxes, indicating the relative levels of these colors present in a fill mix you select.

Finally, below the RGB boxes is the Alpha indicator box. The Alpha indicator box allows you to change the level of transparency of a fill, from completely transparent (a value of 0%) to completely opaque (a value of 100%).

Changing the Color of a Line or Fill

First, select the Stroke Color box or the Fill Color box, depending on whether you plan to change a line or object outline, or the color of an object's fill. Clicking on the icon (the Pencil or the Paint Can) allows you to use the Color Selection area to choose a customized color. Clicking on the selection box to the right of the icon reveals a series of swatches for color selection.

If you choose to use the Color Selection area, first click on the Pencil or Paint Can icon. Next, move the mouse pointer over the different colors in the Color Selection area. As the pointer passes over different mixes of color, the color selected appears in the Color box next to the Pencil or Paint Can icon. At the same time, the Red, Green, and Blue levels appear in the RGB boxes to the right. Click the left mouse button to select a specific color. You can then adjust the color by using the sliders next to the RGB boxes. For example, clicking on the Down arrow next to the R (Red) box reveals a vertical slider. Dragging that slider up increases the level of red in the color mix. Dragging the slider down decreases the level of red in the color mix. Finally, the transparency of the fill color you have selected can be altered using the Alpha box. Either enter an Alpha level directly into the box (with 0% indicating complete transparency and 100% indicating complete opacity), or change the Alpha level using the slider accessed through the arrow to the right of the Alpha box.

The Character Panel

In Flash, there are many possible combinations of font, color, and style for text. Text is modified using the Character panel.

First, make sure that the Character panel is displayed on your screen. Do this by clicking on Window>Panels>Character, as shown in Figure 9.11. If there is already a check mark next to the Character panel when you click Window>Panels>Character, then the panel is already being displayed, usually to the right of the work area.

To modify text that you have already typed, first click on the Text Tool button, and then click inside the text box. You can now directly modify the text. Highlight the text you want to change by clicking directly to the left of that text and dragging the mouse until the text is highlighted. The Character panel will show the font type you are using, as well as other information about the text, such as its size and fill color. All of these elements can be changed using the Character panel.

Note: Make sure that you click directly on the text box you want to modify. If you click outside that text box, you will create a new text box.

The Paragraph Panel

The Paragraph panel allows you to format some elements of the way text is laid out in a text box. You can change the paragraph's alignment, left margin indent, first line indent, right margin indent, and line spacing, as shown in Figure 9.12.

To change a paragraph's alignment, first select some text in a text box, using the Text tool. Only the area of text that you select will be affected by this procedure. Next, click on the alignment button you choose. Left Alignment aligns the text to the left margin; Center Alignment centers the text in the text box; Right Alignment aligns the text to the right margin; Full Justify spaces the text so that it is aligned to the right and left margins.

The Left Margin box indents a selected area of text from the left margin. You can either directly enter the number of pixels to indent or use the slider to the right of the box.

The Indentation box indents the first line on a paragraph of selected text. You can either directly enter the number of pixels to indent or use the slider to the right of the box.

Note: For the Indentation box to work, you must first fix the width of the text box by dragging on the circle in the upper-right corner of the box and setting a width. Once you have set a width for the box, the circle in the upper-right corner becomes a square, and the text box has a fixed width. If the width of the text box is not fixed, text will not wrap around as you write, and the text box will keep getting longer as you type more text. With a fixed text box, text will wrap to the next line when you reach the end of the box.

The Right Margin box indents a selected area of text from the right margin. You can either directly enter the number of pixels to indent or use the slider to the right of the box.

The Line Spacing box determines the amount of vertical space between each line in some text. After selecting some lines of text, either enter the number of pixels to space the lines directly into the box or use the slider to the right of the Line Spacing box.

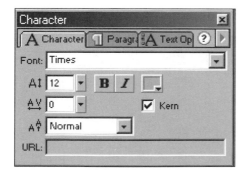

FIGURE 9.11   The Character Panel.

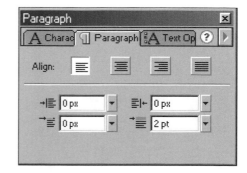

FIGURE 9.12   The Paragraph Panel.

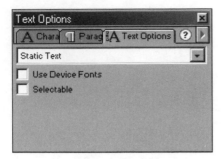

FIGURE 9.13   The Text Options Panel.

The Text Options Panel

The Text Options panel (see Figure 9.13) is used for advanced Flash procedures including creating input boxes that allow a user to communicate with a linked database. The default selection of Static Text will allow normal text presentation in Flash animations.

Conclusion

This chapter provided detailed instructions on drawing and editing objects with Flash. It also showed how to place objects in specific locations on the Flash stage. The next chapter covers how to animate objects and how to create interactive multimedia presentations with Flash.

10 Animation and Interactivity Tools in Flash

Flash provides an extremely versatile environment for creating animations that can be used as Flash films or exported into other formats such as animated .gifs. Flash also allows you to include a high level of interactivity in presentations as the viewers can start and stop sequences of events themselves. This chapter covers basic animation and interactivity tools. Then it concludes with a project: creating an interactive, online set of study flashcards.

Tweening

Tweening is the process Flash uses to make objects appear to move smoothly across the stage. It also allows you to change the size and shape of objects.

With Motion tweening, an instance of a symbol (such as a graphic, a button, or a movie) changes from one position or shape, at one keyframe, to another position or shape, at another keyframe. Motion tweening will not work with objects that are not symbols. In addition, one instance of a symbol can only tween into another location or shape; one instance of a symbol cannot tween into another symbol.

To create a motion tween, first create a keyframe on a layer, by clicking on the point on the layer where you want the object to appear, and then selecting Insert>Keyframe or pressing F6. If you want the object to appear at the beginning of the animation, this step is not necessary, because the first frame in a layer acts as a keyframe.

Next, insert an instance of a symbol. You can create a symbol by drawing an object, selecting it with the Arrow or other selection tool, and selecting Insert>Convert to Symbol. If you already have a symbol you want to use, select it from the Library.

Drag the symbol onto the area you want it to be on the stage. You will notice that the keyframe for that layer now has a black dot in it, indicating that there is now an object on that layer at that keyframe point. This is illustrated in Figure 10.1.

Next, choose the point later in the time line where you want the motion to end. Add a keyframe in that frame, by clicking on the frame and choosing Insert>Keyframe or pressing F6.

Click on the first keyframe again. Move the instance of a symbol to the point where you want it to begin during the animation.

Click on the second keyframe again. Move the instance to the point where you want it to end, during the animation, as shown in Figure 10.2.

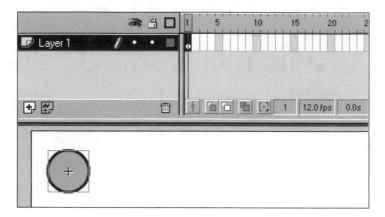

FIGURE 10.1   Inserting an Instance of a Symbol at the Beginning of a Layer.

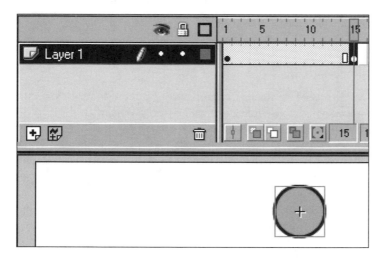

FIGURE 10.2   Moving an Instance to the Keyframe Marking the End of the Tween.

Finally, create the motion tween. Do this by clicking the right mouse button on the first keyframe again, and selecting Create Motion Tween. An arrow will appear between the first keyframe and the last keyframe, indicating that the symbol is undergoing a motion tween. Figure 10.3 shows a circle that will go through a motion tween moving it from left to right.

You can now test the motion tween in two ways. You can either select Control>Test Movie or drag the playhead to advance through the movie.

The Frame Panel and Motion Tweens

The Frame panel (see Figure 10.4) allows you to label a frame and modify the characteristics of a motion tween. The Frame panel options follow.

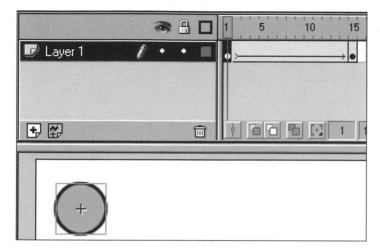

FIGURE 10.3   A Completed Motion Tween.

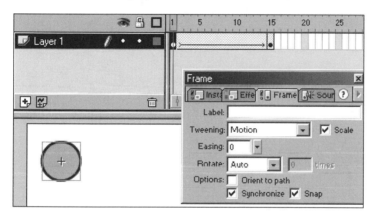

FIGURE 10.4   The Frame Panel and a Motion Tween.

- The Label box allows you to give a specific keyframe a label name, instead of simply using the frame number. This is useful in some advanced Actionscript programs.
- The Tweening box allows you to specify a motion tween, a shape tween, or no tween.
- The Scale box is used in motion tweens if you change the size as well as the location of the object. Checking Scale tweens the size of the object as well as its movement.
- Easing determines whether a tween happens most quickly at the beginning of an animation, evenly throughout the animation, or most quickly at the end of the animation. Values of less than 0 will cause the motion tween to begin slowly and accelerate at the end. Values of greater than 0 will cause the motion tween to begin quickly and decelerate at the end. A value of 0 produces even motion speed throughout the tween.
- Rotate allows you to rotate the object a specified number of times through the motion tween.

- Orient to path causes the tweened object to turn itself according to its path, the way a car moves along a winding road. If Orient to path is not selected, the object will follow the tween direction, but will point in one direction for the entire tween.
- The Synchronize option should be selected. It ensures that the motion tween will loop correctly through the animation.
- Snap causes the object in a motion tween to attach easily to a motion guide path.

Motion Guide Layers

Ordinary motion tweening moves an instance of a symbol in straight lines between locations of that instance at different keyframes. Motion guide Layers allow you to plot out the path of an object in great detail. For example, you might want to show an object moving in a circular path. Without a motion guide layer, you would have to create a series of keyframes moving an object around in a roughly circular path. But the path would actually be a large number of straight lines, as the object tweens between each keyframe.

Motion guide layers take care of the need to have more complex paths. With a motion guide layer, you use any of the drawing tools Flash provides, such as the Pencil, Circle, or Rectangle tool, to draw a path. An instance of a symbol is then linked to that path. An example of a rectangular symbol following a curved path appears in Figure 10.5.

To create a motion path, follow these steps:

- Put an instance of a symbol into a layer, either at the beginning of the layer or at a point where you have inserted a keyframe.
- Insert a keyframe at a later point in the layer.
- Create a motion tween for that instance by right clicking on the first keyframe and selecting Create Motion Tween, as shown in Figure 10.6. A solid line will appear between the two keyframes.

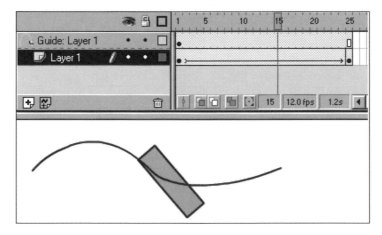

FIGURE 10.5   A Rectangle Following a Motion Guide Layer.

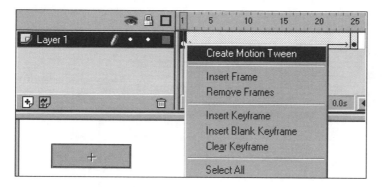

FIGURE 10.6   Creating a Motion Tween.

- Now insert a motion guide layer above the first layer. Do this by right clicking on the label area of the first layer, and selecting Add Motion Guide. As shown in Figure 10.7, a new layer will appear, with the symbol for a motion guide in the layer.
- In the motion guide layer, draw the path you want the object to follow as the film advances between the two keyframes in the object's layer. You can draw the path with any drawing tool you choose, such as the Pencil, Brush, Circle, or Rectangle.
- Once you have drawn the path, click on the first keyframe in the object's layer. Drag the object to the beginning of the path, as shown in Figure 10.8. If you have selected Snap in the Frame panel, described previously, the rectangle will "snap" to the beginning of the path when you drag it near enough to the path.
- Then click on the final keyframe in the object's layer. Drag the object to the end of the path, so that the crosshairs at the center of the object touch the path, as shown in Figure 10.9.
- Now, if you test the movie, either by moving the playhead or by choosing Control> Test Movie, you will see the object move along the path you drew.

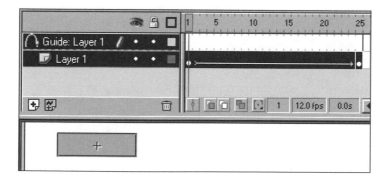

FIGURE 10.7   Creating a Motion Guide Layer.

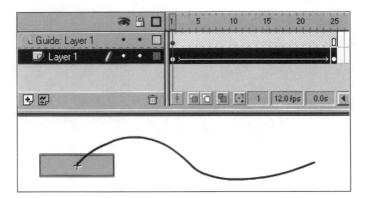

FIGURE 10.8   A Rectangle Snapped to the Beginning of the Motion Path.

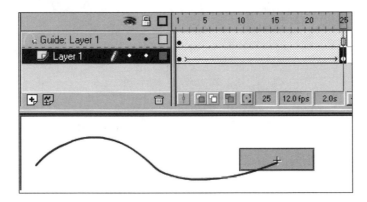

FIGURE 10.9   A Rectangle at the End of the Motion Path.

Shape Tweens

Shape tweens change the shape of an object across an animation. The process of creating a shape tween is similar to that of creating a motion tween. The main difference is that motion tweens involve the change of only one instance of a symbol, whereas shape tweens involve one object changing into another object. Figure 10.10 shows an example of a square undergoing a shape tween into a circle.

To create a shape tween, follow these steps.

- Insert a keyframe on a layer where you want the object to appear in its first shape.
- Select that keyframe, and draw the first object—in this example, a square—at that point, as shown in Figure 10.11.
- Next, insert a keyframe later on the time line. Delete the first object, the square, at that second keyframe. Draw the second object in the second keyframe. In this example, a circle is drawn, as shown in Figure 10.12.
- Now click on the first keyframe, so that the square appears on the stage again.

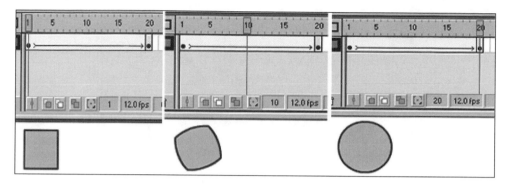

FIGURE 10.10   A Shape Tween.

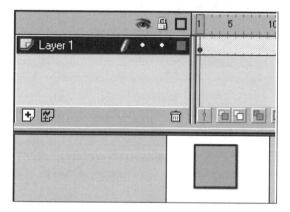

FIGURE 10.11   A Square at Keyframe 1.

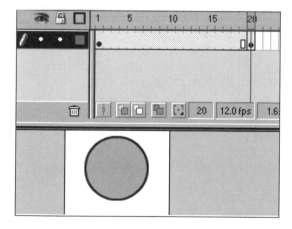

FIGURE 10.12   A Circle at the End Keyframe.

- Activate the Frame panel by choosing Window>Panels>Frame.
- Select Shape Tweening. A solid arrow will appear between the beginning and end keyframes, as shown in Figure 10.13.

    The Frame panel allows some options for shape tweening.

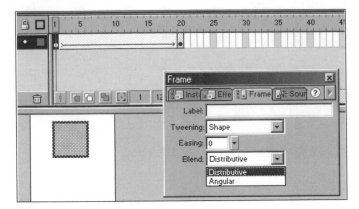

FIGURE 10.13   Creating a Shape Tween with the Frame Panel.

The Easing option, as with motion tweening, determines whether the greatest rate of change occurs at the beginning of the tween, at the end of the tween, or if there is an equal amount of change throughout the tween. Negative values for Easing cause high levels of change at the beginning of the tween, positive values cause high levels of change at the end of the tween, and a value of 0 causes steady change throughout the tween.

The distributive versus angular option determines the smoothness of the tween. Distributive shape tweening produces smoother, rounded edges as the tween takes place, whereas Angular shape tweening maintains edges that are more similar to the original objects throughout the tween.

■ Now, if you test the movie, either by moving the playhead or by choosing Con-trol>Test Movie, you will see the square change into a circle.

Shape Tweening with Symbols

Shape tweening cannot take place with instances of symbols. If you take a symbol from the Library, or import an image that becomes a symbol in the Library, it is necessary to break it apart before shape tweening can take place. Follow the same steps described above for shape tweening, but instead of drawing objects, drag them there from the Library. Each time you drag an instance of a symbol onto the time line, make sure to highlight it and choose Modify>Break Apart. When the symbol is broken apart, it can then be shape tweened.

Note: Sometimes Modify>Break Apart must be chosen repeatedly before a symbol is truly broken apart. When a symbol is broken apart, it will take on a more grainy appearance, like an object that has been selected with the Arrow tool.

The Instance Panel

The Instance panel (see Figure 10.14) is used in more advanced Flash programming. At some times, you may want a specific instance of a symbol to behave as some other type of symbol. For example, you may want a button to simply serve as a graphic. The Instance panel is used for these purposes.

The Effect Panel

The Effect panel works with motion tweens to change the color and transparency of an instance of a symbol. For example, if you wanted the color of a leaf to change from green to orange over the course of an animation, one way to do it would be to use the Effect panel along with a motion tween.

The Effect panel works with instances of symbols, so to use it you first have to create a symbol or take one from a Library. Create a layer for the symbol, insert a keyframe where you want the symbol to first appear, and place the symbol into the work area. This creates an instance of the symbol.

Next, choose a point in the animation time line by which you want the symbol to have completely changed color or transparency. Insert a keyframe there. Now go back to the first keyframe and create a motion tween for that symbol's instance, by clicking on the keyframe with the right mouse button and choosing Create Motion Tween. A solid arrow will appear between the two keyframes.

Finally, click on the second keyframe again. Now activate the Effect panel by choosing Window>Panels>Effect.

You may now choose an effect from the Effect panel (see Figure 10.15). The Effect panel allows you to make the symbol's instance change brightness, color, transparency, or a combination of these effects.

None is the default value for the Effect panel. Selecting None leaves the instance of the symbol unchanged across the motion tween.

Brightness changes the brightness of the instance, making it darker or brighter across the motion tween. Dragging the Brightness bar down to –100% will make the object completely black. Dragging the Brightness bar up to 100% will make the object completely white. The midpoint of the Brightness bar, 0%, leaves the color unchanged. Interim values make the color change to be slightly brighter or darker.

Tint changes the color of the instance from its original color at the first keyframe to a color you select at the second keyframe. When you select Tint, a box with a percentage value and a slider appear next to the Tint title. Use the slider to set the amount of change in color that will take place over the motion tween, from no change (0%) to complete change (100%). Change the color using the color grid at the bottom of the Effect panel, by changing the Red

FIGURE 10.14   The Instance Panel.

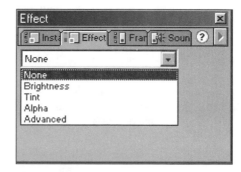

FIGURE 10.15   The Effect Panel.

(R), Green (G), and Blue (B) values with the slider, or by choosing a color from the Color box next to the Tint Color label.

Alpha changes the transparency level of the instance. Ordinarily when you draw an object or create a symbol, it is completely opaque, blocking out all objects behind it. The Alpha setting makes the object more or less transparent. Change the transparency level using the slider, which allows a range of 0% (completely transparent or invisible) to 100% (completely opaque).

The Advanced selection allows you to change the levels of red, blue, green, and transparency simultaneously. The boxes on the left (closest to each color or Alpha) are used to decrease that color or Alpha level by a given percentage. The boxes on the right increase or decrease the color or Alpha level by a constant amount.

The Sound Panel

Adding sound to a Flash animation will make it more interesting. In addition, sound can be used to provide information for the user. For example, a high or low beep can be added to indicate whether a person has given a correct or incorrect response to a question. Because sounds are built into a Flash animation, it is very easy to create Flash pages using sound, and people with current browsers will have no problem hearing sounds in Flash animations.

Inserting a Sound into a Flash Animation

The first step to adding a sound in Flash is to import the sound from another source. Flash itself provides a limited number of sounds that may be accessed through the Common Sound Library, discussed later.

To import a sound, choose File>Import and then navigate to the folder that contains your sound files. Flash can import a wide range of sound files, including .wav files and .mp3 files. Double-click on the sound you want to import.

The sound will now appear in the library for that Flash file. You can view the Library by choosing Window>Library or pressing Control + L.

Note: Flash cannot be used for editing sound files—for example, to shorten them or add effects such as an echo, to slow them down, or to speed them up. Before importing a sound into Flash, it is a good idea to do any necessary editing of the sound using Windows Sound Recorder or other editing software. For example, if you have a five-minute recording that you want to use only two or three seconds of in the Flash animation, you cannot clip out the two or three seconds using Flash. Flash will store the entire sound in the Flash file, making it unnecessarily large.

Once a sound is in the Flash library, you can test what it will sound like by selecting it and pressing the Play arrow in the Library. To add a sound to the Flash animation, it is best to create a separate layer first for sounds. Do this by clicking on the layer area and choosing Insert>Layer, or right clicking and choosing Insert Layer.

Next, add a keyframe to that layer at the point in the animation when you want the sound to play. Click on that keyframe.

Finally, drag the sound from the Library onto the work area. You will notice that a graphic of the sound wave will appear to the right of the keyframe in the layer you created for the sound. Now, whenever the animation reaches that point on the time line, the sound will play.

It is also possible to insert sounds into an animation using the Sound panel. In addition, once a sound has been inserted, you can use the Sound panel to change the characteristics of the sound, such as how loud it plays, what speaker or speakers it will come from, and how many times the sound repeats.

To use the Sound panel, first make sure that it is visible on the work area by choosing Window>Panels>Sound. The Sound panel will appear on the screen, as shown in Figure 10.16. If you click on a keyframe containing a sound, that sound's name will appear in the Sound box on the Sound panel. If you click on a keyframe that does not contain a sound, the Sound box will be blank. If you click on a frame that is empty and not a keyframe, the Sound box will be grayed out. The Sound panel has several functions.

The Sound box allows you to choose a sound to add to a keyframe. Clicking on the Down arrow to the right of the Sound box will display all of the sounds that are in your Library, even those that are already in use in your animation. Clicking on one of these sounds will add that sound to the keyframe you have selected.

Note: Sounds from the Common Sound Library will not appear in the Sound box unless they are in use in your animation. Once a sound has been inserted into your animation from the Common Sound Library, it will also appear in the Library for your Flash animation. Sounds from the Common Sound Library may also be dragged into your Flash Library for later use.

The Effect box in the Sound panel allows you to choose from a series of simple sound effects. None makes the sound play through both speakers, according to the standard stereo format. Left Channel and Right Channel cause the sound to be played only through either channel. Fade Right to Left and Fade Left to Right cause the sound to move from one speaker to the other as it plays. Fade In causes the sound to increase in volume as it plays, and Fade Out causes it to decrease in volume as it plays. Finally, Custom allows you to use the Sound Editor to produce your own changes in volume for each channel. The Edit button also allows you to change sound volumes in each channel across the duration of the sound.

The Sync button affects when the sound begins in the animation. The default value, Event, causes the sound to play in its entirety when a certain event occurs in the animation, such as when the keyframe a sound is attached to is reached, or when a button the sound is attached to is pressed. Start is used with Stop, described next. Whereas Event causes sounds to play in entirety, Start and Stop can be used together to play only part of a sound.

Stop causes a sound in the layer to stop playing. To stop a sound from playing at a certain point, first insert another layer above the layer the sound is in. Insert a keyframe at the point where you want the sound to stop. Select the sound that you want to stop from the Sound box, and select Stop on the Sync button. Now that sound will stop playing when the animation reaches that keyframe. Streaming synchronizes the sound to the animation for use in Web presentations. Essentially, Streaming causes the

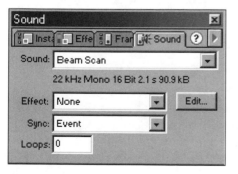

FIGURE 10.16   The Sound Panel.

animation to skip frames if necessary, as it is playing on the Web, to keep pace with the sound that is playing.

The Loops button controls how many times the sound plays once it has begun. A loop value of 0 or 1 will cause the sound to play once. Loop values higher than 1 will cause the sound to play the loop value entered. For example, a loop value of 4 will cause the sound to play four times in succession.

Note: If the animation is designed to repeat itself over and over, you should be careful not to set the loop value so high as to cause the sound to play for longer than one entire cycle of the animation. Otherwise, the loops will begin to overlap each other as the animation cycles, interfering with sound clarity.

Creating a Button

One of the major steps to creating interactivity in a Flash animation is creating and inserting buttons that allow a viewer to control the action in the animation. Flash provides many buttons in the Flash Library, but it is useful to know the different parts of a button and how to create one. The following steps show how to create a button.

While in a Flash movie, first select Insert>New Symbol. The Symbol Properties box will appear, as shown in Figure 10.17. Select the Button option, and enter a name (such as Round Button) in the Name text box. Click OK.

A new Flash work space appears. Notice that the time line is different from the usual Flash time line, as shown in Figure 10.18. The beginning of a button time line is divided into four frames, called Up, Over, Down, and Hit. Each of these frames corresponds to one instance of a button. Up is what the button will look like when it is simply on the stage. Over is what the button looks like when the mouse pointer is moved over the button. Down is the appearance of the button when someone clicks on it. Finally, Hit is the area on or around the button that is active. The Hit area is the area that action (such as moving the cursor over the Hit area) will cause the button to respond.

To create a button, you follow the same steps you would follow to create a movie with four keyframes in it. First, select the Up frame. You can draw an object in this frame, or insert a symbol or even a movie, if you want your button to be animated. For a basic button, simply draw a circle with a blue fill, as shown in Figure 10.19.

Note: Make sure that you center the button on the crosshairs in the middle of the work area. Centering the button in each frame (Up, Over, Down, and Hit, if you use Hit) ensures that the button does not appear to move in an unwanted direction when it is pressed or released.

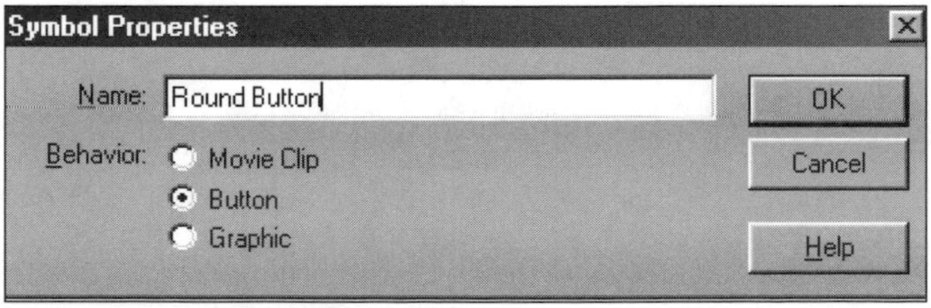

FIGURE 10.17   Naming a Button Symbol.

Next, click on the Over frame and insert a new keyframe by right clicking on the Over frame and selecting Insert Keyframe. To change the appearance of the button when the pointer is passed over it, change the object or symbol in the Over frame. For this example, use the Paint Bucket to change the circle's fill to green, as shown in Figure 10.20.

Next, click on the Down frame and insert a new keyframe. You can now change the appearance of the button when it is being "pressed" by clicking on it. Change the button to red for the Down position, as shown in Figure 10.21.

FIGURE 10.18   The Button Time Line.

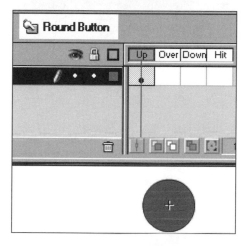

FIGURE 10.19   A Blue Circle for the Button Up Position.

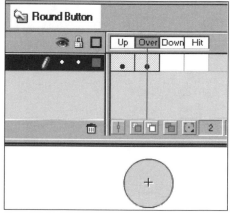

FIGURE 10.20   A Green Circle for the Button Over Position.

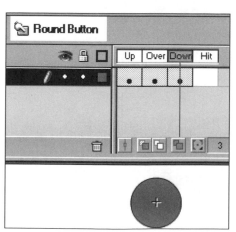

FIGURE 10.21   A Red Circle for the Button Down Position.

Finally, you can specify the area on the stage that the button responds to by inserting an image into the Hit frame. If you do not insert an object or symbol into the Hit frame, the area that Flash will treat as a button will be the shape of the object or instance that is in the Down frame, or whatever the most recent keyframe is in the sequence of frames. If you want to specify the area that Flash will treat as the button, insert a keyframe into the Hit frame, and draw or insert a new object into the work area. Generally the Hit area is the same as the button, so there is no need to modify the Hit area.

You can now drag the button onto your animation. Once it is in the animation, you can test it by selecting Control>Enable Simple Buttons.

Basic Actionscript Commands

Actionscript is the programming language used in Flash. Actionscript commands perform functions such as causing different actions to occur when a specific frame is reached or when a button is pushed. Actionscript is an advanced programming language, but some of the commands available in Actionscript are relatively simple to use. They greatly increase the interactivity of Flash animations.

Frame Actions

Frame Actions are actions that take place when a certain frame in a time line is reached. To explore some basic commands, first open a new Flash file and insert a keyframe in Frame 10 on Layer 1. Click on that keyframe.

Activate the Actions panel by selecting Window>Actions. The Frame Actions panel will appear, as shown in Figure 10.22.

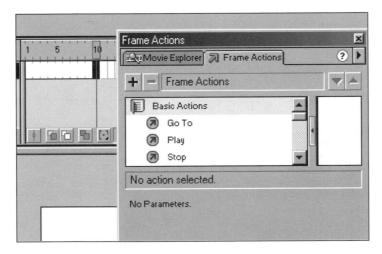

FIGURE 10.22   The Frame Actions Panel.

A series of Basic Actions appear. Choosing one of these basic actions will cause the animation to execute the action when the keyframe in Frame 10 is reached. The most essential Frame Actions in Flash are Go To and Stop. You will notice that when you select an action in the Frame Actions panel, an italic letter *a* will appear in that frame. This indicates that an Actionscript command is associated with that frame.

The Go To Command

Selecting Go To tells Flash to go to a new frame or scene when that frame is reached. When you click on Go To, a series of options appear, as shown in Figure 10.23.

- The Actionscript box to the right shows the actual Actionscript code that is produced by your commands.
- The Scene option allows you to select what scene the animation will go to, if the animation has multiple scenes in it.
- The Type option allows you to select specific locations for the animation to go to, such as a specific frame, a labeled keyframe, or another option. In this example, the command is to go to a specific frame number.
- The Frame command allows you to pick a certain frame. In this example, the film will return to Frame 1 once it reaches Frame 10.
- The Go to and Play option determines what will happen when the animation reaches the frame. Because the Go to and Play box is checked, in this example, the movie will go to Frame 1 and play. If the Go to and Play box was not checked, the movie would go to Frame 1 and stop.

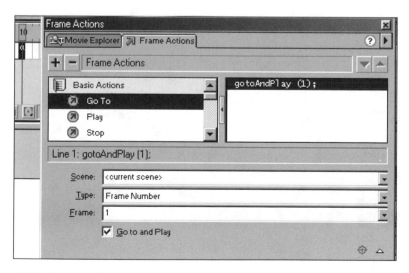

FIGURE 10.23   The Go To Command.

The Stop Command

The Stop command instructs Flash to stop when it has reached a specific frame. Usually this is used in conjunction with another Go To command associated with an Object Action, such as a button push, which will be described next.

Object Actions

Object Actions are actions that are carried out when a button is pushed or some other object is used. To explore some basic commands, first open a new Flash file and insert a button from the Common Libraries into Frame 1 on Layer 1. Click on the button.

Activate the Actions panel by selecting Window>Actions. The Object Actions panel will appear, as shown in Figure 10.24.

A series of Basic Actions appear. Choosing one of these basic actions will cause the animation to execute the action when some command is carried out with the button, usually pressing and releasing it. The most essential Object Action in Flash is Go To.

The Go To Command

Selecting Go To tells Flash to go to a new frame or scene when the button is released. When you click on Go To, a series of options appear, as shown in Figure 10.25.

- The Actionscript box to the right shows the actual Actionscript code that is produced by your commands.
- The Scene option allows you to select what scene the animation will go to following the mouse event, if the animation has multiple scenes in it.
- The Type option allows you to select specific locations for the animation to go to, such as a specific frame, a labeled keyframe, or another option. In this example, the command is to go to a specific frame number when the button is released.

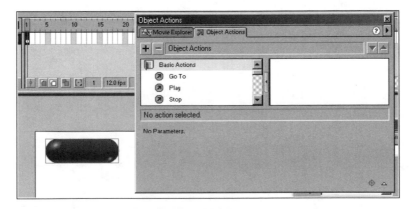

FIGURE 10.24   The Object Actions Panel.

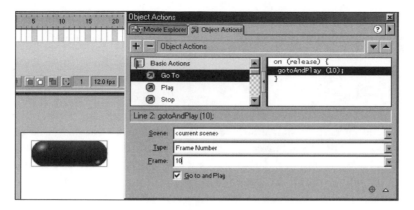

FIGURE 10.25   The Go To Command.

- The Frame command allows you to pick a certain frame. In this example, the film will advance to Frame 10 when the button is pushed.
- The Go to and Play option determines what will happen when the button is released. Because the Go to and Play box is checked, in this example, the movie will go to Frame 10 and play. If the Go to and Play box was not checked, the movie would go to Frame 10 and stop.

Exporting the Final Flash Animation

When you create a Flash animation, the file you work with is a Flash, or .fla, file. The .fla file contains the library of images and sounds you have created and imported, along with all of the animation instructions you produce for the movie. The .fla movie can be edited using Flash, and you can view the final Flash animation using the .fla movie. Once you are done creating the Flash movie, it must be exported into a format that can be viewed on the Web or on some other media, such as a floppy disk, CD-ROM, or DVD. Flash provides several options that you can choose from for final export.

For use in web presentations, the Flash Player movie, which is saved as an .swf file, is the most common choice for Flash animations. A Flash Player movie retains all of the characteristics of the original Flash animation, but can be very small, taking up very little bandwidth and allowing very quick downloads. Every time you test the Flash animation by choosing Control>Test Movie, Flash creates a Flash Player movie and saves it in the same directory as the Flash animation. The Flash Player movie has the same name as the Flash animation, but it has an extension of .swf instead of .fla. You could use this Flash Player movie as your final product, but Flash allows you to select several options to customize the Flash Player movie through the Export function.

To create a Flash Player movie using the Export function, follow these steps.

- Open the Flash animation you want to export into a Flash Player movie.
- Choose File>Export Movie and name the Flash Player movie. The default value for the file type is Flash Player (.swf). Keep this value.

Note: If you are going to use the Flash Player movie on the Web, you should use the standard guidelines for naming it. This includes making the name fewer than eight characters long and not including any spaces.

The Export Menu

Once you have named the Flash Player movie and chosen the Save option, an Export Flash Player menu appears, as shown in Figure 10.26. This menu allows you to customize the characteristics of the Flash Player movie.

Load Order controls which layer appears first, as the Flash Player movie downloads onto a computer screen. The Bottom Up choice makes the bottom layer in your film appear first. The Top Down choice makes the top layer in the film appear first. Because the background is usually on the bottom layer, it is generally best to use the default value, Bottom Up.

Several options are available.

- Generate Size Report produces a text file that indicates the size of the Flash Player at each frame in the animation.
- Protect from Import prevents people who view the Flash Player file from importing it themselves and editing it as a Flash movie.

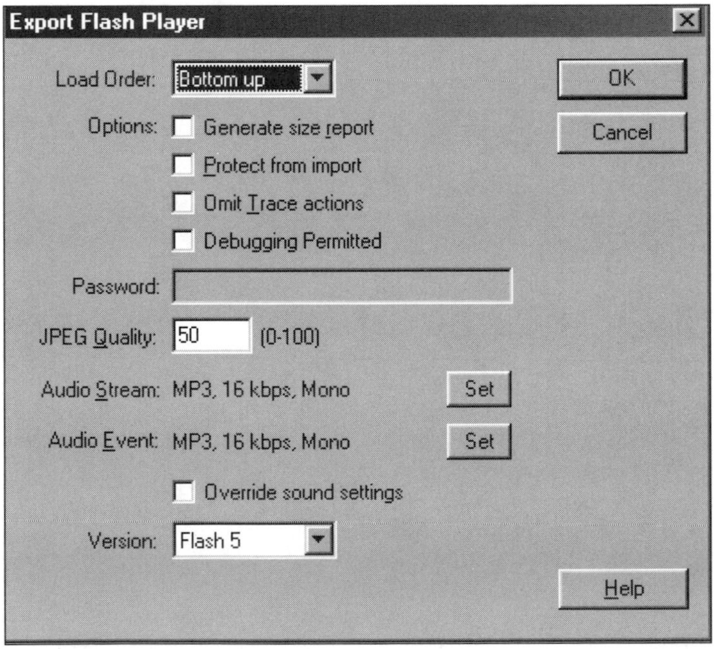

FIGURE 10.26   Export Flash Player Menu.

- Omit Trace actions, Debugging Permitted, and the Password option are advanced Flash procedures that permit a user who accesses the Flash movie online to control its operation.
- JPEG Quality is a very important option when exporting a Flash Player movie. Setting the JPEG quality affects the final size of the Flash movie. One of the most useful characteristics of Flash is that Flash Player movies can be very small, yet are very compelling multimedia. Lowering the JPEG quality not only reduces the size of the Flash Player movie, allowing faster downloads, but also decreases the graphic quality of the presentation. Increasing the JPEG quality increases the size and quality of the movie, causing slower downloads. Experimenting with different quality levels is the best strategy for determining the trade-off between size and quality you prefer.
- Set Audio Stream and Set Audio Event allow you to specify the quality of the sounds that play in the Flash Player movie. As with the JPEG quality option, there is a trade-off between sound quality and sound size. For the smallest size files that still provide adequate sound quality, MP3 compression is often the best choice. Further specifications available include the bit rate and the quality, with higher bit rates and higher quality producing better sounds, but larger files. Once again, experimenting with different options is the best strategy for determining the trade-off between size and quality you prefer.
- Override Sound Settings allows you to override the settings you initially created for the Flash Player movie, should you want to export a second version with a higher quality.
- The Version setting allows you to export the Flash Player movie in different versions, such as Flash 4. Exporting the movie in the most current format ensures that all of the actions that take place in a complex movie will work perfectly. Exporting it in an earlier format may cause problems with some actions that were not supported by earlier formats. However, if the Flash movie is relatively simple, there is a benefit to exporting it as an earlier version. If people who are accessing your web pages have an older version of the Flash Player plug-in installed, they may not be able to view a new animation without installing the newest Flash plug-in. If you export the film as an earlier version of Flash, more people will be able to view it without updating their Flash plug-ins.
- Choose OK after specifying the Export options. Now, you have created a Flash Player movie that can be inserted into a web page.

Creating a Web Page for a Flash Player Movie

Many programs that create web pages, such as Adobe GoLive and Macromedia Dreamweaver, allow you to insert a Flash Player movie directly the same way you would insert any graphic file. Flash also gives you the option to create a web page that includes your Flash Player movie. Then you can later edit that page further with a web page editing program, if necessary. To create the web page, simply choose File>Publish. Flash will create a Flash Player movie and an HTML web page that includes the movie. Both the Flash Player movie and the web page will have the same name as the Flash movie you are working with, but with different extensions (.swf and .html).

Creating a Stand-alone Flash Player

You may also want to create a version of your Flash movie that can be distributed on disk instead of on the Web. Flash allows you to create a Flash Projector file, which is an .exe file in Windows. This file includes all of the necessary software to run the Flash movie without a web browser or the Flash plug-in. To create a Flash Projector file, first save your Flash movie as a Flash Player movie. Next, play the Flash Player movie. While it is playing, choose File>Create Projector. You can then name and save the Projector file.

Other Export Options

Flash also allows one to export the Flash movie in a variety of other formats, such as a Quicktime movie, an animated .gif file, and an AVI file. These options are useful if you are creating non-Flash multimedia. However, each of these options has limitations that do not exist with Flash Player movies and Flash projectors. For example, animated .gif files created by export from Flash will lose any sound effects and interactivity. However, animated .gifs and other multimedia formats exported from Flash will still be very appealing.

A Project: Flashcards for the Web

In this project, you will make a set of flashcards for learners to use online. The user will navigate through a series of flashcards and answers using buttons.

First, create a Flash animation by starting Flash and saving the file. Do this by choosing File>Save. Name the file Flashcards.

Define the size and background color of the movie by selecting Modify>Movie. For this example, the movie will have a width of 550 pixels and a height of 400 pixels, and a background color of white.

Creating the Flashcards

Each flashcard will be a symbol of the graphic type. To create Question Card 1, follow these steps.

Choose Insert>New Symbol. The Symbol Properties box will appear, as shown in Figure 10.27. Enter the name Card 1Q (for Card 1, question), and designate the symbol as a graphic.

You will now be able to create the symbol. Because you will be drawing rectangular cards, it may be useful to make the grid and rulers visible by selecting View>Grid>Show Grid and View>Rulers.

Figure 10.28 shows how Card 1Q should look. Label Layer 1 by double-clicking on the Layer 1 label, which will become highlighted. Enter Background in the Layer Label box.

Using the Rectangle drawing tool, draw Card 1 in Layer 1, the Background layer.

Select a fill for the rectangle by clicking on the Paint Bucket button and then the Fill Color button. Because the fill for the rectangle will be the background of the flashcard, use a light color. Position the paint bucket over the rectangle and click to fill the rectangle.

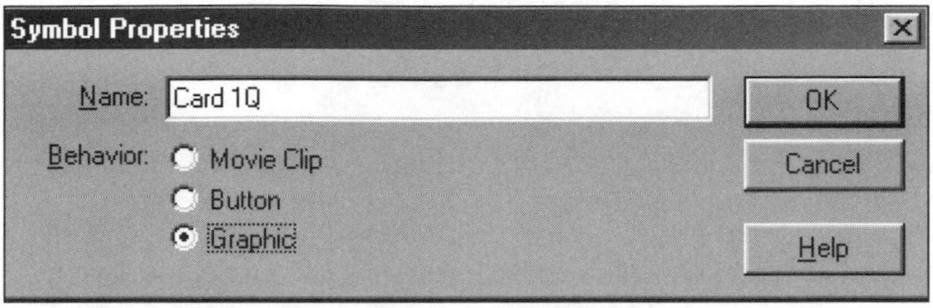

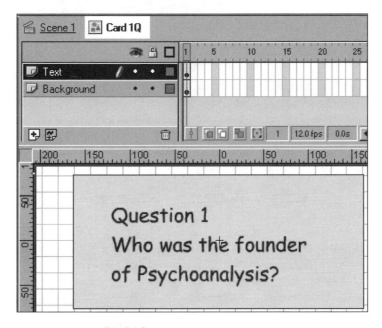

FIGURE 10.27   Inserting a Symbol.

FIGURE 10.28   Card 1Q.

Next, add another layer to the graphic. This layer will contain the text of the question. Add the layer by clicking on Layer 1 on the work area and then select Insert>Layer. Layer 2 will appear. Label Layer 2 Text.

Make sure that the Text layer is active by clicking on the Text layer label. The area around the label will become black, and a pencil will appear next to the label.

Add a text box to the Text layer by selecting the Text button, positioning it over the background rectangle you created, and clicking. The text box will appear. Type in Question 1.

Hit return, and type in a question. For this example, use the question "Who was the founder of Psychoanalysis?"

Now choose a font, font size, and fill that look good. Do this by highlighting the text in the text box and using the Character panel. If the Character panel is not visible, choose Window>Panels>Character. Figure 10.29 shows the Character panel and the text box.

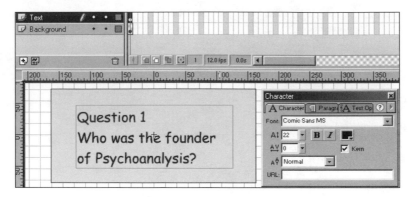

FIGURE 10.29   Card 1Q Character Panel and Text Box.

Using the Character panel and text box options, choose a font, font size, and fill. For this example, the text is Comic Sans MS, 22 points, with black fill.

Now that you have created Card Question 1, you can duplicate it to create all of the question and answer cards. First, make sure your library is visible by clicking Window> Library. At this point, the only symbol available in the Library will be Card Q1, which will appear in the top window of the Library.

Click on Options>Duplicate to make a duplicate of the card. This duplicate will be Card Answer 1. In the Name box, which initially reads Card 1Q copy, enter Card 1A (for Card 1, Answer) and choose OK.

Click on the Arrow tool to allow you to select the text box. Click on the Text Layer to make it active, and double-click on the text box to highlight it. Change the text to read "Answer 1" and "The founder of Psychoanalysis was Sigmund Freud."

Repeat this duplication process to create question Card 2Q, with the question "Who pioneered classical conditioning?" and answer Card 2A, with the answer "Ivan Pavlov pioneered classical conditioning."

Once again, repeat the duplication process to create question Card 3Q, with the question "Who was a major figure in operant conditioning?" and answer Card 3A, with the answer "B. F. Skinner was a major figure in operant conditioning." Your library should now have six graphic symbols in it: Card 1Q, Card 1A, Card 2Q, Card 2A, Card 3Q, and Card 3A.

The next step is to create buttons to advance or back up through the flashcards. First, create a blank button symbol by choosing Insert>New Symbol. The Symbol Properties box will appear. Enter the name Button Next (to indicate that this will be the button that moves a person to the next card), and designate the symbol as a Button. This is shown in Figure 10.30.

The Button work area now appears on your work space. Notice that the Button Layer area is divided into four frames, Up (what the button looks like when it is not pressed), Over (when the pointer is over the button, but it is not pressed), Down (when the button is pressed), and Hit (the area that the button actively responds to). You will make a slightly different image each for Up, Over, and Down. These frames are shown in Figure 10.31.

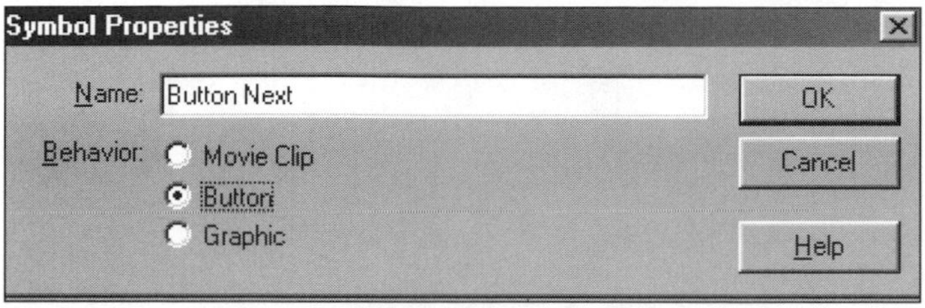

FIGURE 10.30   Inserting a Button.

FIGURE 10.31   Button Frames.

You will notice that the orange playhead highlights the Up frame. There is already a keyframe in the Up frame. First you will make the image of the button that will appear when it is in the Up position.

Label Layer 1 by double-clicking on the Layer 1 label, which will become highlighted. Enter Background in the Layer Label box. Using the Rectangle drawing tool, draw the background, a small rectangle, in Layer 1, the Background layer. Center the rectangle on the crosshairs in the middle of the work area.

Select a fill for the rectangle by clicking on the Paint Bucket button and then the Fill Color button. Because the fill for the rectangle will be the background of the button, use a dark blue. Position the paint bucket over the rectangle and click to fill the rectangle.

Next, add another layer to the button. This layer will contain the text Next. Add the layer by clicking on Layer 1 on the work area and then select Insert>Layer. Layer 2 will appear. Label Layer 2 Text.

Make sure that the Text layer is active by clicking on the Text layer label. The area around the label will become black, and a pencil will appear next to the label.

Add a text box to the Text layer by selecting the Text button, positioning it over the background rectangle you created, and clicking. The text box will appear. Type in Next.

Now choose a font, font size, and fill that look good. Do this by highlighting the text in the text box and using the Character panel.

Using the Character panel options, choose a font, font size, and fill. For this example, the text is Comic Sans MS, 20 points, with white fill. Figure 10.32 shows what the button should look like so far, with the Up frame completed.

Next, you will change the button's appearance for when it is in the Over position. First, insert a keyframe in the Background layer, in the Over frame, by clicking on that frame and choosing Insert>Keyframe or pressing F6. A black dot will appear in the Background layer, Over frame. You should also insert a frame in the Over frame in the Text layer, by clicking on that frame and choosing Insert>Frame or pressing F5. A clear rectangle will appear in the Text layer, Over frame.

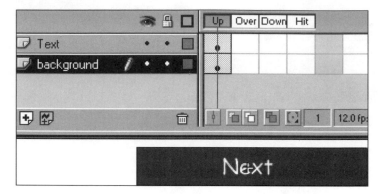

FIGURE 10.32   The Up Frame.

Now change the fill color for the rectangular button, to make it a lighter blue. First, select the Arrow tool, and make the Background layer active. Next, choose the Paint Bucket tool and choose a lighter blue color from the Color box.

Finally, position the Paint Bucket tool over the rectangle (making sure the Background layer is active). Click to fill the rectangle with the lighter blue color.

Next, change the button's appearance for when it is in the Down position. First, insert a keyframe in the Background layer, in the Down frame, by clicking on that frame and choosing Insert>Keyframe or pressing F6. A black dot will appear in the Background layer, Over frame. You should also insert a frame in the Down frame in the Text layer, by clicking on that frame and choosing Insert>Frame or pressing F5. A clear rectangle will appear in the Text layer, Down frame.

Now change the fill color for the rectangular button, to make it red. First, select the Arrow tool, and make the Background layer active. Next, choose the Paint Bucket tool and choose a red color from the Color box.

Finally, position the Paint Bucket tool over the rectangle (making sure the Background layer is active) and click to fill the rectangle with the red color. Now the button will turn red when it is pressed down.

The final step in creating the button is defining the Hit area, which is the area in which the button actively functions when a pointer is passed over it. In most cases, the Hit area should be the same size as the button itself.

To make the Hit area the same size as the rectangular button, first use the Arrow tool to make the background layer active. Next, insert a keyframe on the background layer, in the Hit frame, by clicking on that frame, and choosing Insert>Keyframe or pressing F6. It is not necessary to insert a frame in the Text layer. Figure 10.33 shows how the entire Next button should appear.

You also need a Previous button to move the viewer back through the series of flash-cards. This button can be duplicated from the Next Button in your library.

First, make sure the Library is visible by choosing Window>Library. The Library should show all of the flashcards you created, along with Button Next. Click on Button Next, so that it appears in the window at the top of the Library.

Select Action>Duplicate, and in the Symbol Properties box name it Button Previous and specify that it is a Button. Click OK. Button Previous will now appear in your library.

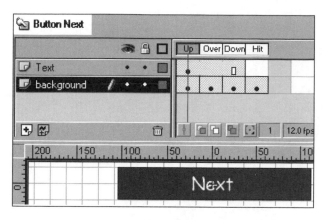

FIGURE 10.33   The Finished Next Button.

Click on it, and then select Options>Edit. The button will appear in the workspace. The only change that needs to be made to this button is to change the text on the Text layer from Next to Previous.

First, use the Arrow tool to make the Text layer active. You will see a pencil appear on that layer.

Next, double-click on the text box that contains the text Next until it is highlighted. The pointer will turn to the Text tool, an A with a crosshairs next to it. Type in the new text: Previous.

You will probably need to realign the text box on the background rectangle. Click on the Arrow tool again, and use it to move the text box so that it is centered on the rectangle.

The buttons are now completed. Now it is time to assemble the parts of the flashcards into a full, interactive Flash animation.

Creating the Interactive Flashcard Animation

First, create layers for the cards, the buttons, and the action commands. Click on Layer 1. Rename it Actions.

While Layer 1 is active, choose Insert>Layer. Layer 2 will appear. Rename that layer Buttons.

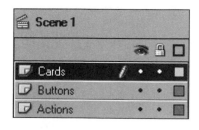

FIGURE 10.34   Layers for Flashcard Animation.

Insert a final layer, by choosing Insert>Layer. Layer 3 will appear. Rename that layer Cards. The final set of layers should be as it appears in Figure 10.34.

Next, set up the first frame for each of the three layers. The Cards layer will have the first question flashcard. The Buttons layer will have a Next button in it, so that the user can advance to the next card, which will be the answer card for question 1. Finally, the Actions layer will have a command to tell Flash to stop each time it advances to the next frame, so that only one card will appear each time a button is pushed. Figure 10.35 shows how the first frame should look.

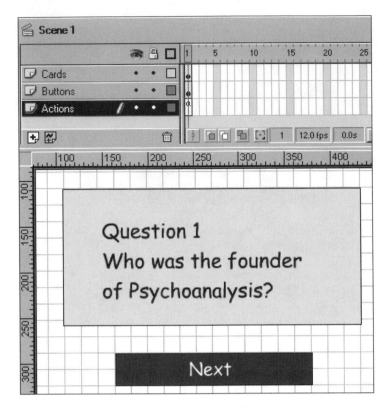

FIGURE 10.35   Frame 1 for Flashcard Animation.

Click on the Cards layer to make it active. From the Library, drag Card 1Q onto the stage, centering it. A black dot will appear in keyframe 1 on the Cards layer, indicating that an instance of a symbol is now in that layer at that keyframe.

Click on the Buttons layer to make it active. Drag Button Next from the Library to the stage, centering it under Card 1Q. A black dot will also appear in keyframe 1 on the Buttons layer.

Click on the Actions layer to make it active. Click in Frame 1 of the Actions layer to work with the keyframe in frame 1. Select Window>Actions to make the Frame Actions panel active. Finally, under Basic Actions, click on Stop. This assigns the frame action of Stop to Frame 1, as shown in Figure 10.36.

Now add an action to the button by clicking on the Buttons layer to make it active, and then clicking on the Next button on the stage. You will notice that the Frame Actions panel switches to Object Actions. Double click on Go To. Some Actionscript code will appear in the window to the right. This code tells Flash to go to another frame when the Next button is released by the user. To make the movie advance to the next frame when the Next button is released, choose Next Frame in the Type selection box. This assigns the object action of Go To Next Frame on Release to the Next button in Frame 1, as shown in Figure 10.37.

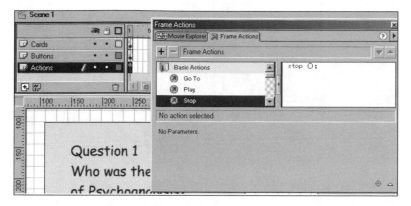

FIGURE 10.36   Frame Action for Frame 1.

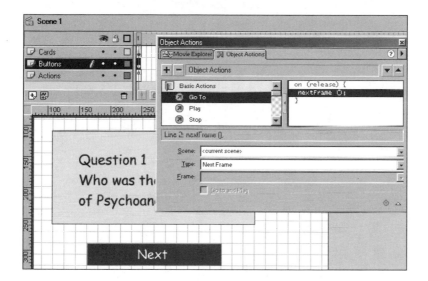

FIGURE 10.37   Object Action for Button in Frame 1.

The next step will be to set up the second frame for each of the three layers. Start by adding blank frames to each of the layers, by clicking on Frame 2 in each layer, and by choosing Insert>Frame or pressing F5. Next, insert a keyframe in Frame 2 on the Cards layer, by choosing Insert>Keyframe or pressing F6.

At this point, it may be useful to activate the Onion Skin option in Flash, which allows you to see previous frames. Onion skinning helps to line up objects from frame to frame. This is shown in Figure 10.38.

Now delete Card 1Q from Frame 2 in the Cards layer by clicking on it and pressing Delete. Replace Card 1Q in Frame 2 with Card 1A, by dragging Card 1A from the Library. Line it up with the onion skin image of Card 1Q.

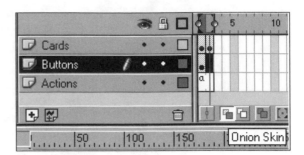

FIGURE 10.38 Onion Skinning across Frames.

Now make the Buttons layer active by clicking on it. Add a keyframe in Frame 2. Move the Next button to the right, to make room for the Previous button that should now be included. Drag an instance of the Previous button from the Library and position it to the left of the Next button. Figure 10.39 shows how the Flash animation should look at this point.

Now add an action to the Previous button (the action associated with the Next button remains active). With the Buttons layer active, click on the Previous button and select Window>Actions. The Object Actions panel will appear. Double-click on Go To. Some Actionscript code will appear in the window to the right.

To make the movie back up to the previous frame when the Previous button is released, choose Previous Frame in the Type selection box. The correct Actionscript is shown in Figure 10.40. No modifications are necessary for the Actions layer.

Next, add the Question 2 flashcard to the animation. First, insert blank frames into Frame 3 for each layer.

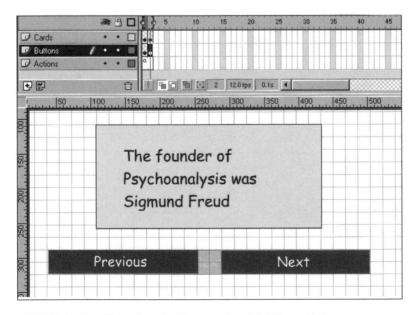

FIGURE 10.39 Changing the Flashcard and Adding a Button.

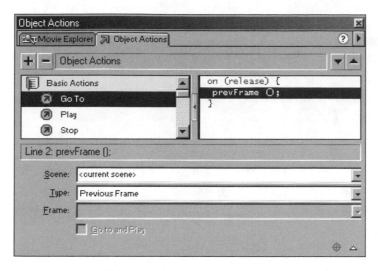

FIGURE 10.40   Object Action for Previous Button.

Activate the Cards layer and insert a keyframe in Frame 3. Delete Card 1A from Frame 3 and drag an instance of Card 2Q into the work area, positioning it over the onion skin of Card 1A. No modifications are necessary for the Buttons or Actions layers.

Next, add the Answer 2 flashcard to the animation. First, insert blank frames into Frame 4 for each layer.

Activate the Cards layer and insert a keyframe in Frame 4. Delete Card 2Q from Frame 4 and drag an instance of Card 2A into the work area, positioning it over the onion skin of Card 2Q. No modifications are necessary for the Buttons or Actions layers in Frame 4.

Next, add the Question 3 flashcard to the animation. First, insert blank frames into Frame 5 for each layer.

Activate the Cards layer and insert a keyframe in Frame 5. Delete Card 2A from Frame 5 and drag an instance of Card 3Q into the work area, positioning it over the onion skin of Card 2A. No modifications are necessary for the Buttons or Actions layers in Frame 5.

Finally, add the flashcard for Answer 3 to the animation, and end the animation. Figure 10.41 shows the completed flashcard animation.

First, insert blank frames into Frame 6 for each layer. Activate the Cards layer and insert a keyframe in Frame 6. Delete Card 3Q from Frame 6 and drag an instance of Card 3A into the work area, positioning it over the onion skin of Card 3Q.

Activate the Buttons layer and insert a keyframe into Frame 6 of the Buttons layer. Click on the instance of the Next button in the keyframe in Frame 6 of the Buttons layer and delete that button (because there is no next card).

Center the Previous button under the flashcard. Notice that the onion skins of the previous buttons are still visible. They will not be visible during the actual Flash animation.

The Flash animation is now complete! You may test it by choosing Control>Test Movie. Figure 10.42 shows the Flash Player movie.

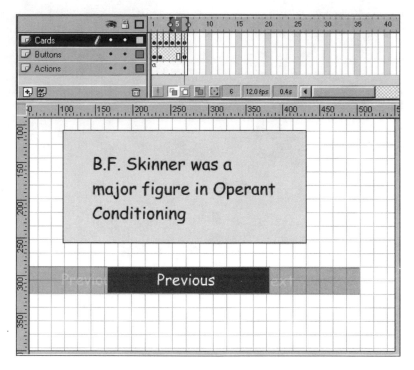

FIGURE 10.41   Completed Flashcard.

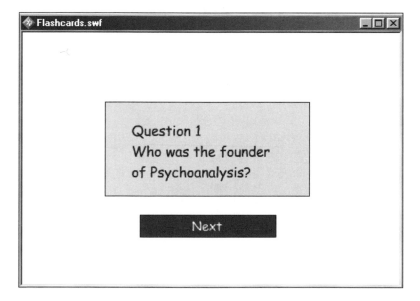

FIGURE 10.42   Flash Player Movie.

Export a Flash Player movie of your flashcards by choosing File>Export Movie and choosing any export options. This will create a Flash Player movie named Flashcards.swf.

Create a web page that contains the flashcard movie by selecting File>Publish. This will create the Flashcards.swf file, and an HTML file called Flashcards.html that contains the HTML code necessary to embed the movie and play it on the Web.

Finally, you can create a stand-alone projector file of the flashcards.

1. Start the Flashcards.swf file by navigating to it using Windows Explorer and double-clicking on it.
2. Choose File>Create Projector. This will create a stand-alone Flash movie called Flashcards.exe that can be distributed and played offline, without the need for a web browser or any other software.

11 Introducing JavaScript

HyperText Markup (HTML) pages are essentially pages that describe where text and graphics are placed on a web page. Once placed, the page stays as the HTML code has described it, and other than links, everything stays put. JavaScript adds a dynamic component to an HTML page by providing it with objects that will change depending on what the user (page viewer) does with the mouse, keyboard, or some other input device, such as a stylus. For example, when the mouse pointer passes over a graphic on a web page, JavaScript can cause the graphic to change in some way. The change may be subtle, such as a change in color, or the change may display a completely different graphic.

For the user who encounters these changes, a sense of interaction takes place. The user's actions have created a *response* from the web page. Information entered into a web page form, such as the user's name, can be passed to a variable for different types of processing. For example, the name can be displayed on the screen with a greeting. Other information entered into a form can be calculated and then displayed in another part of the page to show a different value. A common use would be adding tax and shipping costs to an initial purchase price.

Writing JavaScript Programs

One of the many nice features of JavaScript is the ability to integrate scripts written in JavaScript in HTML pages with the HTML markup language. You do not need a special processor or compiler to create JavaScript code. All you need is a text editor such as Note Pad, which comes with computers using Microsoft Windows, or SimpleText, supplied free with Macintosh operating systems. In most respects, you can think of JavaScript as a scripting language that supercharges HTML pages.

JavaScript programs or scripts are read by your browser—generally Netscape Navigator or Internet Explorer. The browsers read or *parse* the scripts to *interpret* what they mean. The parser needs to see certain key elements and the words used in JavaScript to know what to do so that it can correctly interpret the script. Unfortunately, Netscape Navigator and Internet Explorer interpret JavaScript in slightly different manners, so that certain JavaScript programs work differently on each browser. Because we are concentrating on the basic features of JavaScript, few problems will arise because of the different interpretations that Netscape and Microsoft have built into their browsers. The next chapter examines how to get around some of the more common problems arising because of differences in the browsers.

Getting Started

If you have never written HTML or any other computer language, you must remember that computers are literal machines. That is, you must include all of the marks and words that you see in the scripts in this book. Even a tiny difference can cause a script to fail. In some respects creating a good script is like talking to an infant. Computers need explicit instructions including all the steps they must take to accomplish a task. If you are familiar with computer languages, once you get used to the formatting conventions, you will probably find writing scripts to be creative and logical.

JavaScript programs (or scripts) reside within HTML pages. So the first step in setting up a JavaScript program is to create tags that let the browser know that the code is JavaScript and not HTML. For example, the following shows a simple line of JavaScript within an HTML page:

```
<HTML>
<BODY bgcolor = white>
<SCRIPT language="JavaScript">
greeting= "<B>Hello </B> from JavaScript.";
document.write(greeting);
</SCRIPT>
</BODY>
<HTML>
```

When you load the script into your browser, you will see,

Hello from JavaScript

In and of itself, seeing text on a web page is nothing to turn heads, but you can see that the manner in which it is done is nothing like HTML. First, the line of text is placed into another word called greeting. The word *greeting* is a variable assigned the value <B>Hello</B> from JavaScript—the code that could go into a standard HTML page. However, HTML cannot deal with variables, and JavaScript can. The importance of variables lies in the fact that the users can supply information for variables. For example, the following script gets information from the user and then combines it with a greeting variable to provide a unique welcome for those viewing the web page.

```
<HTML>
<body bgcolor="white">
<script language="JavaScript">
var yourname;
var greeting="Welcome, ";
yourname=prompt("Enter your name:","Name");
document.write(greeting + yourname);
</script>
</body>
</html>
```

Type in the script and save it as **NewWelcome.html.** If it is copied correctly, you will see the web page do something you cannot do with HTML alone. When you respond to the prompt, the word you respond with appears written on your web page.

Setting Up JavaScript

When you enter JavaScript, with a few exceptions, you must enter it in a JavaScript "container" as the initial examples show. The JavaScript container looks like the following:

```
<script language="JavaScript">
Your JavaScript goes here
</script>
```

You can enter your JavaScript in the head area of an HTML page, or you can do it within the body. The head area is in the `<HEAD>` . . . `</HEAD>` container of an HTML page. When you write functions in JavaScript, you want to put them into the head area because that part of the HTML page loads first. So when your page first calls a function to execute, the function is fully loaded and all ready to go.

Case Sensitivity

JavaScript is case sensitive. That means that the JavaScript parser (interpreter) pays attention to upper- and lowercase letters in words. For example, a variable named "Ralph" is different from a variable named "ralph." Most of the keywords and statements in JavaScript are in lowercase, but you will find many exceptions. For example, in the statement

```
var alpha = Math.round(55.567)
```

the M in Math *must* be uppercase. Otherwise, the script will not work.

One instance in which case sensitivity is problematic is when JavaScript and HTML have different conventions and rules about a similar object or statement. For example, in HTML, to fire a JavaScript function, you might see lines such as the following:

```
<FORM name="beta">
<INPUT TYPE="button" NAME="alf" value="Click here"
onClick="Jump()">
```

The event handler onClick is conventionally spelled with both upper- and lowercase text. However, in JavaScript, you would write

```
document.beta.alf.onclick=Jump();
```

For the most part, you will not be confronted with mixed choices of HTML and JavaScript renderings. As a rule of thumb, use lowercase text unless a function or object indicates otherwise.

Comments

One of the more important features of just about every programming language is the *comment.* Comments are little reminders and explanations of why you put something in a script. At the time you enter the script, you may know perfectly well what you did and why you did it. However, later when you are going over your script, you may have forgotten. Single-line comments are preceded by double slashes (//), and a container beginning with /* and ending with */ will comment multiple lines. The following example shows how comments are used in JavaScript on both single and multiple lines:

```
<script language="JavaScript">
//This next function is to greet the viewer using the built-
//in alert function
function Howdy() {
  alert("Hi there and welcome to JavaScript")
}
/*The greeting can be placed in the BODY tag of an HTML page
and automatically appears using the HTML onLoad event handler
when the page is loaded */
</script>
```

When learning JavaScript, wait until you have your script working correctly before putting in comments. In that way you can focus on getting your script working properly before reminding yourself how you did it.

Naming Rules

When you name a variable or function, you use an *identifier.* All identifiers must begin with an ASCII letter (a–z, A–Z), a dollar sign ($), or an underscore (_). The other characters in the identifier can be what you want. However, you cannot use reserved words in variable names. Table 11.1 shows a list of reserved words to avoid using in variable or function names.

You should also try to avoid words you will find used in statements, methods, and attributes. For example, "name" and "value" are attributes of forms and should be avoided as well. As you learn more JavaScript, try to avoid using the new words you learn as names for variables and functions.

Literals

Values that appear directly in a program are called *literals.* For our purposes, you can think of three types of literals: strings, numbers, and Booleans. Each is briefly discussed.

TABLE 11.1   Reserved Words

abstract	final	public
boolean	finally	return
break	float	short
byte	for	static
case	function	super
catch	goto	switch
char	if	synchronized
class	implements	this
const	import	throw
continue	in	throws
debugger	instanceof	transient
default	int	true
delete	interface	try
do	long	typeof
double	native	var
else	new	void
enum	null	volatile
export	package	while
extends	private	with
false	protected	

String Literals.   Both characters and *nothing* enclosed in double (") or single (') quotation marks are considered strings. You delimit a string with *either* a single or double set of quotes but not both in a single delimit. The following are examples of string literals:

```
" "
"A word is worth one word."
"1234"
"first line \n second line"
"I do 2."
'A quote from e. e. cummings'
'rose="Red Enough" '
```

With string literals, you can use the backslash (\) with certain characters to include limited formatting. For example, to make a new line appear—as the fourth example above does—place a "\n" character between the two elements of the string that you want on two different lines. For example, the following script places the "\" to display an apostrophe in a word:

```
<html>
<head>
<script language="JavaScript">
document.write("Bill\'s Place")
```

```
</script>
</head>
<body bgcolor=#abcdef>
</body>
</html>
```

The special characters are *escape sequences*. Table 11.2 shows the primary JavaScript escape sequences.

Numbers. Numbers are recognized as data with which mathematical calculations can be made. For example, 576 is a number and "576" is a string, and if you attempt to perform calculations with "576" you will not get a calculated result, as you will with a number. Both integers and floating point numbers are treated as floating point, so there is no need to write different types of scripts for the two different types. Thus the integer and floating point numbers

```
34
34.567
```

use the same format. The only difference is that the floating point literal has a decimal point.

However, octal and hexadecimal values are different from decimal ones and need special characters. If you are working with octal (base 8), you place a zero and the values 0 to 7. For example,

```
012
```

is the octal representation of the decimal number 10.

A number system you are more likely to deal with in JavaScript than octal is hexadecimal, or base 16. Colors in HTML are often represented by six-character hexadecimal

TABLE 11.2 Escape Sequences

Escape Sequence	Character or Format
\b	backspace
\f	form feed
\n	new line
\r	carriage return
\t	tab
\'	single quote or apostrophe
\"	double quote
\\	backslash

values with characters ranging from 0 to F. For example, the color red is FF0000. Hexadecimal numbers are preceded by zero-X (or zero-x). For example,

```
0xBEC001
0Xffa2b4
0xFF00FF
```

are all valid hexadecimal *literals* in JavaScript.

Booleans.   Boolean values are either *true* or *false.* Typically, you will find Boolean values in conditional statements in which the script will branch or not based on the Boolean outcome of true or false. For example, the following Boolean is based on two variables being unequal:

```
if (apples != oranges) {. . . .
```

Boolean values can also be treated as numeric values 0 and 1. False equals 0 and true equals 1. The following script shows that a Boolean "true" value can be treated as a "1" and used in a calculation. The variable "a" is given the value "true" or "1" because the expression "7 > 5" means "7 is greater than 5." That is true, of course, and it is also equal to the numeric value 1.

```
<html>
<head>
<script language="JavaScript">
  a=7>5
  b=a+1
  document.write(b)
</script>
</head>
<body bgcolor=#ffff00>
</body>
</html>
```

Variables

As the name implies, variables vary or change. Like other scripting and programming languages, variables are containers that hold literals or expressions. The following are some examples of variables:

```
var willie="Bill";
var tax = 12.95 * .06;
```

Variables are *assigned* a value by the equal (=) operator. Also in JavaScript, variables are declared using the **var** keyword. You need only declare a variable once in a script and even if its value changes, it remains declared. You can declare a variable without assigning it a value and then later assign it a value. For example, the following script declares a couple of variables, but it does not assign them a value right away:

```
<html>
<head>
<script language="JavaScript">
  var item;
  var tax;
  item=234.78;
  tax=.06;
  var total= item + (item * tax);
  document.write(total);
</script>
</head>
<body bgcolor=#fedcba>
</body>
</html>
```

Unassigned variables are usually held in reserve until another variable or set of variables gathers information and then assigns the unassigned variables with their values.

Variables are considered either *global* or *local*. Global variables are defined over the entire script, whereas local variables are defined only within and used in functions. Another way of putting it is that global variables have *scope* over the entire script whereas local variables have scope only within a function. If a local variable within a function changes, it will not affect a global variable with the same name. For example, the following script first declares and assigns a value to a global variable. Then, in a function, a local variable with the same name is assigned a different value and printed to the screen. Finally, the global variable is printed to the screen, and you can see two different values.

```
<html>
<head>
<script language="JavaScript">
var showMe="Global in nature.";
function watchThis() {
var showMe="Local kind of guy.";
document.write(showMe);
}
watchThis();     // displays local variable on screen
document.write(showMe); //displays global variable
</script>
</head>
<body bgcolor="moccasin">
</body>
</html>
```

When you run the script, you will see two different outcomes on the screen as

```
Local kind of guy.Global in nature
```

The first phrase, "Local kind of guy," is sent from the local variable that was unaffected by the definition of the global variable *in the function*. Likewise, the global variable was unaffected by the value of local variable and displayed `Global in nature`.

Operators

A compound or complex *expression* is a combination of strings, numbers, Boolean values, or variables connected with *operators*. Simple expressions are single variables, arrays, literals, or functions. For example, the following script contains a variable named "average" made up of different variables and operators:

```
var average=(test1 + test2 + test3) / 3
```

The operators in that variable definition include the equal sign (=), the plus sign (+), the slash used for division (/), and the parentheses ( ).

Table 11.3 is a list of the operators used in these chapters on JavaScript. The bitwise operators and some others you will not be using were not included in the list.

Not surprisingly, you use a set of operands with the operators. Because strings are words, you will not use math calculations. For example,

```
"Bees" * "Flowers";
```

does not make any sense because multiplying the word "Bees" by the word "Flowers" is not mathematically possible. However, you can *concatenate* strings (join them into one string) in JavaScript using the addition sign (+). Therefore, the expression

```
"Bees" + "Flowers";
```

would result in `"BeesFlowers"` and although that may not appear very useful, you can do it. More useful would be concatenating string variables or literals such as first and last names.

If you mix numbers and words using concatenation, the number will be transformed into a string as part of a new variable. For example, the following script results in the string "apple5":

```
<html>
<head>
<script language="JavaScript">
var aString="apple"
var bNumber=5
var cBoth=aString + bNumber
```

```
document.write(cBoth);
</script>
</head>
<body bgcolor="lightseagreen">
</body>
</html>
```

Launching JavaScript Scripts

Whereas this chapter has shown examples of functions to clarify different operations in JavaScript, the next chapter contains a detailed discussion of using functions. For the time being, think of functions as a collection of operations, commands, and statements that JavaScript "packages" in a term—something like a variable but very different. The function packages can be launched at different places in an HTML page.

TABLE 11.3   Common Operators Used with JavaScript

Symbol	Operation
+	add (and concatenate)
–	subtract
*	multiply
/	divide
%	modulus (remainder)
++	increment
−−	decrement
<	less than
>	greater than
<=	less than or equal to
>=	greater than or equal to
&&	logical AND
||	logical OR
!	logical NOT
==	test for equality
!=	test for inequality
=	assignment
+=	add and assign
−=	subtract and assign
*=	multiply and assign
%=	modulus and assign
/=	divide and assign
( )	function arguments
.	structure member (called a Dot) in structure or property
,	multiple evaluation
[ ]	array elements (access, index)

Immediate Execution

When the JavaScript is not in a function, it executes or "runs" as soon as the script is encountered in the browser. For example, the following script fires off as soon as it is interpreted (parsed):

```
<HTML>
<head>
<title>Immediate Mode</title>
<script language="JavaScript">
document.write("Do it now!")
</script>
</head>
</html>
```

Even when the JavaScript is written in the head area and the web page has no body area (in the <BODY> container), the script will write a message on the page.

Deferred Mode

The deferred mode in JavaScript waits until the user does something to fire a JavaScript function. For example, the following script waits until you close the page by quitting or going to another link to initiate a built-in alert function.

```
<html>
<body bgcolor="indianred" onunload="alert('see you later')">
<h2> Quit to fire the JavaScript</h2>
</body>
</html>
```

Only when you leave the page does the built-in alert function provide you with an appropriate message. Figure 11.1 shows what the viewer sees,

More commonly, the deferred mode is initiated by a function, as shown in the following script:

```
<html>
<head>
<script language="JavaScript">
function clickToFire() {
alert("I waited until you asked!")
}
</script>
</head>
<body bgcolor="#008888">
<p><p><p><center>
```

```
<h2>Click the link to launch JavaScript</h2>
<a href="#" onClick="clickToFire()";>Click here when ready</a>
</center>
</body>
</html>
```

Figure 11.2 shows the screen as soon as the link has been clicked.

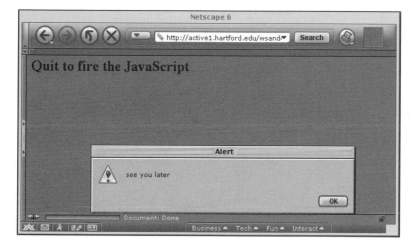

FIGURE 11.1   Alert Box That Appears Only When the Page Is Unloaded.

FIGURE 11.2   The JavaScript Program Launched by Clicking on Hotspots on the HTML Page.

Conclusion

Even with a little JavaScript added to an HTML page, the character of the page changes dramatically. From being a static page with no dynamic components, a web page with JavaScript is transformed into a page with not only a dynamic elements, but also elements that are controlled by the viewer. The deferred function in JavaScript enables the designer to hold back any actions triggered by JavaScript until the user (or viewer) decides to take an action. Because the action is controlled by the viewer, the design can be interactive in that the designer can program responses to the viewer's actions.

12 JavaScript Fundamentals

The previous chapter introduced JavaScript as a dynamic language that can be placed in an HTML page and used to enhance the interactivity of web pages. This chapter explores the fundamental structures in JavaScript and how they might be used in an interactive page to enhance getting a point across. If you are at all familiar with programming languages, you will see familiar structures in JavaScript similar to other languages. Readers for whom this is their first work with programming will find it both challenging and interesting.

Functions

Several examples in the last chapter using functions illustrated different ways a JavaScript program could be launched, but functions themselves have not been defined as a structure in JavaScript. Essentially, a function is an encapsulated set of statements or commands that can be launched by different events in an HTML page. A user function begins with the keyword `function`. A name follows along with a set of parentheses that may contain an optional argument. Function has the form

```
function functionName(optional argument) {
   Statements, variables, objects and commands
}
```

For example, the following script uses a function with a no argument taking data from a form and then adding tax to the amount found in the form.

```
<html>
<head>
<script language ="JavaScript">
function addTax() {
var item=document.calcTax.purchase.value;
item = parseInt(item);
item += (item * .07);
alert("Total=$" + item);
}
```

```
</script>
</head>
<body bgcolor=#face00>
<p>
<form name="calcTax">
<input type="text" name="purchase"><b>: Enter amount of
item</b><p>
<input type="button" value="Click for total:"
onClick="addTax()">
</form>
</body>
</html>
```

The script is not fired until the button is pressed. The deferred launching of the script allows the user plenty of time to enter a value to be calculated in the form window.

Basic Structures in JavaScript

All programming languages have three basic structures:

- Sequence
- Branch
- Loop

Sequence

A *sequence* occurs when a program executes one line of code after the other, beginning at the top and continuing downward. Probably the majority of lines in a JavaScript program are simple sequences, whether they are declarations of variables or statements to be executed one at a time. For example, the following is a simple sequence:

```
<script language ="JavaScript">
var greeting="Hello";
var welcome="Welcome to JavaScript";
document.write(greeting + "! " + welcome);
</script>
```

In creating sequences in JavaScript, you must have the correct order for the script to work properly. In the above example, first each of the variables was declared and defined. These variables have to be first declared in the sequence before they can be used in the `document.write()` function. For example, if the line

```
var greeting="Hello";
```

were placed below the line

```
document.write(greeting + "! " + welcome);
```

the variable would not be defined when the parser reached the document.write() function and would be declared "undefined" in the output to the screen. The sequence requires that variables be defined before they can be used in a statement elsewhere in the program.

Branch

The *branch* structure goes out of sequence by skipping over and not executing lines that do not meet certain conditions established in the program. Such lines are called *conditional statements* because they set up the conditions under which a line will execute. For example, the following script compares two variables and executes a line *only* if the two variables are equal:

```
<script language ="JavaScript">
var itemA=250;
var itemB=250;
if (itemA == itemB) {
   document.write("The values are equal");
}
</script>
```

Because the two variables, itemA and itemB, both have a value of 250, the line

```
document.write("The values are equal");
```

executes, and "The values are equal" appears on the screen. Had the two values been different, nothing would have appeared on the screen. Further on in this chapter when conditional statements are examined more closely, the different conditions for which JavaScript can test will be discussed.

Loop

The final major structure in JavaScript is the *loop*. A loop statement repeats itself until it meets an established condition. When that condition is met, the loop stops. Rather than having to write repetitive code, loops allow the programmer to write a single statement or set of statements and then repeat it several times. Loops are especially useful for dealing with array variables (introduced in a later section). The following example shows a simple loop that writes numbers to the screen.

```
<script language ="JavaScript">
lineBreak="<BR>";
   for(counter=15;counter<25;counter++) {
```

```
document.write(counter+lineBreak);
}
</script>
```

Instead of having to write `document.write(counter+lineBreak)` ten times in the script, it has to be written only once. The variable named `lineBreak` is defined as an HTML tag that results in a line break or carriage return. Either a tag or a variable containing a tag can be part of the output statement.

Conditional Statements

As one of the basic structures in programming, conditional statements allow the program to "think" by making decisions. This section examines the different types of conditional statements in JavaScript and some examples of how they might be used. In an environment in which a response needs to be evaluated and a response given, conditional statements are used a great deal. In fact, all learning and training environments rely heavily on conditional statements to guide the learner or trainee.

if

JavaScript and most other languages have a conditional structure based on the `if` statement. The fundamental order of the `if` statement is

```
if(condition) {
Do this or that
}
```

The actions or statements within the curly braces are executed if the condition is met, and they are not executed if the condition is not met. You can have as many statements as you want between the curly braces. For example, the following script contains three different outcomes if the condition is evaluated as true. ("True" is used here in the Boolean sense that a "true" or "1" is generated. Thus, in a negatively stated condition, as the following script has, if the *false* condition is met; then the outcome is *true*.)

```
<script language ="JavaScript">
var Nancy="Smart";
var Becky="Fun";
var lineBreak="<BR>";
if (Nancy != Becky) {
  document.write("Nancy and Becky " + lineBreak)
  document.write("are very different " + lineBreak)
  document.write("but still best friends.")
}
</script>
```

Multiple Conditions

Sometimes more than a single condition or one or more options are available in a situation. For example, in looking at job applicants an employer may want education *and* experience in the person she is looking to hire. The double ampersand operator (&&) is the symbol used when two or more conditions must be met—the logical AND. For example,

```
<script language ="JavaScript">
var college="graduate";
var experience=5;
if ((college=="graduate") && (experience >= 3)){
  document.write("You're hired!")
}
</script>
```

results in a "true" outcome because both variables are met. Notice that in the above script three sets of parentheses are required to encompass the conditional. The outer set encompasses both conditionals, and each condition has its own set of parentheses. You may have as many conditions as you want in an `if` statement.

Besides the logical AND, you may also use the logical OR, represented by the double "pipes" operator (| |). In order for a condition to be true, *only a single* condition needs to be met. The following script uses both the logical OR and the logical AND. Essentially, the script (constructed by a desperate matchmaker) evaluates three conditions using the logical OR and a single condition using the logical AND. Only *one* of the logical OR conditions must be true *plus* the single logical AND condition.

```
<script language ="JavaScript">
var looks="odd";
var status="poor";
var personality="interesting";
var health="breathing";
if ((looks=="attractive") || (status=="rich") ||
(personality=="interesting") && (health=="breathing")){
  document.write("Call the preacher!")
}
</script>
```

else

The statement can have a second outcome if the condition is false. In other words, it provides two options in the following format:

```
If (condition) {
Do this
} else {
```

```
Do that
}
```

Under these circumstances, the script branches no matter what the condition. For example, the following script shows how a response to a correct or incorrect answer to an online quiz might look:

```
<script language ="JavaScript">
  var answer="Ottoman Empire";
if(answer=="Ottoman Empire") {
  alert("That's correct. Very good.")
}
else {
alert("No, the correct answer is the Ottoman Empire");
}
</script>
```

When you run the script, you will always get the alert box shown in Figure 12.1.

Change the variable to "British Empire" and run the script again. You will see the alert box shown in Figure 12.2.

else if

Under some circumstances, you will need more than a single else statement, and JavaScript provides for this set of circumstances with the else if statement. The general format is

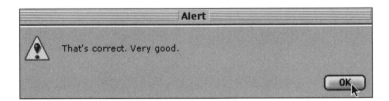

FIGURE 12.1   The True Condition Message.

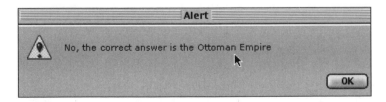

FIGURE 12.2   The False Condition Message.

```
If (condition) {
Take path 1
}
else if (this other condition) {
Take path 2
}
else if (still another condition))
Take path 3
}
else {
Take path 4
}
```

The important arrangement in using the else if statement is that *after* the last else if you need an else statement. Thus, you have the following arrangement of the conditional statements when the else if statement is employed:

```
if
else if
else if
else
```

You can use as many else if statements as you want as long as the first follows if and the last one is followed by else. The following example shows how you might use this structure in a JavaScript program:

```
<html>
<head>
<script language ="JavaScript">
var choice="socket wrench";
if(choice=="screwdriver") {
  alert("Look in Bin 124.")
}
else if (choice=="hammer") {
  alert("Look in Bin 438");
}
else if (choice=="socket wrench") {
  alert("Look in Bin 952");
}
else {
  alert("We do not have that product.");
}
</script>
</head>
<body bgcolor=#660000>
```

```
</body>
</html>
```

Using `else if` allows you to write very complex conditions so that the user is not limited to a few choices or has to make several choices as a set of conditional statements burrows its way to a solution.

switch

The final statement that can be used to filter through several choices is the `switch` statement. When you have a single condition and several choices, you might find it easier and more efficient to use `switch` instead of writing several `else if` statements. The basic format of `switch` is

```
switch(beta) {
case alpha:
  Take path A
  break;    // skip the rest and stop if case==beta
case beta:
  Take path B
  break;    // skip the rest and stop if case==beta
default:   //if no matches execute this
Tell user that nothing matches
}
```

The switch statement sets up the selection criteria for matching a case statement. If the expression in the `switch` statement matches the value in the `case xxx:` statement, the program executes the code in that `case` block. By placing a `break` statement after each block of code in a `case` block, the rest of the `cases` can be skipped to save processing time and avoid an error of attempting to execute more than one element in the `switch` block. The `default:` block has no identifier but is simply executed if *none* of the cases meet the switch expression value. To see how it works, the JavaScript program in the `else if` example has been rewritten using `switch`.

```
<html>
<head>
<script language ="JavaScript">
var choice="socket wrench";
switch(choice) {
case 'screwdriver':
  alert("Look in Bin 124");
  break;
case 'hammer':
  alert("Look in Bin 438");
  break;
```

```
case 'socket wrench':
  alert("Look in Bin 438");
  break;
default:
alert("We do not have that product.");
}
</script>
</head>
<body>
</body>
</html>
```

Placing the break at the end of every case within a switch statement is optional, but doing so is good practice to save processing time and protect against errors.

Loops

JavaScript has four loop structures, three of which we will examine in detail in this section. Each loop structure has an optimal use, and depending on what you need done with JavaScript, one is more appropriate than another.

for

When you have a known number of loops, the easiest to use is the for loop. The for loop has the following general structure.

```
for(begin; test; increment/decrement) {
Do this or that
}
```

The "begin" or initialize portion of the for statement is the beginning value of the counter. The "test" or condition portion tests to see if the countervariable meets the test condition, and the increment portion adds or subtracts from the countervariable. For example, the following loop counts backward to a blastoff:

```
<html>
<head>
<script language ="JavaScript">
lineBreak="<BR>";
for(var counter=10;counter>=0;counter--) {
document.write("<center><h3>"+counter+lineBreak+"</h3></
center>");
}
document.write("<center><h1>Blast Off!</h1></center>");
```

```
</script>
</head>
<body bgcolor=lightseagreen>
</body>
</html>
```

while

The `while` loop looks for a certain condition, and as long as that condition is present, it continues looping. This type of loop is valuable for those cases in which you are unsure as to the number of times the loop must be made. For example, you might create a question that has one right answer, and unless that right answer is entered, the loop keeps on looping. The `while` loop is similar to the `for` loop except it does not contain a built-in counter variable, and the loop does not have a beginning countervalue.

```
while (condition) {
   statements, commands, definitions
}
```

To see how the loop might work, this next example uses the prompt() function. If the answer is incorrect, the prompt keeps repeating the question. Note that the variable named "answer" is shifted to all lowercase using the string method, `.toLowerCase`. The change of all responses to lowercase is to ensure that the respondent's answer is accepted even if the respondent uses uppercase characters in his or her response.

```
<html>
<head>
<script language ="JavaScript">
var answer;
while(answer!="zebra") {
answer=prompt("What is a black and white striped animal found
in Africa that looks like a horse?"," ");
answer=answer.toLowerCase();
}
document.write("That is correct!")
</script>
</head>
<body bgcolor=#00face>
</body>
</html>
```

As you can see when you run the program, you can take as many or as few tries as you want using the `while` loop. Unlike the `for` loop, no automatic increment occurs, and the only changes in the value of the test variable are those entered by the user.

do while

In comparing the do/while loop with the while loop, the differences may not appear obvious or even useful; however, the do/while loop has definite applications different from those of the while loop. First, the do/while loop has the test condition at the end of the loop, which means that it *must iterate the loop at least once.* The while loop may encounter the exit condition immediately and be out of the loop before issuing any of the commands, but the do/while loop always runs the full gamut of code before exiting. The format of the do/while loop terminates, not with a curly brace, but with the while test condition.

```
do {
   statements, commands, definitions
   }
while(condition);
```

One of the most useful applications of do/while loops is to search through an array to find and display a given element. The next section covers arrays, and in it you will find a do/while loop at work.

Arrays

One of the key objects in JavaScript is the array object. An array is something like a collection of variables using a common name but each with a separate identifying mark. Each of the *elements* of an array contains its own data. For example, an eBusiness may want to group customers into an array rather than having separate variables for each customer. Using an array, customers could be in the same "place" but in different compartments.

Several methods are available in JavaScript to declare an array, but only two are discussed here. First, you can declare an array with no values and then add the values such as is shown in the following example:

```
var customer= new Array();
customer[0]="Jones";
customer[1]="Smith";
customer[2]="Jackson";
customer[3]="Washington";
```

Alternatively, you can put all of your values into a dense array as shown in the following:

```
var customer = new Array("Jones", "Smith", "Jackson",
"Washington");
```

Both methods result in identical arrays. The first element of an array in JavaScript is always 0 instead of 1 if no element values are assigned, as is the case in the second example of declaring an array. Hence the *first element's value* is `"Jones"` and is identified by the element (`customer[0]`). For example, try out the following script:

```
<html>
<script language ="JavaScript">
var customer = new Array("Jones", "Smith", "Jackson",
"Washington");
document.write(customer[2]);
</script>
<body bgcolor=#00ffff>
</body>
</html>
```

If all goes according to plan, you should see `"Jackson"` on the screen. Beginning with 0 for Jones, 1 for Smith, the element number for Jackson would be 2. In the `document.write()` function, the array element `customer [2]` calls up the value `"Jackson."`

Arrays and Loops

As noted in the previous section, arrays are often associated with loops. The reason for this association is that loops iterate through a number of elements. Because each element has a number and numbers can be represented by variables in JavaScript, sequentially iterating through a loop, all of the values in an array can be identified with very little code. For example, the following script segment would display the fourth element in an array named "parts."

```
var counter = 3;
document.write(parts[counter]);
```

To find any one element in an array based on the element's value can be done easily with a loop. Instead of numeric literals, you can use a counter variable to go through all of the array elements. Even better, use a loop finding a match in one array and bring out other information from another array that matches the found element, something like searching a database. For example, the following two arrays are parallel. The first array is a set of names, and the second array is a set of telephone numbers. To find a telephone number, you can enter the name, and the array searches the name array to find the element number with the search name. It then takes the element number and opens the element with the same number in the phone array to match a person and his phone number. The following script uses the `do loop` to accomplish this task:

```
<html>
<head>
<title>Search Loop </title>
<script language ="JavaScript">
function findIt() {
  var customer = new Array("Jones", "Smith", "Jackson",
  "Washington");
```

```
    var phone = new Array("555-7865", "555-3214","555-2270",
    "555-1944");
    var counter=0;
    do {
         var search=document.people.ID.value;
         counter += 1;
         var match=(counter-1);
} while(search !=customer[match]);
    alert(search + " phone number =" + phone[match]);
}
</script>
</head>
<body bgcolor=#00ffff>
<p>
<form name="people">
Enter the last name:
<input type="text" name="ID">
<p>
<input type="button" value="Press to find phone number."
onClick="findIt()">
</form>
</body>
</html>
```

Figure 12.3 shows how the screen appears when a match has been made.

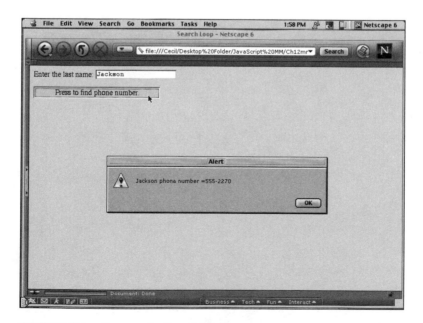

FIGURE 12.3   Output of a Search Script.

Conclusion

Using the basic structures of JavaScript, you can not only do more with the language to create interactive multimedia, but you can also do it with less work. Using loops and arrays together, for example, you can repeat a series of commands to add robust features of interactivity but actually use less code. The loop repeats the steps, and the array stores data entered using the loop, and so rather than having to individually assign values to variables, loops and arrays are shortcuts to the same results.

13 JavaScript Interaction

In the previous chapter, some forms were used in the examples, and Chapter 11 briefly discussed forms. This chapter looks at the different ways that forms in HTML and JavaScript work together to create an interactive environment on the Web. The form windows are the source of user input, and by using JavaScript to respond to the input, you are able to create an interactive format.

The Form Object

In referencing a form using JavaScript, think of the form as an object with different properties. In the hierarchy of a form object, the document (web page) is at the top, followed by the form, the elements in the form, and finally the properties of the elements. Visualized, the hierarchy looks like the following:

```
Document (object)
    Form (property of document)
        Element (property of form)
            Element properties (property of element)
```

In JavaScript, you reference a form in that hierarchy. For example, if your form is named "dogs" and an element is named "breed," the value of the element would be expressed as

```
document.dogs.breed.value;
```

If the element "breed" is a text window, the value of "breed" would be whatever the user types into the window. For example, if the user types in "Irish Wolfhound," then "Irish Wolfhound" becomes the value of `document.dogs.breed.value;`. That value can be placed into a variable and used in the script for any purpose the designer wishes. The following script is designed to provide some practice using forms and JavaScript together and to show how to pass variables from a JavaScript program to the output windows.

```
<html>
<head>
```

```
<script language="JavaScript">
function showProp() {
  var alpha=document.basic.length;
  document.basic.first.value="Length of form=" +alpha;
  var beta="Second element";
  document.basic.second.value=beta;
  var gamma="Third element";
  document.basic.third.value=gamma;
  }
</script>
</head>
<body bgcolor="powderblue">
<p><center>
<h1>Basic Form</h1>
<form name="basic">First:
<input type=text name="first"> Second:
<input type=text name="second">Third:
<input type=text name="third"><p>
<input type=button value="Click to make it happen."
onClick="showProp()">
</form>
</center>
</body>
</html>
```

Figure 13.1 shows what the screen looks like after the button to launch the JavaScript function is pressed.

Besides having element properties, form objects have other properties as well. For example, the form object has a length. The length is made up of the number of elements between the `<form>` and `</form>` tags—the form container. In the above example, the length of the form is placed into a variable (alpha) and then defined as the value of the element named "first." The output shows that the form has four elements—the three text windows and the button. Further on in this chapter, other types of form elements beyond text windows and buttons are covered.

As can be seen from the example, to pass data to a form, use the following format:

```
document.form.element.value=variableName (or literal)
```

To pass data from a form to a variable, use the reverse order:

```
variableName=document.form.element.value
```

The important structure to keep in mind when passing data between forms and JavaScript variables is that *in JavaScript* all forms are considered objects. By using the object hierarchy of forms, you can easily construct scripts that use the data in both the forms and JavaScript.

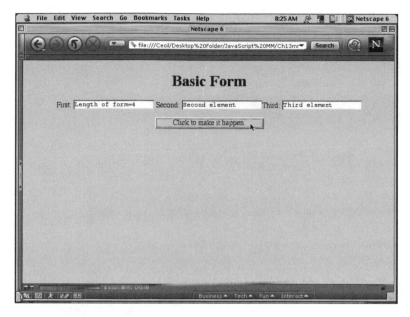

FIGURE 13.1   Data Passed between Form Elements.

The Form Array Object

Whenever you put a form in an HTML page, you create an array object as well as a form object. The first defined form in an HTML page is forms[0], and the first element of a form is elements[0]. (Both use the *plural* as array elements.) You need not know the names of either the forms or their elements in an array object—just the order they appear on a page. The advantage of treating a form object as an array object is that you can write JavaScript statements used with any other array. For example, you can loop through one form to reformat data using input for another form. The following example shows how JavaScript treats two forms by referencing their array values on an HTML page, moving data from one form to the other. A third form contains nothing by a button to fire the JavaScript function.

```
<html>
<head>
<script language="JavaScript">
function moveIt() {
for (var counter=0;counter<document.forms[0].length;counter++) {
document.forms[1].elements[counter].value=document.forms
[0].elements[counter].value;
   }
}
</script>
</head>
```

```
<body bgcolor="lightsteelblue"><p>
<h2>First Form</h2>
<form name="primary">
<input type=text name="firstName"> First Name:<br>
<input type=text name="lastName"> Last Name:<br>
<input type=text name="Address"> Address:<br>
<input type=text name="City"> City:<br>
<input type=text name="State"> State: <p>
</form>
<h2>Second Form</h2>
<form name="secondary">
<input type=text name="firstName2">
<input type=text name="lastName2"> Name:<br>
<input type=text name="Address2">
<input type=text name="City2" >,  
<input type=text name="State2" size=2 > Address: <p>
</form>
<form>
<input type=button value="Click to Transfer Data:"
onClick="moveIt()">
</form>
</body>
</html>
```

Figure 13.2 shows the data moved from the first form to the second form.

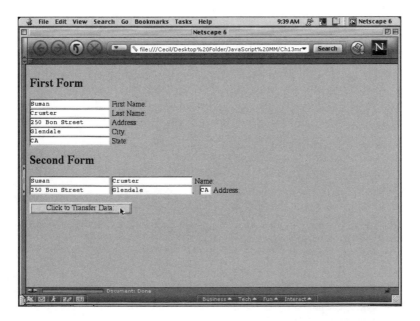

FIGURE 13.2   Form Data Transfer.

Structuring Question Forms

A common type of social interaction is called the Q–A sequence. The sequence begins with a question, the listener responds to the question, the questioner evaluates the response, and further questions and answers make up the bulk of the interactive sequence. In a web page, a Q–A sequence can be used to elicit action on the part of the viewer and the page designed to respond to the answer. Several techniques can be used with forms, and JavaScript to create anything from quick responses to entire quizzes or examinations. Both answers and responses to answers can use forms.

Short Answers and Text Fields

The first type of question-and-answer interaction examined is the short answer response to an open-ended question. The query expects the user to fill in a text box with a response to a question. The viewer responds and in turn receives a response in a form window. The list of "correct" responses can be placed into an array. A search variable is made up of the contents of the query window (the input text box named Question). A loop compares all of the values in the array for a match. If a match is found, a find variable is flagged with a message. If no match is made, the find variable is flagged with another message. Finally, the find variable is sent to the response window and the viewer has his or her answer. For example, the following script might be used in a kennel web page.

```
<html>
<head>
<script language="JavaScript">
function askQ() {
   var breeds=new Array("collie","hound","setter",
   "pointer","sheltie");
   var search=document.QA.question.value;
   var find=null;
   for(var counter=0;counter<breeds.length;counter++) {
     if(search.toLowerCase()==breeds[counter]) {
         find="Yes we do have " + search +"s.";
         }
     }
   if (find==null) {
   find="Sorry we do not have that breed.";
   }
document.QA.response.value=find;
}
</script>
</head>
<body bgcolor="palegoldenrod">
<p>
<h1>Breed Form</h1>
<form name="QA">
```

```
<input type=text name="question"> What kind of breed are you
seeking? <p>
<input type=text name="response" size=35> Response.<p>
<input type=button value="Click here to send query"
onClick="askQ()">
</form>
</body>
</html>
```

The array works like a minidatabase, and if the array parallels another array, it can work like a relational database. Because the user enters data in an open-ended context, having a finite loop through the array is important. Otherwise, the user could end up with an infinite loop as the program keeps searching for a string not in the array. Figure 13.3 shows the page with a successful search.

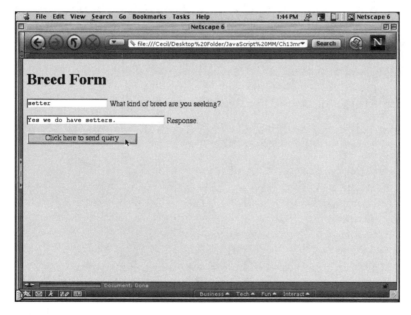

FIGURE 13.3   A Response Form.

Radio Buttons and Check Boxes

HTML has two types of buttons that can have a "checked" status—radio buttons and checkboxes. Radio buttons are designed to give the user a *single* choice from a variety of selections, whereas checkboxes are designed to provide the user with several selections.

Radio Buttons

Because radio buttons are form properties, they must be placed into a form container in HTML. They have the format

```
<input type=radio name="nm" value="val" Checked=Boolean>
```

This format is like any other form object properties with two important exceptions. First, the radio button can have a "checked" status. The checked status is a Boolean literal, or true or false. If the checked status is true, the button appears with the button indicating a checked status on the screen. Second, radio buttons are part of a set that can have only a single one in the set checked. To achieve this state, all of the radio buttons are given the same name, even though they can have different values. For example, a set of radio buttons in a form may look like the following in a real estate page:

```
<form name "singleFam">
<input type=radio name="houses" value="ranch">
<input type=radio name="houses" value="victorian">
<input type=radio name="houses" value="colonial">
<input type=radio name="houses" value="raised ranch">
<input type=radio name="houses" value="split level">
</form>
```

The viewer would be asked to accept one type of house, and depending on which style was selected, the script would select web pages with houses of the selected type. Radio buttons have a "checked" property, and JavaScript can use a conditional statement to query whether a button is checked by using the format

```
if (form.element.checked) {
    flag=up
}
```

However, because all of the radio buttons have the same name, how is it possible to write a JavaScript statement that will isolate the one that is checked? Fortunately, forms are array objects, and even though all of the radio buttons have the same name, *each has a different element value*. Thus, the first radio button in a form is element[0], the second element[1], and so on to the last element in the form.

Even though radio buttons in a set must have the same name, they may have different values. The values can be passed to variables or evaluated as values in a form object. The following script shows how the web page viewer can select a radio button and have the value of that button passed on. In the following example, the checked radio button value is passed to a text window to illustrate how checked radio buttons are evaluated and their values extracted.

```
<html>
<head>
<script language="JavaScript">
function radioCheck(form) {
for(var counter=0;document.computers.length;counter++) {
if(document.computers.elements[counter].checked) {
document.computers.feature.value=document.computers.elements
[counter].value ;
                }
```

```
            }
      }
      </script>
      </head>
      <body bgcolor="honeydew">
      <form name="computers">
      <h4>Which of the following is the most important <br>
       in the purchase of a computer?</h4>
      <input type=radio name="components" value="price" >
      Price<br>
      <input type=radio name="components" value="performance" >
      Performance<br>
      <input type=radio name="components" value="brand name">
      Brand    name<br>
      <input type=radio name="components" value="ease of use">
      Ease of use<p>
      <input type=text name="feature">
      <input type=button value="Check" onClick=
      "radioCheck(this.form)">
      </form>
      </body>
      </html>
```

An important feature of this script is the use of `form` as an argument and `this.form` to specify the form argument. Note that the button tag with the value `Check` contains the event handler to fire the `radioCheck()` function. The argument supplied in the function is `this.form`. The self-referent is possible because the button is within the form that the function is to evaluate. Had the button been in a different form, then the argument would specify the full form name. Figure 13.4 show a radio button value passed to a text form.

Checkboxes and Multiple Choices

Although radio buttons with the same name are mutually exclusive, checkboxes are not. You can have several checkboxes named the same, and they can all be checked simultaneously. When a checkbox is checked *or unchecked,* a click event is recorded. The first time a checkbox is clicked, it becomes checked. When a checked checkbox is clicked, it becomes unchecked; however, a click is still recorded. In the following example, each time you click a checkbox, the background color changes. The `bgColor` property is one document property that can be changed just about anywhere in an HTML script, and all of the JavaScript is right in the HTML tag.

```
      <html>
      <head>
      <Title>Check Box </title>
      </head>
```

```
<body bgcolor="slategray">
<form name="computers">
<h4>Select a background color: </h4>
<ul>
<input type=checkbox name="red"
onClick='document.bgColor="red' " > Red<br>
<input type=checkbox name="green"
onClick='document.bgColor="green' "> Green<br>
<input type=checkbox name="blue"
onClick='document.bgColor="blue' "> Blue<br>
<input type=checkbox name="purple"
onClick='document.bgColor="purple' "> Purple<p>
</ul>
</form>
</body>
</html>
```

Notice in the input tags how the event handler `onClick` uses single and double quotes to issue a JavaScript statement. In JavaScript and HTML, you have two levels of quotations. If a line begins with single quotes and you need quotation marks within the first set of quotes, you can use double quotes. (You can do the opposite if you begin with double quotes.)

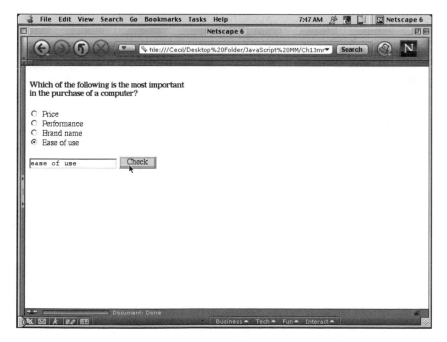

FIGURE 13.4   Radio Button to Pass a Variable.

Quiz Project

A fundamental purpose of a form is to generate feedback. Feedback can go to two different places—to the user who sees it on the screen and/or to someone else (e.g., web site owner) who will see the results when it arrives via email. The following script incorporates three types of form input—checkboxes, radio buttons, and text windows—and shows one way to evaluate quiz data. The feedback to the web page viewer who takes the quiz is immediate in a text box window, and the feedback to the web page designer via email occurs after a submit button is pressed. Because this next script is fairly long, numerous comments in the script explain what the different parts of the JavaScript program do. However, before jumping into the entire script, the following sections review the key elements of the program.

Checkbox Function

Before any other steps are taken in the JavaScript portion of the script, a global variable named "score" is declared. All three functions use that variable and so declaring it prior to beginning the functions is important.

The checkbox questions are multiple choice, so you need to look at all of them to record which ones are selected (clicked) and which ones have the correct answer. The heart of the scoreOne() function is the following conditional statement:

```
if(document.quiz.elements[ques].checked && ans=="*") {
```

As part of a loop structure, the same conditional statement queries whether the current form element (1) is checked and (2) has a correct answer. Both conditions are important because a viewer can check and then uncheck a response. Because only a single click is required to load the value of a checkbox form, if the form is *unselected* after being selected, the second click does not change the value of the element. Therefore, to get around that problem, the condition must also query whether the form element is still checked.

Radio Button Function

Because radio buttons have only a single correct answer in a group, only one of the entire group will be selected with the answer. Therefore, the conditional statement

```
if(document.quiz.boole.value=="*")
```

can be employed using the form element's name instead of number. If the Boolean is true (the answer is correct), then the score variable increments by 4. Otherwise, nothing is added to the score. The reason that (4) four is added to the score value is that each of the questions with radio buttons or checkboxes has four choices. Because the multiple-choice question using checkboxes can be partially correct, the value of each question must be a total of 4 so that calculations of the final score are correct.

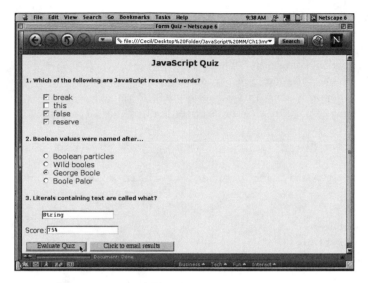

FIGURE 13.5   A Calculated Outcome in a Quiz.

Input Text Function

To evaluate the response to the open-ended question is relatively simple. Because only a single correct answer is acceptable, only a single matching condition is required. However, to make sure that a response is not rejected because of the case of the letters in the response, all characters inserted into the variable are changed to lowercase using the following line:

```
var ans=document.quiz.word.value.toLowerCase();
```

Now when the condition (`ans=="string"`) is queried, no problems of case arise. Once all three of the functions are complete, they are all placed into a complex function [`scoreIt()`] that allows all of them to be fired simultaneously. Figure 13.5 shows how the page appears on the scree.

The Quiz Form Script

```
<html>
<head>
<Title>Form Quiz </title>
<style type="text/css">
body  { font-family:Verdana}
</style >
<script language="JavaScript">
```

```
//Declare global variable for use with all functions
var score=0;
//Function to score multiple choice
function scoreOne() {
for (var ques=0; ques<4; ques++) {
   var ans=document.quiz.elements[ques].value;
  if(document.quiz.elements[ques].checked && ans=="*") {
     score +=1;
      var hitFlag=1;
      }
//Check to see if an incorrect score is selected
if(hitFlag ==1 && document.quiz.elements[ques].checked &&
ans=="-") {
     score -=1;
      var flag=1;
      }
    }
if(flag!=1 && score==3) {
score=4
 }
}

//Function to score single choice
function scoreTwo() {
 if(document.quiz.boole.value=="*") {
   score +=4;
 }
}

//Function to score open-ended question
function scoreThree() {
var ans=document.quiz.word.value.toLowerCase();
if(ans=="string") {
 score +=4;
   }
}

//Combine functions into single function
function scoreIt() {
//Reset score value
score=0;
scoreOne();
 scoreTwo();
scoreThree();
//Generate the total into percent
```

```
score= ((score/12) * 100) + "%";
document.quiz.score.value=score;
}
</script>
</head>
<body bgcolor="whitesmoke" onLoad="document.quiz.reset()">
<h3><center>JavaScript Quiz</center><h3>
<form name="quiz" method=post
action="mailto:yourName@domain.com?subject=Quiz"
enctype="text/plain">
<h5>1. Which of the following are JavaScript reserved
words? </h5>
<ul>
<input type=checkbox name="one" onClick='one.value="*' "
>break<br>
<input type=checkbox name="two" onClick='two.value="*' "
>this<br>
<input type=checkbox name="three" onClick='three.value="*' "
>false<br>
<input type=checkbox name="four" onClick='four.value="-
' " >reserve<p>
</ul>


<h5>2. Boolean values were named after . . . </h5>
<ul>
<input type=radio name="boole"  onClick='boole.value="-
" ' >Boolean particles<br>
<input type=radio name="boole" onClick='boole.value="-" '
>Wild booles<br>
<input type=radio name="boole" onClick='boole.value="*" '
>George Boole<br>
<input type=radio name="boole" onClick='boole.value="-" '
>Boole Palor<p>
</ul>
<h5>3. Literals containing text are called what? </h5>
<ul>
<input type=text name="word">
</ul>
Score:<input type=text name="score"><p>
<input type=button value= "Evaluate Quiz "
onClick="scoreIt()">
<input type=submit value="Click to email results">
</form>
</body>
</html>
```

HTML Features

The HTML portion of the script has a number of elements worth noting. First, a little stand-alone JavaScript is in the `<BODY>` tag. The event handler line

```
onLoad="document.quiz.reset()"
```

fires a form reset as soon as the quiz loads. This has the effect of clearing the form on reload commands from the browser.

To send the results to a designated addressee requires action and method commands in the `<FORM>` tag. The line

```
  <form name="quiz" method=post
action="mailto:yourName@domain.com?subject=Quiz"
enctype="text/plain">
```

directs the form to be sent to the specified address when the submit command is issued by a submit button in the form. The email address, which you should change to your own, along with the subject line is part of the "mailto:" action. The encryption type is important to specify as "text/plain" or the information is passed in a format that requires special interpretation. When the data arrive in an email with the "text" encryption, they appears as follows:

```
one=*
two=*
three=*
four=-
boole=on
word=string
score=83.333333333333334%
```

As can be seen, the results are somewhat cryptic, but the score value generated by Java-Script and placed into the Score text window is clear and complete. The other values are the values in the form elements.

14 Organizing Multimedia

Successful development of any interactive media requires careful planning, mastery of the technologies used, and competent, comprehensive production management. Most large multimedia projects are the result of an integrated team effort by a group of highly skilled professionals. Organizing and managing such a group requires patience, skill, and effort. This chapter will explore some of the issues associated with organizing and planning the production of interactive media in a team environment and how you can assess whether your development efforts resulted in overwhelming success.

Human Resources

Within a multimedia production team, several key roles must be assigned. Although it is truc that somc of the software packages discussed in this book provide individuals with the capability to produce simple, yet effective, interactive media modules, the production of high-quality mass-produced multimedia titles requires the participation of an entire production team. Take a look at the credits for any interactive game on the market. The list is quite extensive. Some of the key players in a multimedia production team might include:

- Production manager
- Graphic artist
- Instructional designer
- Digital video technician
- Videographer
- Audio technician/recording specialist
- Programmer
- Content specialist

For any high-quality production, the team must be organized by the production manager. The role of the production manager is to coordinate, facilitate, and dictate the production schedule for the multimedia project. This might include securing funding for the project from the prospective client, identifying and securing equipment and facility needs, coordinating the efforts of the members of the team and most important—determining the scope and purpose of the project. Although detailed knowledge of the authoring environment and the techniques involved are desirable, the production manager does not necessarily need to possess these skills. The key skill that the production manager must possess is "people skills." The production manager must be an expert at bringing people together, which may often be a difficult task. Dealing with temperamental personalities can be a full-time job in itself.

The roles of the other members of the team are briefly outlined here.

1. **Graphic artist.** The graphic artist is responsible for producing the look and the feel of the project. This individual should be proficient with both bitmap and vector editing tools. A solid background in design principles is also desirable.
2. **Instructional designer.** This is an essential role in the corporate or educational training development environment. This individual is responsible for determining the learning outcomes of the multimedia project. The instructional designer must also be familiar with current technologies and educational practices.
3. **Audio/video experts.** These individuals are essential for projects that involve narration or digital video. A solid background in audio and/or video recording and editing is required to fulfill the jobs of these individuals.
4. **Computer programmer.** The computer programmer's task is to pull all of the elements produced by the other team members and make them work together in the authoring environment of choice. A solid background in object-oriented programming and scripting languages is a plus for this individual.
5. **Content specialist.** The content specialist is responsible for collecting accurate content for use in the project. This individual must be aware of any and all changes that could potentially make the available content out-of-date.

Technical Resources

Identifying the technical resources needed to complete the project successfully is the job of the project manager. Considerations that must be made when identifying these needs include necessary computer equipment and software, digital video creation and editing equipment, sound capture and editing equipment, digital images, and so on. In general, the best available computer equipment is required to begin the production process. This includes securing computers with the fastest available CPUs, the most available RAM, and the largest hard drives that fit into a given budget. Large monitors are also a major plus when working with complex authoring programs such as Macromedia Director. When working with digital video, hard drive space becomes an even greater concern. Large amounts of disk space are no longer a luxury when it comes to producing video-intensive multimedia. A rule of thumb also dictates that the latest version of your authoring software should also be used to produce the final version of the project.

Planning the Project

As described in Chapter 5, initial planning is an essential component of producing an effective, quality multimedia application. The planning process begins by defining the goals of the project. What should this multimedia title do? Whom should it be designed for? What type of hardware will be required to run this application? When should this project be completed by? When considering commercial applications, all of these questions should be answered with the close cooperation of the client. Any miscommunication with the client at this point will surely lead to major problems during the development cycle of the project.

During the initial planning process, the goals of the project should be defined up front. These include projected outcomes of the completed project. An integral part of defining project goals is the identification of project objectives. Objectives are specific, measurable outcomes that will result when the project is complete. These should be demonstrable. Finally, to achieve the project objectives will require identifying actual activities within the project. Activities will be those actions that work to bring about successful achievement of the project outcomes and goals.

In general, the project planning process can be broken up into the following components:

- Define the project concept
- Diagram the program
- Develop a project storyboard
- Develop accompanying text and narration
- Develop a time line

As discussed in Chapter 5, a project storyboard and time line are key pieces to making sure all of the team players are on the same page and work together to achieve successful completion of the project (success = on-time + on-budget). Once all of these pieces are in place, the project manager will then have the job of making sure everyone is doing his or her job.

Assessment

The four applications discussed in this book were all initially created for slightly different uses, yet they can all do many of the same things—some better than others. Each of the applications has very strong and some not so strong parts to it. As the producers of these applications fight for bigger and bigger sales volumes, the packages will grow closer and closer together. It seems natural for application developers to seek to add new and expanded functionality to their products. Eventually it is likely that, with the exception of JavaScript, these applications will become nearly indistinguishable.

JavaScript is really a control language that adds considerable functionality to HTML and some server-side language such as ASP and Perl. JavaScript is probably the most advanced tool of the four we survey in this text. Although it is likely that JavaScript will expand in the future, it is even more likely that it will become integrated with more and more other applications so that you will start to see JavaScript capabilities in PowerPoint and Flash and Director in the future.

The latter three are likely to become more and more alike, so that you will see more of the functionality of each become more and more incorporated and refined in the others. Each has remarkable strengths.

Table 14.1 summarizes some of the strengths and weaknesses of the four applications detailed in this text. All of them can really accomplish most of the things they have been measured on, but sometimes not without considerable effort and expertise. In some cases, one of the applications is so much stronger on a dimension than the others that it simply is not a fair comparison.

As you can see from the table, there are some interesting differences. For novice users who want to make charts and graphs, none of the other applications even comes close to PowerPoint. But PowerPoint is limited in the kinds of interactivity that you can include, and it has a reputation of being slow on the Internet.

If bandwidth is your primary concern and you want incredible drawing ability, animation, and rich interactivity, Flash has to be your choice. There is no better package available for including a wide range of animations, and it is an absolute bandwidth miser. Also, Flash is an excellent front end to use with most server-side languages such as ASP, PHP, and Perl.

Director's real strength is its ability to bring together a wide range of resources into a neatly packaged stand-alone application. Rich and very sophisticated multimedia can be created with Director for distribution on CD-ROM. It is not a choice for Internet applications except in a limited number of situations in which the Director movie contains very limited video and sound.

TABLE 14.1   Summary of Key Differences

Task	PowerPoint	Flash	Director	JavaScript
Creates stand-alone applications	Yes	Yes	Superior	No
Includes animation	Yes	Yes	Yes	Yes
Creates animations	No	Superior	Yes	Animate HTML layers
User-paced applications	Yes	Yes	Yes	Yes
Includes diverse interactivity	No	Yes	Yes	Yes
Creates charts and graphs	Superior	With Generator	Yes	With tables
Has advanced audio mixing capabilities	No	Yes	Yes	No
Has advanced drawing capabilities	Limited	Superior	Yes	No
Has bandwidth properties	Has improved, but still weak	Superior	Marginal	Excellent
Required expertise	Novice can get great results	Technically sound	Technically sound	Expert for wide range of results

INDEX